The CIMA Handbook of Strategic Management

C I *m* A

Published in association with
the Chartered Institute of
Management Accountants

Books in the CIMA Professional Handbook series
Series Editor: Rob Dixon

IT Management Handbook
Edited by Rob Dixon and Ray Franks

Management Accounting Handbook
Edited by Colin Drury

Quality Management Handbook
Edited by Max Hand and Brian Plowman

Strategic Management Handbook
Edited by John Thompson

The CIMA Handbook of Strategic Management

Edited by John Thompson

BUTTERWORTH
HEINEMANN

1131480/X

Butterworth-Heinemann Ltd
Linacre House, Jordan Hill, Oxford OX2 8DP

 A member of the Reed Elsevier plc group

OXFORD   LONDON   BOSTON
MUNICH   NEW DELHI   SINGAPORE   SYDNEY
TOKYO   TORONTO   WELLINGTON

First published 1995

British Library Cataloguing in Publication Data
Strategic Management Handbook – (CIMA
Professional Handbook)
  I. Thompson, John L. II. Series
  658.4012

ISBN 0 7506 1906 6

Printed in England by Clays Ltd, St Ives plc

Contents

Contributors

David Allen (CBE, M.Phil., FCMA, JDipMA, FCIS, FRSA) is a past president (1983-4) of the Chartered Insitute of Management Accountants, and a past chairman (1987-92) of the Financial and Management Accounting Committee of the International Federation of Accountants. He was associated for many years with the Cadbury Schweppes group, holding directorships of various subsidiary companies, notably Cadbury Limited. However, his primary role now is as chairman of S.F.M. Limited, consultants in Strategic Financial Management, where his assignments have included both public and private sectors. He is also the CIMA industrial professor at the University of Loughborough, and a member of the Review Panel of the U.K. Financial Reporting Council. He is a regular contributor to the professional press, and the author of a number of books, the most recent being *Strategic Financial Management* (*Financial Times*), *The Cost of Capital* (Hawksmere) and *Strategic Financial Decisions* (Kogan Page). He is a non-executive director of Solihull Healthcare NHS Trust.

Andy Bailey (BSc MSc) is a research officer in the Centre for Strategic Management and Organizational Change at Cranfield School of Management. He is a psychologist by background and has researched in the area of cognitive styles and decision-making. He has spent the past 3 years undertaking a major research project on the processes of strategy development. His current research includes an exploration of the links between the strategy development process and organizational context and an international comparison of strategy formulation. He has worked with the senior managers of a number of organizations in the area of strategy process.

Robin Bellis-Jones is a Director of Develin & Partners, Management Consultants. He holds a Bachelor of Science degree in Mechanical Engineering and a Bachelor of Commerce degree – both from the University of Birmingham – and an MBA from the Cranfield School of Management. He held senior positions in finance and engineering before moving to consultancy more than 14 years ago. He has wide experience in the financial services sector, and in the engineering, manufacturing, retail, distribution, oil, and electronics industries, specializing in activity-based cost management and in organizational and overhead effectiveness studies. With Nick Develin, he is co-author of *Activity Based Cost Management*, an Accountants Digest for the Institute of Chartered Accountants in England and Wales. He is a member of Council and Fellow of the Chartered Institute of Management Accountants, and has chaired the Institute's Research and Technical Committee and its Activity Based Management working group. Also, he lectures widely on the full range of activity-based techniques and how they support both strategic and tactical decision-making.

Linda Bennett holds undergraduate and postgraduate degrees in English, Anglo-Irish Literature and Bibliography as well as an MBA. She has written widely for literary reviews and worked extensively in the book trade. Since 1994 she has been Sales and Marketing Director of T. C. Farnes, a library supply company based in Dumfries. She has previously lectured in strategic management at the University of Huddersfield, where she carried out research into the publishing industry.

Peter J Buckley (BA, MA, PhD) is Professor of Managerial Economics at the University of Bradford Management Centre and Visiting Professor at the Universities of Reading and Paris I (Panthéon-Sorbonne). He has published fourteen books in English and one in German, together with many widely cited articles on the multinational enterprise and the global economy. He was Vice-President of the Academy of International Business (1991-2) and was elected a Fellow of the Academy in 1985 for 'outstanding achievements in international business'. His current research concerns the management of cooperative strategies (ESRC-funded), the role of management in international joint ventures and alliances and projects on Asia-Pacific economies.

Dr Nigel Campbell is the Director of the Greater Manchester Centre for Japanese Studies and a Senior Lecturer at Manchester Business School.

Sir Graham Day was born in Canada and his early career blended management posts in companies such as Canadian Pacific with a professorial position in Business Administration in his native Nova Scotia. He has spent 15 of his last 20 working years in the UK; he has recently retired from full-time executive employment, and has returned to Canada to live.

He first came to the UK to be chief executive of Cammell Laird, and this was followed by the post of Chairman and Chief Executive of British Shipbuilders. He held a similar post at Rover, which at the time was the only European car company to increase sales and market share during an economic recession. He served on the board at British Aerospace after that company bought Rover; and he has been Chairman of Power Gen and Cadbury Schweppes.

Peel H. Holroyd set up his own consultancy in food and agriculture after retiring from Marks & Spencer plc, where, for nearly 20 years, he was a senior food technologist. He was active in the development of this company's poultry, veal, beef and pork products. He earlier studied in both the UK and Canada. He has served as Director General of the British Poultry Federation, and he is a visiting lecturer at the Royal Agricultural College. His work regularly takes him to America, Australia, New Zealand and South Africa.

Gerry Johnson is Professor of Strategic Management and Director of Research of Cranfield School of Management. After graduating from University College, London, he worked for several years in management positions in Unilever and Reed International before becoming a management consultant. He has also taught at Aston University Management Centre, where he obtained his PhD, and Manchester Business School. He took up his appointment at Cranfield in 1988.

Professor Johnson is author of *Strategic Change and the Management Process* (Blackwell, 1987), co-author of *Exploring Corporate Strategy* (Prentice-Hall, 3rd edition, 1993), and editor of *Business Strategy and Retailing* (Wiley, 1987) and the *Challenge of Strategic Management* (Kogan Page, 1992). He is also author of numerous papers on strategic management, and is a member of the editorial board of the *Strategic Management Journal*. His research work is primarily concerned with processes of strategy development and change in organizations. He has also worked as a consultant at a senior level on issues of strategy formulation and strategic change with a number of UK and international firms.

Simon Littlejohn is now Group Community Affairs Executive for Yorkshire Water plc, having proposed and gained board-level support for a corporate community investment policy. He joined the company in 1990 as Human Resources Adviser to the Managing Director, where his role was to review policies and propose new initiatives post-privatization. From 1985, as the first personnel manager for the Japanese volume electronic component manufacturer Alps Electric (UK) Ltd, Simon set up a greenfield manufacturing operation in Milton Keynes, which trebled in size over a 3-year period. Before that, he worked for nearly 20 years in several corporate and business level positions in the Plessey Company. He has an honours degree in biological sciences, and is a Fellow of the Institute of Personnel Management and a Member of the Institute of Management.

Brian Plowman is a Director of Develin & Partners, Management Consultants. He holds a Bachelor of Science degree in Mechanical Engineering from Brunel University. His industrial experience includes production engineering appointments in the UK and Europe, and he was director of a plastics products manufacturer. He has sixteen years' consulting experience covering all aspects of corporate transformation. During the last six years, he has specialized in the development of methodologies for Total Quality and Business Process Management, and has applied these successfully in the financial services, research, energy, transport, retail, manufacturing and food industries. He is a Chartered Engineer, and a Member of the Institution of Mechanical Engineers. He is also a Fellow of the Association of Quality Management Consultants, a Fellow of the Institute of Management Consultants, and a founder member of the Institute of Business Process Re-engineering. He is co-editor and contributor of *Quality Management Handbook* in the CIMA series of books, and is the author of *High Value, Low Cost* published by Pitman Publishing in August 1994. He is also a regular speaker at conferences around the world.

Dr Bill Richardson (PhD, MSc, ACIB, ACIS, DCA, MBIM) is Subject Leader of Management Strategy and Business Decision-Making at Sheffield Business School. He is the author of more than fifty books and articles on the subject of strategic decision-making and has extensive experience of consultancy particularly in the small and medium-sized enterprise context. Previously he worked in the banking, travel and local-authority professions.

Tom Sheridan is an Oxford MA, and Fellow of both the Chartered Institute of Management Accountants and of the Institute of Management Consultants. He has over 35 years' experience of management accountancy and has held every job in financial management from Cost Accountant to Finance Director.

After 25 years as Managing Consultant with PA Consulting, he left in 1992 to run his own consultancy and to concentrate on the latest developments in controllership and financial management. He is a member of CIMA's MPD and Europe Committees, and is CIMA's representative on the CCAB FEE Consultative Committee (and its management accounting working party). He is a Director of the UK Accounting Institutes' Foundation for Accountancy and Financial Management, and is currently engaged in advising a major Central European country on how to develop management accountancy.

He is a well known writer and lecturer on management accountancy and his book on international management and accounting, costing and budgeting, *Finanzmeister*, was published by Pitman in 1991.

Dr Denis Smith (BEd, MSc, MBA, PhD, DASE, FIPD, MIOSH) is Professor of Management at Durham University Business School. Prior to taking up his post at Durham he was Director of Liverpool Business School at Liverpool John Moores University, where he was also head of the Centre for Risk and Crisis Management. He has previously held academic posts at the University of Manchester, Nottingham Trent University and DeMontfort University. He is Visiting Professor of Strategic Management at the University of Sheffield and has been Visiting Professor of Human Resource Management at Kobe University in Japan. He has been the editor-in-chief of *Business Strategy and the Environment* and is currently the joint book reviews editor of *Industrial and Environment Crisis Quarterly*. He serves on the editorial advisory boards of *Disaster Limitation and Management; Disaster Management; European Environment; Iconoclastic Papers; Journal of Contingencies and Crisis Management* and *Technology Analysis and Strategic Management*. In addition to his mainstream academic activities he has held a series of Company Directorships and is currently a non-Executive Director of Mersey Regional Ambulance Trust.

John Thompson (BA, MBA) is Head of Management Strategy and Director of the part-time MBA programme at the University of Huddersfield. He has worked in retailing and in the steel industry and he retains close links with a variety of organizations through consultancy and Teaching Company Schemes. He is author of the textbook *Strategic Management; Awareness and Change*, now in its second edition, and a new strategy book for the executive market, *Strategy in Action*. Both books are published by Chapman and Hall. He is also author of a number of articles and case studies.

Introduction –
Strategic management: content, process and dilemmas
John Thompson

Strategic management is a complex and fascinating subject, with straightforward underlying principles but no 'right answers'.

Companies succeed if their strategies are *appropriate* for the circumstances they face, *feasible* in respect of their resources, skills and capabilities, and *desirable* to their important stakeholders – those individuals and groups, both internal and external, who have a stake in, and an influence over, the business.

Companies fail when their strategies do not meet the expectations of these stakeholders or produce outcomes that are undesirable to them.

To succeed in the long term, companies must compete effectively and outperform their rivals in a dynamic, and often turbulent, environment. To accomplish this, they must find suitable ways for creating and adding value for their customers. A culture of internal cooperation and customer orientation, together with a willingness to learn, adapt and change, is ideal. Alliances and good working relationships with suppliers, distributors and customers are often critically important as well.

Organizations must deploy and utilize their resources to create, implement and change strategies. Some changes will be gradual and continuous – emergent in an environment of 'competitive chaos' and uncertainty. On other occasions some companies must face the need for major discontinuous change – strategic regeneration – or simultaneous changes to strategies, structures and styles of management.

This book has been created as an eclectic collection of original papers that reflect a variety of perspectives on the key strategic issues and questions for the 1990s. They vary in style and approach and we hope they will prove to be both interesting and thought-provoking. Different topics lend themselves to different treatments, ranging from the academic to the conceptual and the very practical. To accommodate this and satisfy the differing needs of a variety of readers we have deliberately invited contributions from both broadly based strategic thinkers and specialists, with papers from experts in financial management and human resource management. Some of the writers are established academics; others are practising managers and consultants. A number of the papers are based on primary research and can be classified as applied theory; the remainder are reflective on the critical issues. All of them are forward-looking and relevant for the 1990s.

It is not the intention of this handbook to reproduce views that have been well-aired in previous publications on strategy, or to attempt to be prescriptive and offer what appear to be ready-made solutions to complex strategic problems, but rather to discuss strategic issues, dilemmas and challenges which are relevant for organizations as they strive to compete effectively and prosper in the uncertain 1990s.

In this introductory chapter we look briefly at what is meant by *strategic management* and present a framework for the twelve papers in the collection. Specifically we:

● define strategy and strategic management;
● examine the requirements for strategic success in the 1990s; and
● consider the essential aspects of the strategic challenge for organizations.

Strategy and strategic management

Strategies are means to ends, and these ends concern the purpose and objectives of the organization. They are the things that businesses do, the paths they follow, and the decisions they take, in order to reach certain points and levels of success.

Strategic management is a process that needs to be understood rather than a discipline that can be taught. It is the process by which organizations determine their purpose, objectives and desired levels of attainment; decide upon actions for achieving these objectives in an appropriate timescale, and frequently in a changing environment; implement the actions; and assess progress and results. Whenever and wherever necessary the actions may be changed or modified. The magnitude of these changes can be dramatic and revolutionary, or more gradual and evolutionary.

The three essential elements of strategic management are:
● **awareness** – understanding the strategic situation
● **formulation** – choosing suitable strategies
● **implementation** – making the chosen strategies happen.

On their own, good ideas are inadequate. They must be made to work and bring results.

Levels of strategy

There are three linked and interdependent levels of strategy.

Competitive strategy is concerned with creating and maintaining a competitive advantage in each and every area of the business. It can be achieved through any one function, or a combination of several. For each functional activity, such as production, marketing and human resources, the company will have a **functional strategy**. It is critical that these functional strategies are designed and managed in a coordinated way, such that they interrelate with each other and, at the same time, collectively allow the competitive strategies to be implemented properly.

Successful functional and competitive strategies **add value**, which is perceived as important by the company's stakeholders, especially its customers, and which helps distinguish the organization from its competitors. An individual functional area can add value. Internal linkages and cooperation between functions can also add value.

External networks that create synergy (beneficial emergent properties) by linking a company closely with its suppliers, distributors and/or customers are also a source of added value, but these are an aspect of the corporate strategy.

Corporate strategy, then, is deciding what businesses the organization should be in, and how the group of activities should be structured and managed. An organization may choose to focus on a single product range or service, concentrate on products or services that are related, say through technology or marketing, or diversify into unrelated businesses. Conventional wisdom appears to favour concentration, but successful conglomerates such as Hanson and BTR are testimony to the fact that diversification can be successful when the strategic control of the organization is appropriate.

The elements of strategic management

Figure 1 shows how strategic management needs **awareness** of how successful and strong the organization and its strategies are, and of how circumstances are changing. At any time, previously sound products, services and strategies are likely to be in decline. As this happens new 'windows of opportunity' are opening for the vigilant and proactive competitors.

New strategies must be created. Sometimes this will be part of a formal planning process; at other times the changes will emerge as managers try out ideas.

The processes of designing and carrying through the changes must be managed, monitored and controlled. Proper **implementation** is critically important.

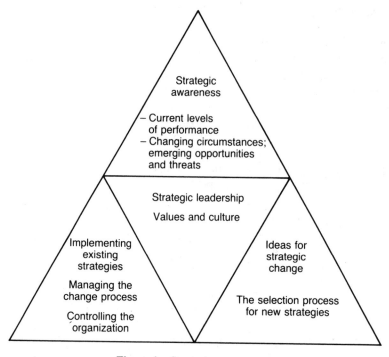

Figure 1   *Strategic management*

The relative success of an organization in dealing with these strategic issues will be dependent upon the corporate culture and values, and the strength and style of the strategic leader. Consequently these are shown at the very heart of the triangle in Figure 1, impacting on – and ideally blending together – the other issues.

Simply, it is this 'heart' that determines the ability of the organization to **learn** from its own successes and failures, from external stakeholders, and from changes in the environmental forces; and, as a result of this learning, to act positively at the appropriate time.

It is important to remember that environments spring surprises and that for many companies the environment represents a form of 'competitive chaos'. Changes by any single competitor at any time impact upon rival organizations, all of which may be forced to react to defend their positions. Their reactions introduce further changes to the competitive environment, which may, consequently, be in a state of perpetual flux. Clearly some competitors will be more proactive than their rivals, attempting to *manage their competitive environment*; and some will be in a position to react more quickly and positively to threatening changes.

A competitive industry environment suggests that the most positive companies will be continually seeking opportunities both to innovate and improve existing products and services and to find important new competitive opportunities ahead of their main rivals. It is important to recognize that *future* competition may not only come from existing rivals. Newcomers may attempt to break into a market; and it is quite feasible that if a newcomer does succeed in this way, it is because it is offering customers something new and different, and thereby changing the competitive situation dramatically.

Stakeholder trade-offs

Success appears to require an organizational structure and culture that welcome change rather than fight it, and an understanding of priorities and strategic needs. This implies a corporate juggling act, whereby the organization must succeed in dealing with three potentially conflicting influences:

- The performance requirements of **shareholders**, which, if met satisfactorily, will tend to be relatively stable and consistent. The problem occurs when their needs and expectations are not met. The survival of the business can be under threat; shareholders may be willing to sell out. They will certainly look for changes to strategies, and possibly of strategic leadership.
- The needs, expectations and aspirations of **customers**, who are also targeted by competitors.
- **Competitors**, which, like the organization, should be looking for new ways of adding value and creating competitive advantage.

When shareholders impose short-term financial performance demands, more speculative investments, aimed at securing long-term competitive advantage, may have to be constrained. Equally, while competitor benchmarking is essential, focusing too much on what competitors are doing, and might do, can lead to defensive strategies, or a reluctance to act until competitors have been seen to be doing something similar. It is original and innovatory ideas that develop new market opportunities.

Two things are clear:

1 Shareholder expectations **must** be met, both in the short- and long-term.

2 This aim cannot be achieved without satisfying customers, which in turn needs cooperation and support from suppliers and distributors and from

people inside the organization. Neither of these can be achieved without some regard for competition.

Many would also contend that shareholder expectations *should not* be achieved at the expense of ethical or socially responsible behaviour.

The tools of strategic success

Adding value

A business must add value if it is to be successful. As supply potential has grown to exceed global demand in the majority of industries, adding value has become increasingly important. In simple terms the extent of the value added is the difference between the value of the outputs from an organization and the cost of the inputs or resources used. It is therefore important to use all resources efficiently and properly; it is also critical to ensure that the potential value of the outputs is maximized by ensuring they fully meet the needs of the customers for whom they are intended. An organization achieves this when it sees its customers' objectives as its own objectives and *enables its customers to easily add more value* or, in the case of final consumers, *feel they are gaining true value for money*.

The important elements are:

- understanding and being close to customers
- a commitment to quality
- a high level of all-round service
- speedy reaction to competitive opportunities and threats
- innovation.

Core competencies and capabilities

Core competencies and capabilities concern the way that resources are managed for strategic effectiveness.

Successful companies develop **strategic abilities** that can be used to satisfy and exploit the key success factors in their targeted markets and industries. These can be features of the actual strategy or the structural processes.

Core competencies (Hamel and Prahalad, 1990) are *distinctive* skills, normally relating to particular products, services or technologies – Honda, for example, has such skills in engine technology – which help a company to differentiate its products or services and thereby create competitive advantage.

The more distinctive and hard to copy are these skills, the greater the advantage. These competencies are often very basic and at the heart of the business; they are then exploited in a range of different end products. Honda engines can be seen in cars, motorcycles, boats and lawnmowers.

Simply having the skills is not enough, though. They have to be carefully managed and exploited, and they need improving all the time. Competitors are always going to try to match them.

Strategic capabilities (Stalk et al., 1992) are conceptually similar, but they are really process skills as distinct from core technologies and products. They can again be used to create competitive advantage because they add value for customers.

The ability to develop new products quickly is an example. Skills and best practice developed in one area of a business can be transferred to others if there is a deliberate attempt to learn and share. Information management – harnessing the potential of new technologies – is an increasingly critical skill.

Architecture and synergy

Internal architecture refers to the linkages and interdependencies between the various functions in a business and between the businesses in a large organization. It would be unusual if there were no benefits (synergy) to be gained from sharing knowledge and skills, and working together on occasions. In a diverse organization, attaining the potential synergies depends a great deal upon the way corporate headquarters manages the businesses and seeks to both control and integrate the various parts.

External architecture is equally important and relates to the added value or supply chainlinking suppliers, manufacturers, distributors and finally customers. This is a second network of mutually interdependent partners and again organizations can benefit from establishing and nurturing close links. Japanese companies are particularly successful in achieving links and benefits. Partners have to support each other, though, and understand each other's various needs and expectations.

Competitive advantage

Competitive *advantage* implies a distinct, and ideally sustainable, edge over competitors. It is more than the idea of a competitive strategy, which may or may not prove distinctive.

Porter (1985) has shown how companies can seek broad advantage within an industry or focus on one or a number of distinct segments. Porter argues that advantage can accrue from:

1   **Cost leadership**, whereby a company prices around the average for the market (with a 'middle-of-the-road' product or service) and enjoys superior profits because its costs are lower than those of its rivals.

2   **Differentiation**, where value is added in areas of real significance for customers, who are then willing to pay a premium price for the distinctiveness. A range of differentiated products (or services), each designed to appeal to a different segment, is possible, as is focus on just one segment.

Speed (say quicker new product development) and fast reaction to opportunities and threats can provide advantage, essentially by reducing costs and differentiating.

Real competitive advantage implies companies are able to satisfy customer needs more effectively than their competitors. Because few individual sources of advantage are sustainable in the long run, the most successful companies innovate and continually seek new forms of advantage in order to open up a competitive gap and then maintain their lead. Successfully achieving this is a cultural issue.

Achieving competitive advantage

Competitive advantage, then, does not come from simply being different. It is achieved if and when *real* value is added for customers. This often requires companies to **stretch their resources** to achieve higher returns (Hamel and Prahalad, 1993). Improved productivity may be one way; ideally employees will come up with **innovations**, new and better ways of doing things for customers.

This innovation can result in lower costs, differentiation or a faster response to opportunities and threats, the bases of competitive advantage; and it is most likely to happen when the organization succeeds in harnessing and exploiting its core competencies and capabilities.

It also requires that employees are **empowered**. Authority, responsibility and accountability will be decentralized, *allowing employees to make decisions for themselves*. They should be able and willing to look for improvements. When this is managed well, a company may succeed in changing the rules of competition. Basically organizations should seek to encourage **ordinary people to achieve extraordinary results**.

This will only happen if achievement is properly recognized, and initiative and success rewarded. Some people, though, are naturally reticent about taking risks.

3M (Post-It Notes), Sony, Hewlett-Packard and Motorola are four organizations recognized as being highly creative and innovative. In each case employees are actively encouraged to look for, and try out, new ideas. In such businesses the majority of products in the corporate portfolio will have only existed for a few years. Effective empowerment can bring continual growth to successful companies and also provide ideas for turning around companies in decline.

Competitive advantage is also facilitated by good internal and external communications – achieving one of the potential benefits of linkages. Without this, businesses cannot share and *learn* best practice. Moreover information is a fundamental aspect of organizational control. Companies can learn from suppliers, from distributors, from customers, from other members of a large organization – and from competitors.

Strategic regeneration

Organizations have to deal with dynamic and uncertain environments, as we have seen already. They should actively and continuously look for opportunities to exploit their competencies and strategic abilities, adapt and seek improvements in every area of the business – gradual change, building on an awareness and understanding of current strategies and successes. One difficulty is the fact that organizations are not always able to clarify exactly why they are successful.

At the same time it is also valuable if they can *think ahead discontinuously*, trying to understand future demand, needs and expectations. By doing this they will be aiming to be the first competitor with solutions. Enormous benefits are available to the companies that succeed.

In a sense this process is an attempt to invent the future, and the resources of the organization, its people and technologies, will need to be applied creatively. Caution is necessary when ideas are implemented because markets and customers are likely to resist changes that seem too radical.

In summary, organizations are searching for:

- long-term product or service leadership, which is dictated by the **environment**;
- long-term cost leadership, which is **resource** dependent;
- product and service excellence, doing things faster than competitors without sacrificing quality – essential **values**.

Strategic regeneration refers to simultaneous changes to strategies and structures (organizational processes) in this search.

Strategies have to be reinvented. New products and services should be created by questioning how and why existing ones are popular and successful, and looking for new ways of adding extra value. Electronic publishing and CD-Rom technology, for example, have enormous potential for dramatically changing the ways people learn. Rewards are available for those companies that learn how to exploit these *environmental opportunities*.

Structural changes are designed to improve *resource efficiency* and *effectiveness*. The current trends are:

1   down-sizing – splitting the organization into small, autonomous, decentralized units;
2   delayering – using the power and potential of information technology for reducing the number of layers of managers, in order to speed up decision-making; and
3   process re-engineering – reviewing and redesigning processes in order that tasks can be performed better and faster.

Simply, changes are required to the structure of the organization, the nature and scope of jobs and the network of communications.

Empowerment and teamworking are also seen as essential for creating the values necessary to enable this degree of change.

On paper the idea of strategic regeneration can be justified as essential, exciting and rewarding, but, not unexpectedly, there are likely to be major barriers when applying the ideas. The most obvious hurdles are:

- the quality of leadership required to provide the necessary drive and direction;
- an inability to create an internal culture of change – the most powerful inhibitors will be experienced, established managers who have become out-of-date;
- uncertainty about changing needs and competitor activities.

Sony's mini disc (small compact discs), for example, are competing with Philips' digital compact cassettes (DCCs) to be a leading recorded music format in the second half of the 1990s. Which of the two formats consumers will eventually favour is still unresolved, but the uncertainty did not inhibit these two innovative organizations.

Pascale (1992) uses the word *transformational* to describe organizations that succeed with simultaneous strategic and structural change. They become **learning organizations** which 'encourage continuous learning and knowledge generation at all levels, have processes which can move knowledge around the organization easily to where it is needed, and can translate that knowledge quickly into changes in the way the organization acts, both internally and externally' (Senge, 1991).

Strategy creation

All managers plan. They plan how they may achieve objectives. Planning is essential to provide direction and to help ensure that the appropriate resources are available where and when they are needed for the pursuit of objectives. Sometimes the planning process is detailed and formal; on other occasions planning may be informal, unstructured and essentially 'in the mind'. In the context of strategy formulation a clear distinction needs to be made between the cerebral activity of informal planning and formalized planning systems.

Formal strategic planning systems are most useful in stable conditions. Environmental opportunties and threats are forecast, and then strategies are planned and implemented. Strategies that are appropriate, feasible and desirable are the ones to help the organization achieve its mission and objectives.

Where the environment is more turbulent and less predictable, strategic success requires flexibility, and the ability to learn about new opportunities and introduce appropriate changes continuously. Planning systems can still make a valuable contribution but the plans themselves must not be inflexible.

In addition, is is important not to discount the contribution of visionary strategic leaders who become aware of opportunities – and on occasions, create new opportunities – and take risks based on their awareness and insight of markets and customers.

Planned strategies

Formal planning implies determined actions for achieving stated and desired objectives. For many organizations these objectives will focus on sales growth and profitability. A detailed analysis of the strategic situation will be used to create a number of strategic alternatives, and then certain options will be chosen and implemented.

Planning systems are useful, and perhaps essential, for large groups having a number of businesses which, although possibly independent, need integrating on occasions. There are, though, a number of possible approaches. Head office can delegate the detailed planning to each division, offering advice and making sure the plans can be coordinated into a sensible total package. Alternatively, the planning system can be controlled centrally in order to establish priorities for resource allocation.

While the discipline of planning and setting priorities is valuable, the plans must not be inflexible and incapable of being changed in a dynamic competitive environment. During implementation it is quite likely that some plans will be discarded and others modified.

Visionary leadership

Planning systems imply that strategies are selected carefully and systematically from an analytical process. In other instances major strategic changes will be decided upon without lengthy formal analysis. Typically such changes will reflect strong, entrepreneurial leadership and be visionary and *discontinuous* – 'I have seen the future and this is it!'

To an outsider it can often appear that the organization is pursuing growth with high risk strategies, which are more reliant on luck than serious thought. This view can underestimate the thinking that has gone on, because quite often these visionary leaders have an instinctive feel for the products, services and markets they are concerned with, and enjoy a clear awareness and insight of the opportunities and risks.

This mode of strategy creation is most viable when the strategic leader has the full confidence of the organization, and he or she can persuade others to follow his or her ideas and implement the strategies successfully. Implementation requires more detailed planning and incremental changes with learning – initially it is the broad strategic idea that is formulated entrepreneurially.

Adaptive strategic change

In dynamic and turbulent competitive environments detailed planning is problematical. The plans are only as good as any forecasts, which must be uncertain. It can make sense therefore not to rely on detailed plans, but instead just plan broad strategies within a clearly defined mission and purpose.

Having provided this direction, the strategic leader will allow strategies to emerge in a decentralized organization structure. Managers will be encouraged and empowered to make changes in their areas of responsibility, and, ideally, rewarded for their initiatives. The implication is that functional changes will impact upon competitive strategies in a positive way as the organization adapts to its changing environment.

Learning is at the heart of this mode. Managers must learn about new opportunities and threats; they should also learn from the successes and mistakes of other managers. Managers must be willing to take measured risks; for this to happen understandable mistakes and errors of judgement should not be dealt with harshly.

Change is gradual and comes from experimentation; new strategies bring in an element of trial and error. The success of this mode is very dependent upon communications. Managers must know of opportunities and threats facing them; the organization must be able to synthesize all the changes into a meaningful pattern, and spread learning and best practice.

It is quite feasible to find all three modes in evidence simultaneously in an organization, although of course there is likely to be one dominant mode. *Moreover different managers in the same organization will not necessarily agree on the relative significance of each mode; their perceptions of what is actually happening will vary.*

Strategic issues and dilemmas

We have seen that organizations must compete in uncertain, dynamic and turbulent environments where pressures for change are continuous. New opportunities and threats appear at short notice and require a speedy response. As a result there are a number of major strategic issues or dilemmas for organizations in the mid-1990s. A selection of these are as follows:

The strategic environment

● Recognizing that the past and the future may not be related directly. Continuous improvement and gradual, emergent change – while essential – may be inadequate. Discontinuous strategic change could be necessary.

Corporate objectives and strategies

● Balancing the expectations of shareholders (sometimes focused on short-term financial success) with the longer-term needs of other stakeholders such as customers, while paying constant attention to competition – the corporate juggling act.
● Whether the corporation should be *diversified*, and whether this should be related (marketing or technology) or unrelated, or *focused* on either core competencies or specified products.
● The geographic scope: from global to single continent or country.
● The timing of investments to stimulate growth. The dilemma of needing to invest in a recession (when current revenues do not justify spending) to be ready for expansion at the right time.
● When investing, finding the right balance between spending levels and understanding. Speculative investment in the long term is risky because spending precedes understanding; avoiding such risks, and spending only when there is understanding, may imply inadequate investment for building a future for the organization.

Competitive strategies

- Should the products and services be targeted at the mass market or selected niches?
- Balancing the potential from differentiation (adding value for customers with special features) with the price advantages that can result from low costs – thus adding value in a different way.
- Realizing that competition will continue to come from existing rivals but also from newcomers to the industry – newcomers with fresh competitive ideas.

Structural issues

- Centralization (for control) versus decentralization and empowerment (which yields greater flexibility and the ability to change more quickly).
- The need to encourage businesses in a corporation to compete for scarce resources, and thus avoid slackness and complacency, while encouraging them to cooperate and achieve internal synergies.
- Related to this, coordinating the various activities while being able to separate them sufficiently for the corporation to discern how profitable each discrete product and business is.
- Deploying people in the most appropriate places in the organization. One could argue that people should be flexible and the strongest managers readily moved out of moribund businesses into the best growth opportunities.

Values

- The need to be both proactive and reactive simultaneously – staying up with existing competitors while looking to change the rules of competition.
- The need to act quickly in response to opportunities and threats – and possibly to crises – but not at the expense of either control, consistency or product and service quality.

Conclusion

A view of strategy

This introduction has outlined a number of key themes which are developed in the individual chapters. The underlying ideas have been summarized in Figure 2.

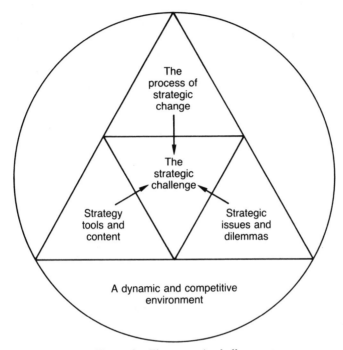

Figure 2 *The strategic challenge*

The strategic challenge for organizations lies in developing decision-making processes for harnessing and exploiting the various strategic tools (the content of strategy) to deal with the issues and dilemmas they face in a changing and competitive environment. To be effective, they must develop and sustain a range of important competencies.

The chapters

The chapters in Part One **Strategic management** examine the important underpinning ideas of positioning and capability and then explore adding value and strategic relationships in greater detail. They relate to the *strategic tools and content* segment of Figure 2.

Part Two, **Strategy development** discusses the processes of *strategy creation and strategic change*. Detailed papers on the techniques for strategic planning have been deliberately omitted, as this aspect of strategy is well documented elsewhere.

Parts Three and Four deal with selected strategic issues and dilemmas. Part Three **Strategic issues and challenges** contains chapters on leadership, the global environment, ethics and the management of strategic crises, and Part Four presents three perspectives on **Strategy evaluation and control**. The first looks at corporate governance, the second at control itself and the third argues the case for a multi-competency approach to strategy evaluation.

The final part, Part Five **Strategic change**, contains just one chapter, which describes and evaluates the strategic regeneration at Yorkshire Water since privatization.

The objective of this handbook, and the consequent rationale for the selection of the individual papers, is a discussion of contemporary strategic issues, dilemmas and challenges for organizations as they strive to compete effectively and prosper in the uncertain 1990s.

References

The material contained in this introductory chapter is largely an edited version of sections taken from Thompson, John L (1995) *Strategy in Action*, Chapman and Hall.

Specific references:

Hamel, G and Prahalad, C K (1990) The Core Competence of the Corporation, Harvard Business Review, May–June.

Hamel, G and Prahalad, C K (1993) Strategy as Stretch and Leverage, *Harvard Business Review*, March–April.

Pascale, R T (1992) Paper presented at the Strategic Renaissance Conference, Strategic Planning Society, London, October.

Porter, M E (1985) *Competitive Advantage: Creating and Sustaining Superior Performance*, Free Press.

Senge, P (1991) *The Fifth Discipline: The Art and Practice of the Learning Organization*, Doubleday.

Stalk, G *et al.* (1992) Competing on Capabilities – The New Rules of Corporate Strategy, *Harvard Business Review*, March–April.

Part One STRATEGIC MANAGEMENT

The first three chapters concentrate on the content of strategic management. Chapter 1, **Positioning and capability**, introduces the keys to strategic success in terms of managing today's products and services and provides a framework for addressing future changes. It is a pithy and insightful summary of established principles.

Robin Bellis-Jones and Brian Plowman stress the importance of meeting customer needs on a continuing basis, implying continuous improvement, while always monitoring competition. At the same time the need to anticipate discontinuous change pressures, and future competition from unexpected sources, should not be overlooked. The secret lies in an appropriate organizational structure and the creative and effective use of the organization's strategic resources. The arguments presented in this chapter relate closely to the E–V–R congruence model (*environment–values–resources*) described in Chapter 11 on performance evaluation.

Strategically effective organizations add value for their customers in a search for a distinctive competitive advantage. They achieve this by differentiating and introducing valuable features, and by good cost management to provide better value for money through competitive pricing. Chapter 2 looks at the strategic importance of adding value, which is defined here in terms of values perceived as important by customers – a qualitative view that leads on to financial benefits. In this respect we are not simply seeing adding value as the difference between the revenue from outputs and the cost of inputs, although, strictly speaking, this is the acknowledged quantitative measure. Adding value requires organizations to focus on quality and customer service.

Michael Porter's value chain (Porter, M E (1985) *Competitive Advantage: Creating and Sustaining Superior Performance*, Free Press) is widely recognized as a useful framework for analysing adding value, and it has been covered extensively in strategy texts. Porter stresses the importance of looking at every area of the business in the search for cost benefit and differentiation opportunities, and the strategic contribution of linkages both inside the organization and between the various members of the supply (or added value) chain. Peel Holroyd applies these ideas in a descriptive and anecdotal paper on adding value in the food and agriculture industries (Chapter 2). This particular industry sector was chosen deliberately, as it pervades all our lives and the ideas are easily recognized and appreciated.

Chapter 3, **Understanding strategic relationships**, develops further the importance of linkages and alliances. Nigel Campbell argues that the management of strategy is the management of interactive behaviour. Well-managed relationships constitute a competitive strength.

His paper considers the various forms of strategically important external alliances and networks and internal, cross-functional and cross-business, relationships. The knowledge and information aspects, together with the need for sound management to ensure that there are benefits for all the partners, are emphasized. We return to internal and external inkages in Chapter 7, which looks at their ethical implications.

Chapter 3 draws heavily on the author's experience of Japanese strategy and practice, where alliances and networks are seen as very important. Japanese management is also discussed briefly in Chapter 12, which looks at strategic regeneration, the final aspect of strategy content described in the introduction to this handbook.

1

Positioning and capability

An introduction to strategy formulation and delivery

Robin Bellis-Jones and Brian Plowman

Two explorers were trudging across the icy wastes. Suddenly a polar bear reared up from behind a glacier.

'What do we do now?' asked one of the men.

The other man knelt down, removed his snowshoes and took a pair of trainers out of his knapsack.

'It's pointless putting those on', said the first man. 'Those bears can outrun any man.'

I know', said the other, 'but I only have to run faster than you.'

Introduction

Positioning and capability are twinned concepts that can be remarkably powerful in helping organizations grapple with the problems of how best to direct their resources. This chapter describes them briefly, discusses the principles and issues underpinning them and gives some examples of the successes their use can achieve.

Positioning is concerned with external factors. Which products and services are we selling to whom? What are our customers' needs? Who are our competitors and how do we compare with them? What is the legislative framework? What do our shareholders expect?

Capability covers internal factors. Do we have the necessary technology and skills? Do we have the *right* competences? Are our business processes appropriate to our needs? Do they permit failures to occur, or are they error-free? Is our organization responsive? How well do we innovate? Does our culture help us or hinder us?

These points are illustrated in Figure 1.1(a).

Some companies focus inwards, developing their capability without understanding what their customers need or what their competitors are doing.

Others focus outwards, setting objectives their staff cannot meet and creating customer expectations they cannot satisfy. This paper argues that positioning and capability are inextricably linked; to be strategically effective organizations must work on both at the same time.

Changing an organization's positioning and capability is like taking a never-ending journey. In setting out to create its own future, a company will find many factors influencing the direction, the route and the means of getting there. Moreover, the journey is iterative, with continuous checks and modifications on the way. See Figure 1.1(b).

Customers have differing needs. Can the company identify the specific and different internal capabilities that will meet those needs? Does the company have a clear plan for its own actions in relation to the competition for every type of product for every type of customer? Does the company have an organization that can respond to the plan, or is the organization itself a barrier to changing positioning and enhancing capability? Does the company know where it is on the journey, and what to do next?

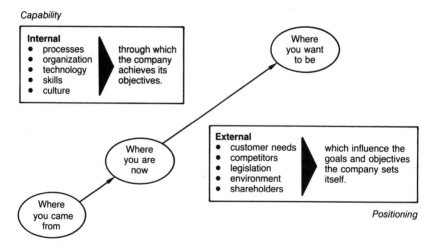

Figure 1.1(a)   *Positioning and capability: twinned concepts*

Answering these questions requires a clear understanding of three elements within the strategy:

- product/customer segmentation *by common capability*;
- competitive stance;
- organizational classification.

We now look at each of these elements in greater detail.

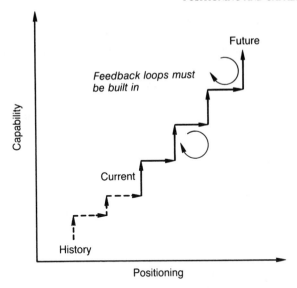

Figure 1.1(b) *Positioning and capability: the journey*

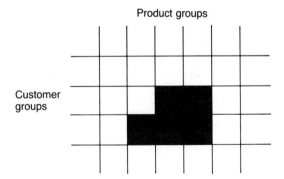

▶ a market segment is a set of customer/product groups with common
characteristics in terms of using
  – the same support functions in the organization
  – the same sales channels
  – the same business processes

Common
capability

Figure 1.2 *Product and customer segmentation*

Product/Customer segmentation by common capability

Figure 1.2 illustrates a product/customer segmentation based on common
capability. The shaded area links all the products and customer groups that
have *common processes from the sales channel through to customer after-care.*

Extending the shaded area vertically brings new customer groups to the process; extending it horizontally introduces new products or new services. Growing common capability in these ways is normally an advantage because it enables existing skills and resources to be applied to new business opportunities. However, careful investigation is required to ensure that the new product or service does not contaminate the service to customers on existing products. If it does, internal processes must be redesigned to meet the different needs.

A typical trap that many companies fall into is to market existing products to a new group of customers who turn out to have needs that are quite different from, and beyond the capability of, the existing process. For example, when one well-known bank introduced a TESSA it offered a telephone enquiry service on the same charge-free telephone number that it used for other products. Although the operators were given the necessary technical training to answer questions from potential customers, the switchboard capacity was inadequate; by overstretching the switchboard's capability, potential customers for all products, not just the TESSA, suffered.

Completing the matrix is therefore seldom straightforward. It requires a thorough understanding of the company's internal business processes.

Competitive stance

Having defined the company's current and potential product/customer segments, we must understand its *competitive* stance on each. Figure 1.3 illustrates four different competitive stances – *new, nurture, defend* and *steal.*

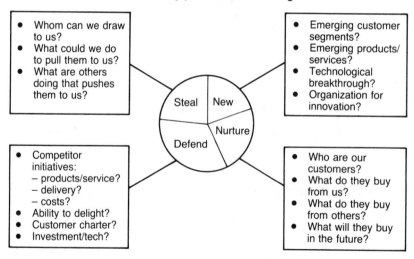

Figure 1.3 *Competitive stance*

A segment may be *new*, created by marketing existing products to a new customer group or new products to an existing group. The new segment may be based on a technological breakthrough that delivers lower unit cost or an improved product/service specification, or on the emergence of a new potential market, such as Eastern Europe.

The competitive stance may be to cross-sell current or new products to existing customers – *nurturing* the existing customer base. This is not cynical exploitation: it means customers buying more from a company because of its record of product and service quality. In order to be able to nurture its existing customer base, a company must know who its customers are and what they are likely to buy in the future. A senior executive of British Telecom is reported to have observed that, at the time of privatization, the only thing that BT knew about its customers was their telephone number, a lack of knowledge that initially presented a significant barrier to future growth.

Companies may have segments in which they must focus on *defending* the customer base. Why are customers going elsewhere? What is attracting them away? What is the company doing that is driving customers away? Some product/customer segments may not be worth defending. How should the company relinquish them without losing other product/customer segments as a consequence?

Stealing customers is the most risky competitive stance. Stealing simply through price reduction – buying market share – will prove embarrassing if the reduced revenue does not fund the level of service needed to retain the stolen customers. It may well prompt retaliatory attacks from stronger competitors.

Conceptually, these four types of competitive stance are simple enough. But unless companies make the effort to think through clearly which they wish to adopt for each product/customer segment, and signal their intentions through the organization, there will be endless confusion and wasted effort.

Organizational classification

Having positioned the company by defining its customer/product segments, and having decided which competitive stance is needed, one must examine how the organization itself can deliver the necessary capability.

Delivering capability is not the simple mechanistic task that some managers believe. Norms of organizational behaviour become deep-seated and extraordinarily powerful. If altering capability demands a change in these norms, it will be a major operation. If the organization fails to recognize the types of barrier it faces, its attempts to change will founder.

In order to recognize barriers, it is useful to think of four major organizational types:

- entrepreneurial
- bureaucratic
- selling
- quality

Each has quite distinct characteristics, summarized in Figure 1.4.

	Entrepreneurial	Selling	Bureaucratic	Quality
Management style	Personal leadership Visionary Participative	Aggressive Reward-driven Directive	Functional/parochial Political Directive Procedure driven	Cooperative Participative Cross-functional Process driven
Culture	Loyal Inspirational Creative Informal	Competitive Fear Divisive Becoming formal	'Efficiency' Fear Protective Formal	Empowering Customer-driven Support/team building Informal
Reward systems	Erratic	Commission	Budgetary Length of service	Company/team profit share
Change	Ad hoc Responsive Opportunity Breakthrough	Limited Reactive Threat	Limited Unresponsive Threat Top down	Continuous improvement Responsive Opportunity Innovation
Resources	Meagre Flexible	Salesmen	Specialist Functional Wasteful	Flexible Adaptive
Decisions	Intuitive Subjective Qualitative	Quantitative	Cost/benefit Quantitative	Quantitative Qualitative Focused
Control/measurement	Loose Instinctive Cash-flow driven	Focused Market share/sales revenue driven	Budgetary Hierarchical Input (cost) driven	Knowledge Understanding Output (service) driven
Communication	Telling Oral Discussion Open	Telling Oral/written Instruction 'Need to know' Centre outwards	Telling Written Restriction/defensive 'Need to know' Functional Tactical	Listening Oral/written Information sharing Open Cross-functional processes Customer-oriented
Horizon	Short-term	Short-term	Short/medium term	Short/medium/long term
Competitive stance	New Steal	Steal	Defend	New Nurture Steal Defend

Figure 1.4 *Organizational classification*

Entrepreneurial organizations tend to centre on individuals who have strong personal leadership. The culture is almost invariably informal and highly participative; staff are creative and loyal; and decision-making is usually focused on a limited range of product/customer segments, and can therefore be responsive and often intuitive. Large companies often create separate divisions or companies to get new products off the ground, encouraging an entrepreneurial style that is deliberately different from the normal company culture.

If entrepreneurial organizations succeed, they tend to evolve into **selling** organizations. Survival depends on an aggressive push for volume and market share, the focus of management attention is on turnover and sales force performance, creativity takes second place to cash flow, and formalized procedures begin to take hold.

If entrepreneurial leaders survive companies' evolution into selling organizations, they are seldom able to live with the overwhelming mediocrity of the **bureaucratic** organization: functional specialism and parochialism start to dominate; internal communications become formal and unresponsive, extending lead times; and the focus moves to medium-term cost/benefit. Growth often outstrips management's capacity to understand what is happening in processes that remain cross-functional. Bureaucratic organizations often retreat into niche markets, but carry administrative overheads and practices that limit their capacity to innovate and respond to changing customer needs.

Surviving the bureaucratic organization means *developing* a culture that combines responsiveness to customer needs with efficiency, that provides direction and control without stifling innovation, and that is adaptive to changing markets and competitive challenges. This is the **quality** organization, which is able to develop its internal capability to meet its strategic market positioning.

Figure 1.5 illustrates how a typical company will alter its organization over time as it grows. The challenge, quite clearly, is to avoid the stifling constraints of bureaucracy and create a flexible, quality organization.

	I	II	III	IV
	Entrepreneurial	**Marketing**	**Bureaucratic**	**Quality**
	Breakthrough	Growth	Niche	Continuous improvement
New	Start-up			Start-up
Steal		Volume		Volume
Defend			Cost	Cost
Nurture				Service

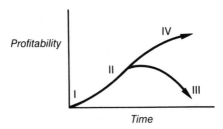

Figure 1.5 *Classifying an organization*

At any one time, a failure to understand the type of organization a company has assumed will mean that attempts to bring cohesion and single-mindedness to its operations will probably be piecemeal and ineffective. Contradictory policies, internal politics and vested interests will conspire to limit the continuous change needed to adjust positioning and keep capability in step. Indentifying a company's organizational characteristics is not therefore simply an interesting academic exercise: it is essential in identifying the barriers to change so that a strategy for dismantling them can be formulated.

For example, an engineering company had become strongly *bureaucratic* in its approach. As it became more and more hidebound by stultifying procedures and standards, overseas competition was growing increasingly innovative in its product developments. Before long, the company was left way behind the market in the features and performance its products offered. It had failed to recognize the positioning it required to meet the demands of a faddish market and the capability needed to respond rapidly to its whims.

The company found that simply placing objectives of faster product development on its managers had little effect. It had to make clear to all involved the new positioning it had to adopt and to challenge fundamentally the procedures by which tasks were planned and performed. Only through the organization's patient but dogged determination did people's approach to their work change and the blindly accepted norms gradually disappear.

The twinned concepts applied

Repositioning means changing capability, as the following four examples from different industries illustrate:

- In the 1960s **Toyota** manufactured a range of medium-sized saloon cars. Within that product/market segment it developed a capability for high quality at low cost. From the formidable position it developed in that specific base, the company has over the last 30 years continuously improved so as to be able to extend its high quality/low cost capability to the luxury car market, and now the Lexus competes direct with BMW, Mercedes and Jaguar.
- **Direct Line Insurance** was established in 1985 by the Royal Bank of Scotland to market motor insurance in the UK. Its main innovation was direct telephone sales to the public, bypassing conventional sales channels that use intermediaries. Direct Line's entry into the market changed the nature of competition in the industry, and the company now has a significant and growing share of the UK motor insurance market. Its competitive capability derived from the delivery of outstanding customer service at low cost, both at the point of sale and in the servicing of insurance claims. Behind this lies a formidable operational capability, which also

delivers comprehensive management information. It has since extended its capability into buildings and contents insurance to the same customer base. Direct Line has an uncompromising attitude to the development of its capability, covering not only the development of its computing and telecommunications systems, but also the development of its people – through training and education in customer needs and, critically, through delegation of responsibility.

Direct Line's success has inevitably affected the longer-established insurance companies very dramatically and forced them to rethink and redesign their competitive strategies.

- **A bus manufacturer** survived a drastic down-turn in its business by focusing not only on the needs of its direct customers – the fleet operators – but on the needs of the *end consumer*, the fare-paying passenger. This meant understanding two sets of needs:

1   *Passengers'* needs for comfort, easy access, personal safety, information, convenient methods of payment, and low cost.
2   *Operators'* needs for a low whole-life cost, reliability, ease of maintenance and cleaning, low running costs, and availability of spares.

Through understanding these needs, the company developed a clear definition of the product/customer segments in which it could excel. It assessed its competitors' capabilities within those segments against its own, and built manufacturing, marketing, selling and distribution capabilities that would differentiate it in its chosen segments.

- **A pensions and life assurance company** that sold its products through intermediaries recognized that its main contact with customers was reactive: it only talked to them when they complained or made enquiries about their policies. Product design had been the preserve of actuaries – sales took no part – and marketing was left with the task of producing brochures. Development of capability was limited to providing an IT system to process new products. Subsequent poor product performance was blamed on sales-force incompetence.

The company's chances of cross-selling to customers was limited by its initial experience of the sale conversion process, a drawn-out saga of quotations, medical examinations, queries, delays, all enmeshed in documents phrased in impenetrable English. Figure 1.6 attempts to illustrate the process. The subsequent support process merely reinforced customers' early convictions.

Change was brought about by researching and quantifying customer needs, measuring and benchmarking competitor performance in terms of product features and customer service, and using technology to streamline conversion and support processes. The company provided its independent sales force with leads, and indicated where potential customers could be found and what they were likely to buy. The sales force was given a voice in the development of new products; and marketing was given ownership of product launch and life-cycle management. Through these changes both positioning and capability were altered. The effects on sales, customer support and costs were dramatic.

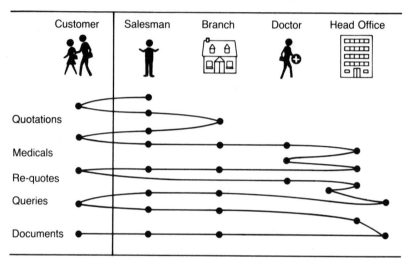

Figure 1.6   *Life assurance: the conventional sale conversion process*

In Conclusion

At senior level, most companies have a pretty good understanding of the current positioning with regard to their customers and competitors. But much more frequently they have only a vague knowledge of their own capability to meet their customers' needs, and to determine what has to change and how to bring that change about.

Establishing a company's true capability, linking it to positioning and implementing an action plan for change, are the difficult steps.

An understanding of corporate capabilities demands not only knowledge, but a *culture* within which people can openly reveal process shortcomings without fear of personal retribution. Devising and agreeing steps to change capability to meet a company's positioning requires teamwork and coopera-tion between managers, and excellent communication with staff.

If this can be achieved, the organization will have focused the efforts of everyone on efficiently meeting the real needs of the right customers. It will have become a potent force in the marketplace.

2

Adding value in the food and agriculture industries
Peel H. Holroyd

Introduction

Value is added as progress is made through the food chain. Value can be added at any stage and in many different forms. The term is used to indicate that by enacting some form of physical change at some stage during production and processing there is every justification to introduce a price or quality differential claim over the original base line. This may be by genuine addition in the form of a physical change, or it may simply be a change in presentation.

Adding value is regarded as a practice that can enable a company to move out of a commodity business by being able to identify something that, in its final product form, makes it distinctive and attractive to the customer. Good examples are to be found with the traditional potato, where it is available in its basic form and also as oven-baked chips, potato crisps and several other products. Similarly, in poultry meat, the ever-increasingly popular chicken is available as a conventional whole, and in fresh, frozen, or portioned forms, together with a legion of recipe dish lines. A comprehensive list of adding value options for poultry is provided in Table 2.1 to illustrate the potential scope.

Taking wheat as an illustration adds a different dimension to the practice. The bread-making variety is used to manufacture many different bread lines and some of course attract added value in presentation forms such as sandwiches, traditional puddings, and smörgåsbords.

However, the feed-wheat variety is used to provide dietary energy in the production of livestock, especially for pigs and poultry. Adding value to feed wheat therefore first starts when it is actually fed to livestock; subsequent value is then accumulated at various stages of the food chain until the housewife finally makes her choice of purchase. One could of course go back a further step in farm production, when feed wheat is grown as part of the crop rotation. Here it helps to upgrade the quality of the soil and, by definition

Table 2.1   Adding value to food products using chicken as the product range

Conventional consistent base	*Adding value*
1 LIVE BIRD	
Conventional farming	• Free range • Speciality breeds • Label specials of specific local communities
Skin colour – white	• Yellow
Bird size – average small medium and large	• Poussin (very small) • Extra large
2 PRIME PROCESSING – whole oven-ready bird	
Wet chilling	• Dry chilling (no added water)
Frozen – under –12°C	• Fresh +0-1°C
Including giblets	• Without giblets
Hand portioning	• Machine-assisted • Fully automatic
Hand de-boning	• Fully automatic e.g. mechanically recovered meat
3 SECONDARY/FURTHER PROCESSING	
Whole	• Portioned breast/leg/thigh/wings • Filleted
Portion	• De-boned (boneless) • De-skinned (skinless) • Chicken pieces
Raw – whole – portioned – pieces – +/– skin or bone – +/– skin and bone – sold as fresh/frozen/canned	• Cooked oven roast • Boiled/steamed • Pan or deep fried • Barbecued/spit roast • Microwaved • Smoked
– sold to retail/fast-food catering/institution	• Crumbed • Enrobed/coated/battered • Marinade • Stuffed
Cooked	• Sandwich filler • Fresh salad packs • Cold pies • Supplemented by sauces, stuffings, flavour enhancers, spices, etc.
Size/shape	• Basically any shape + any size
4 PACKAGING	
Packaging	• Basically anything required • Use of shelf-life extenders, e.g. through gas atmosphere technology • Solid materials, see-through, etc.

therefore, is adding value to the land. The chain really does not stop there as soil cultivation by ploughing, drainage and fertilizing as well as by harvesting, the choice of crops grown and the use of modern set-aside all add value to the biological potential of the soil as a growth medium. Similarly, the modern developments in agricultural machinery, weed control and soil sterilization technology, all contribute to upgrading one of the essential base materials on which the food industry depends.

This chapter uses the example of the food chain to illustrate:

● the complexity of the whole system;
● the infinite number of opportunities that exist for adding value;
● the need for integration among members of the chain if they are to add value and generate synergy.

The chapter also stresses that while organizations are members of at least one added-value chain, they are also individual businesses with individual objectives. The secret lies in the creation of effective networks for the ultimate benefit of all the members of the chain, and of course the customer.

Customer expectations

The food chain illustrated in Figure 2.1 is highly complex but the aim and purpose of all the participants is the definition of products of such quality that they generate repeat purchases by the customer. Without this, no business can survive. In our example of food the ultimate consumer, the member of the public, seeks a value proposition composed of:

● value for money,
● product quality,
● enjoyment from eating the product,
● availability and size,
● convenience and ease of handling,
● quantity and shelf life as stated on the package.

While the marketplace is an ever-changing scene, it is important to recognize that the true consumer reaction to purchasing any item is based on these listed factors. Opportunities for adding value can be found in each of these six components, from the simplest theme of improving the actual or apparent value for money, to the use of high technology in extending the shelf life of perishable products. See Table 2.2

The average consumer responds quickly to changes of quality and improvements in availability, convenience and ease of handing. This can be seen in:

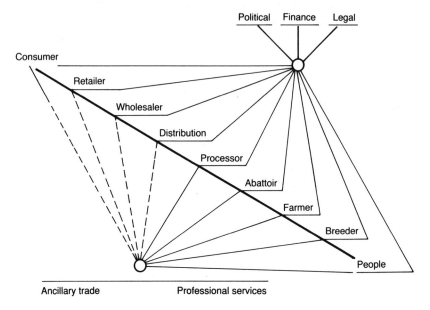

Figure 2.1 *The food chain*

- the choice and potential use of the food,
- the ease with which customers can visit the food store,
- the manner in which food items can be acquired from the shelves,
- service counters, till points and store trolleys,
- access to car parks.

The food market is composed of a wide variety of quality standards, which allow the consuming public the opportunity of selecting both by choice and by price, but within this climate the consumer requirement for 'enjoyment from eating the product' must still be regarded as a priority. All customers and consumers respond positively to those factors that provide and/or create enjoyment: food is no exception. If a higher level of enjoyment can be achieved by adding value in some form, then the opportunity for repeat business is enhanced.

Food plays a part in everyday living, and the quality of the regular daily main meal can provide an air of contentment and satisfaction. Equally it can create the opposite. In the former, it is the food selection and cooking skills that are applauded but, in the latter the source of purchase is invariably considered to be at fault! The challenge to the food industry and to all members of the food chain is therefore one of being able to guarantee full consistency in all aspects of product type and response – to ensure a degree of repeat business that maintains both consumer satisfaction and company profitability.

Table 2.2   Opportunities for adding value

Consumer requirement	Examples of adding value
Value for money	● 100% utilization of the product ● Minimum cooking loss ● Long shelf life
Product quality	● Consistently acceptable ● Brand/own label reputation ● Easy to handle
Enjoyment from eating the product	● Pleasing eating experience ● Full flavour ● No unpleasant after-effect
Availability and size	● Consistent availability ● No wastage ● Good portion control per person
Convenience and ease of handling	● Good packaging + unit size ● Product and packaging hygiene ● Handling off display from store to home.
Quantity Shelf life as stated on the package	● Accuracy ● Safety ● Confidence in brand/own label

Consistency is of special importance to the mail-order business, and with the modern development of such technology as image scanners, house-to-store direct computer links and micro-chip cash exchange, retailing could change its style to one where the consumers grow to trust more products and seek more convenient ways of shopping. Adding value in this way could well become commonplace in the near future.

The global food chain

The food chain is illustrated in its simplest form in Figure 2.1, but it is actually a complex systemic network. People play their part at all stages, and the same people are also part of the country's consuming public. Each sector is the customer of, or supplier to, another member of the chain and, in addition, each producer, processor and food company benefits from companies outside the

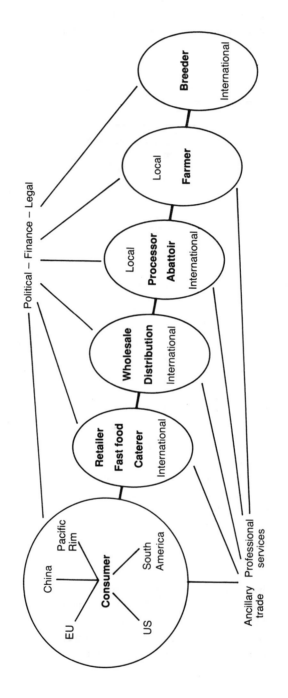

Figure 2.2 *The food chain in detail*

direct chain – including the financial and legal professions on the one hand and the veterinary and other dedicated services on the other. Every sector of the chain has its own, often unique, network of supplying industries, such as packaging, fuel, disinfectants, cleaning materials, clothing, construction, communication and health and safety. These are integral members of the total supply system and quite often through their connections up and down the chain they contribute substantially to the success and global participation of the food industry.

Figure 2.2 is a restated illustration of the food chain, highlighting the extent to which it has become international. The continuing search to bring an ever-expanding and diverse range of foods into the home market is encouraging many British food companies to develop sources of raw material and finished products on a worldwide basis. Modern communication systems, high-technology food manufacture and packaging, combined with a global transport infrastructure, facilitate the ready movement of long and short shelf-life products from any supplier into any retailer's store anywhere in the world. The continued investment in, and the economic emergence of, the Far East will continue to have an important impact on the food industry, creating both opportunities and threats.

The food chain encourages partnerships that can initiate progress. The fluidity of the style and approach to these alliances in the future will clearly be targeted at satisfying the international customer. Membership of the international food chain is another challenge of this decade; not only for providing extra opportunities to add value to an extremely wide range of products and production processes, but also for being able to take part in global competition, influence governments and industrial growth and, above all, for being able to deal successfully with the pressures, demands and opportunities of a changing environment.

It is interesting to recognize one very important subsidiary benefit of international trading. The introduction and application of improved food technology to meet the required customer specifications causes local standards to be upgraded. Improved yields compensate to some considerable degree for the movement of labour out of agriculture, creating an infrastructure that can greatly increase the productive capacity of the local community to meet the demands of an expanding population.

The significance of this is brought out by Table 2.3, which shows the declining proportion of people working in agriculture around the world between 1980 and 1990, and Table 2.4, which charts the speed of growth of world populations. This is an excellent example of how international trading can add value to the business structure of other parts of the world. All organizations in the food chain create very close working relationships up and down the chain, whereby the skills and products of one part of the world can interlink with the skills and processes of another, while everything depends on the detailed infrastructure of communication, transportation and technology transfer.

Table 2.3   Population active in agriculture (%)

	1980	1990
WORLD	49	45
Africa	65	61
North and Central America	15	13
Mexico	37	30
USA	4	3
South America	29	24
Brazil	31	24
Asia	63	58
Japan	11	6
China	74	68
Thailand	67	61
USSR	20	13
Oceania	19	17
Middle East	41	32
Europe	13	9
EC 12	9	6
Central	21	15

Source: EURIBRID Holland

Table 2.4   Population trends 1980–90 (millions)

	1980	1990	Change (%)
WORLD	4450	5288	+19
Africa	481	645	+34
North and Central America	373	428	+15
South America	240	297	+24
Asia	2583	3100	+20
USSR	266	292	+10
Oceania	23	27	+17
Middle East	151	186	+23
Europe	484	497	+3
EC 12 including former GDR	318	350	

Source: EURIBRID Holland

The rapid strides in bio-science will have a major impact but the skills needed to develop the true commercial advantage of such new technology will remain those of the practical farmer, the factory-line member, the transport driver/pilot, and other members of the complete team of people around whom the day-to-day food chain revolves.

In daily practice each member of the chain operates to technical and commercial specifications that are both agreed and regularly updated, with the prime objective of supplying the ultimate customer through the retail trade. The retailers, fast-food businesses, caterers, and the institutional sector all have very strong links with the general public and, as such, it is important that together they provide a very clear and practical specification for any particular product. This specification can then be implemented by farmers, factory processors and the participating ancillary trades. Obviously, without such a specification, and with so many different players in the food chain, it is more difficult to produce and process with any degree of consistency.

Change pressures

Retailing is a very vibrant sector, which must react to, as well as positively create and initiate, change. Change is brought about by many factors, including economic recession, available buying power, health patterns, the size of families and unemployment. The UK demographic picture over a 30-year timescale illustrates such events. See Table 2.5.

Two other examples of change are:

Table 2.5   The United Kingdom demographic change

	1971	1981	1991	2001 (estimated)
Population (millions)	55.5		57.5	59.0
Age profile - over 70s (millions)	8.3		10.9	11.3
People are living longer!				
Nos. of households (millions)	18.3	19.5	21.5	22.7
Average household size (persons)	2.91	2.70	2.50	2.44

Household size is decreasing, but the numbers of households is increasing: 60 per cent are of two persons or less!

One-person households (millions)	3.30	4.20	5.80	6.60

Such demographic change has to be quickly recognized by the retail/supply trade to provide products to meet a similarly rapid alteration in general eating habits and product preference.

- The increase in the number of UK citizens taking holidays overseas. (The British Tourist Authority has estimated that 1.5 million went abroad in 1951, 5 million in 1965 and 23.5 million in 1993.) This, naturally, creates an interest in food products from many other parts of the world. The British consumer quite rightly expects to be able to purchase Continental and Far Eastern dishes in the local High Street.
- The ever increasing number of women/housewives who form part of the UK total workforce. Approximate figures indicate that some 40 per cent of the total workforce are women and that some 70 per cent of women of employable age have some form of gainful employment on a full- or part-time basis. This creates pressure on the time available to shop; and, in turn, an ever-increasing demand for greater convenience, not only in shopping hours but also in the layout of the store; the amount of car-park space; the use of money, credit cards and cheques; and the number of till check-outs.

In addition, the pressure on time available after working hours inevitably means less time for cooking, and consequently convenience in food preparation also has greater emphasis. This, in turn, often influences the type of product purchased.

The decision to create overt added-value lines or processes is made jointly by many members of the chain. For example, in the production of retailer own-label products it is necessary for the retailer, the supplier, and the packaging teams to work closely together to develop a specification that provides the targeted products in a manner that suits all parties and that complies with any appropriate food legislation.

Over the last 20 years there has been an expanding interest in the nutritional content of food. This point is illustrated in the expanding interest in dietary information, and in how diet-related products are widely recognized as added-value lines. Slimming diets are popular and medical advice on dietary content is often sought. Physical fitness is always desired and commercially minded nutritionists present programmes that include advice on such foods as red meat and poultry. The general public does react to such publicity, and comparative values for any range of products are now freely available. This obviously influences consumer buying habits, and of course any professional retailer must react accordingly to maintain customer loyalty. Such change in consumer eating habits will never stop; retailers must always be aware of the potential for change, and in a highly competitive marketplace be prepared to react accordingly back through the food chain.

Table 2.6   Some of the relationships between consumer requirement and production in fresh poultry meat

PRODUCTION FACTORS	APPEARANCE	CLEANLINESS	COLOUR	SHAPE	FLAVOUR	MEAT YIELD	SUCCULENCE	TENDERNESS	WEIGHT	REJECTOR	DOWN GRADING
BIRD											
Quality of chicks				x		x			x		x
Breed			x	x		x			x		x
Sex				x		x	x	x	x		x
Age				x		x	x	x	x		x
DISEASE											
Its prevention					x	x			x		x
Treatment					x				x		x
Disinfection					x				x		x
FACTORY											
Handling of birds	x		x					x	x		x
Plucking	x	x	x				x	x			x
Evisceration	x	x	x			x	x	x	x		x
Chilling	x		x		x		x	x			x
Bagging	x	x			x						x
Despatch	x	x			x						x
FEED		x	x	x	x	x	x		x		x
FARM MANAGEMENT											
Housing					x	x	x		x		x
Brooding						x	x		x		x
Floor type					x				x		x
Litter type					x						x
Litter condition					x				x		x
Ventilation					x	x	x		x		x
Feeders and waterers				x		x	x	x	x		x
BIRD WEIGHT				x		x			x		x
PACKAGING											
Quality	x	x									x
Cleanliness	x	x									x
Sealing	x	x	x		x						x

x = Positive correlation

Satisfying customers

Eating quality is one important aspect of product assessment. Achieving consistency and/or creating new eating experiences are common approaches to adding value. Enjoyment by the consumer obviously stimulates repeat business, as we have said earlier. He/she will expect consistency in product quality, and ultimately enjoyment in eating, recommending to friends and neighbours those products which prove to be particularly satisfying. Equally of course failures in, and dislike of, any food product is likely to be publicized at an alarming speed!

Clearly the many components in producing, processing and manufacturing food can interrelate in a positive or a negative way. There is always the risk of failure, sometimes related to major problems such as food taint, meat toughness, or very short shelf life. Table 2.6 illustrates the complexity of the system linking production and processing with consumer needs and expectations. It shows some of the relationships between the consumer requirements and the production of fresh poultry meat; an 'x' indicates a positive correlation between two factors that will require a complete understanding to prevent a problem or maximize an opportunity. The data behind the preparation of Table 2.6 has been accumulated by the writer over 35 years in the production and retail industries and from the regular monitoring of poultry meat through the very exacting quality-control procedures of formal taste panels. Developing an extensive data bank on the eating quality relationships between the many commercial inputs to food production does provide a positive system of analysing effective 'due diligence' and ensures a positive damage-limitation programme. For example:

On the farm this involves
such aspects as

- Breed of animal/bird
- Feeds used and dietary formulation
- Welfare of all livestock
- Disease-control programme and products used
- Quality of grasses and other vegetation
- Hygiene programmes
- Environmental control
- Effluent disposal and drainage
- Transport

In the feed mill
such aspects as

- Building structure
- Drainage
- Water quality
- Effluent disposal
- Neighbouring factories

- Vermin control
- Hygiene control
- Disinfectants used
- Factory process
- Equipment installed

To all sectors
- People working in the system
- Personal hygiene
- Medical care
- Protective clothing

Quite simply every activity can have a bearing on the process of adding value. As a result, two-way communications are essential between every member of the food chain. One error can quickly destroy consumer confidence, especially if illness or customer complaints emerge.

Consumer protection is very important, with both consumers and their suppliers – retailers, fast-food outlets, caterers and institutional food providers – requiring complete confidence and assurance that modern farming techniques, factory processing and, for example, livestock disease control, are completely compatible with all aspects of human health, aesthetics, and food handling.

The full guarantee of complete food safety is not an option – it is a must!

Food production in its general sense is a high risk business. Risks of any sort cannot be tolerated. The benefit of such an approach is, of course, repeat business, where brand loyalty develops from safe food that is enjoyable to eat and contributes positively to the lifestyle of the ultimate consumer. The four dimensions of food safety are summarized in Figure 2.3.

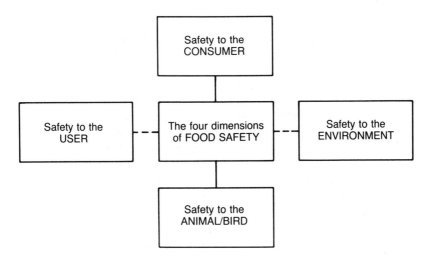

Figure 2.3 *The four dimensions of food safety*

Distribution systems

Disciplined temperature control to minimize risk in the handling and transportation of perishable foods offers another opportunity for adding value to the product range. Distributors have been able to reduce costs and improve efficiencies and turnaround times. For the consumer it has removed the risk and provided a trusted shelf life, as clearly stated on the product label.

A centralized distribution network, while controlling volume, accuracy of recording input and output data and product quality, can also add value by reducing wastage – reducing, for example, pilferage, out-of-life products, product damage and reject packaging.

Composite, multi-temperature food warehouses and trucks can accommodate the need for storing and transporting different food products at different temperatures. Frozen foods need to be kept at approximately –20 degrees centrigrade; cold chilled fresh meat and fish are handled at 0 degrees centrigrade; and fresh produce and provisions should be retained between +5 and +10 degrees centigrade. Grocery products such as biscuits, breakfast cereals, cakes and crisps should be kept at ambient temperature. Historically this has required five different types of truck.

A typical composite distribution warehouse is in the order of 25,000 square feet, with several sections that can be managed individually to take account of different handling and operating procedures. A modern temperature controlled trailer contains flexible bulkhead partitions and can be utilized as one, two or three sections at different temperatures. Usually the coolest would be at –20 degrees C, the middle at 0 degrees C and the third at +10 degrees C.

The management of quality

In an attempt to obtain and maintain the benefits of added-value activities, many food companies have committed themselves to Total Quality Management. Many readers will already be aware that TQM is *total* because it impacts on every aspect of a business and all areas of an organization. *Quality* becomes the primary objective of everyone in the organization by focusing each and every employee on pleasing their internal and external customers. It is *management* in that it sets the long- and short-term direction of an organization and provides ways and means to accomplish the direction by getting the most out of the prime resources of people and machines. Figure 2.4 summarizes the major aspects of TQM and emphasizes the critical importance of people.

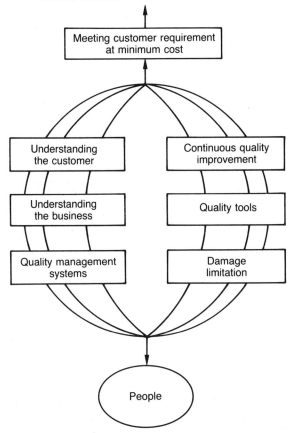

Figure 2.4   *Total quality management (adapted from Munro-Faure and Munro-Faure, 1993)*

The potential benefits are clearly recognizable:

- reduced costs,
- increased sales,
- increased customer loyalty,
- increased competitiveness,
- increased profit.

It is not easy to implement TQM effectively. Success requires a strong commitment and leadership from senior people in the organization.

At the 1994 Australia Poultry Information Exchange Dr Fred H Benoff succinctly summarized the four areas of leadership as:

1   *Customer focus* – where the essence is to work towards having customers brag about the company, the product quality, service, and value.

2   *Systems thinking* – such that operations are oriented to focus the organization on identifying and removing the causes of problems and working as a team both inter- and intra-departmentally.

3   *Visioning and planning* – presenting very clear directions for the future.

4   *People orientation* – interactions with all employees and colleagues in a way that promotes cooperation and a true team spirit. Table 2.7 summarizes this approach.

While quality management is always important, the appropriate TQM programme will be dependent upon the particular supply chain. Figure 2.5, for

Table 2.7   Four areas of leadership

CUSTOMER FOCUS	SYSTEMS THINKING
● Intense awareness of the customer. ● Seeks out and listens to the voice of the customer. ● Monitors and measures customer satisfaction. ● Strives to have customers brag. ● Recognizes the supremacy of the external customer over internal relationships.	● Understands the system and how the parts interact with each other, and works in cooperation with preceding and following stages to optimize the efforts of all stages. ● Breaks down barriers and promotes intra-system communication. ● Understands variation. ● Avoids tampering. ● Constantly searches and eliminates root causes. ● Seeks out and listens to the voice of the process. ● Ensures continuous improvement. ● Ensures the use of the PDSA cycle.*
VISIONING AND PLANNING	PEOPLE ORIENTATION
● Creates, maintains and communicates the vision of the future state of the company. ● Helps identify priorities, opportunities and vulnerabilities. ● Provides long-term direction and long-term goals. ● Models organizational values and integrity.	● Understands that all people are unique individuals. ● Creates trust. ● Serves as coach and council, not judge. ● Is interested in learning if anyone is outside the system, in need of special help. ● Nurtures intrinsic motivation and pride of workmanship. ● Listens and learns. ● Promotes cooperation.

* PSDA cycle . . . Plan-Do-Study-Act cycle.

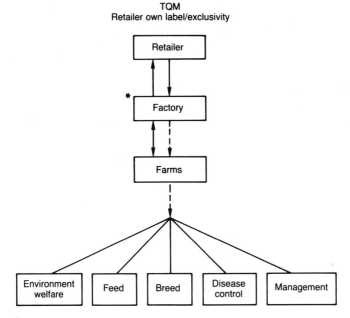

TQM
Retailer own label/exclusivity

*Specification responsibility

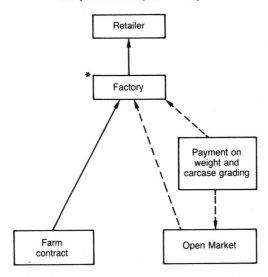

TQM
Factory selection/complete flexibility

*Specification responsibility

Figure 2.5 *Two areas of market style*

example, contrasts the supply chain for own-label products, where the retailer drives the system, and production of food products for specific contracts or the open market, where the retailer is essentially selecting from what is available.

It is important to appreciate that when the supply chain becomes international, it can be increasingly difficult to control quality standards in different countries and cultures. In addition, as illustrated in Figure 2.6, it is all too easy for complacency to set in once initial targets have been achieved. The important message again is consistency.

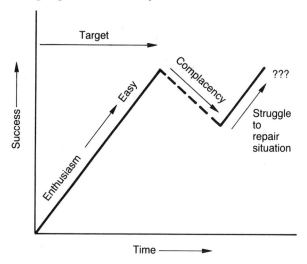

Figure 2.6 *Right mental attitude*

The value-adding network

We have seen earlier how the food chain comprises several stages and several interrelated, interdependent organizations. Together they comprise a network of

Supplier ⟶ (Buyer)
              (Supplier) ⟶ (Buyer)
                              (Supplier)   linkages

with a series of agreements that add value and in aggregate ideally meet customers' expectations. The ultimate purpose of customer satisfaction is not in question, but it must be recognized that:

● The organizations may be members of more than one supply chain.
● Members of the system will have a set of stakeholders exclusive to them.
● Each organization may well have specific objectives that are not always fully compatible with those of the other members of the chain. Compromises and trade-offs will be required.

Value then can be expanded as we progress through the food chain, and each step has the ability to demonstrate this point. However, unless appropriate partners in the chain are involved, the actual benefit may fall below expectations. The proverbial statement that 'one cannot make a silk purse out of a sow's ear' can be very pertinent! One single weak link in the chain can seriously damage the quality of product, company reputation, and chance of generating repeat business for all other members. In this last section therefore we examine the individual components of the complete chain in more detail, in an attempt to clarify those criteria that affect their contribution and the process of adding value.

It should be obvious that certain added-value criteria apply at various stages in the chain, while others are exclusive to specific stages. It should also be apparent that value is affected in aggregate terms by a large number of variables, making for a very complex system, one that cannot be easily controlled. It requires each member to take a holistic and service-oriented viewpoint and at the very least ask: 'Who is my customer's customer?' The outcome should be true quality outputs – comprising accurate quality inputs for the next link in the supply chain. In this way value is added consistently.

Factors such as hygiene, the utilization of modern technology and good management skills can also add value right through the chain, but other factors are more sector specific, namely:

Breeders	Credibility of consistent performance, new product development, health status and customer service.
Farmers	Repeatable performance, speciality skills, direct involvement with other members of the food chain.
Abattoir, further processor	Location infrastructure such as hygiene and temperature controls. Technical efficiency, logistics and computer control.
Distribution	Depots and vehicles to accommodate products with different needs. Hygiene control, fast order processing and exact schedules.
Wholesalers	International trading and currency skills. Knowledge of food legislation.
Retailer, caterer and fast food chain	Image and reputation of brand. Various aspects of service for the final consumer. New product innovation.

Medical and veterinary professionals, together with experts in such fields as vermin control, environmental management and pollution, can all support the adding-value process. They often have extensive experience accumulated through a wide range of contacts throughout the whole industry. They can help spread best practices. Members of the government can also add value, in particular by ensuring that appropriate information is relayed to those people in the food chain who can benefit from it, and by encouraging suitable responses, say, to changes in European legislation.

The above criteria merely illustrate the vast array of variables impacting on the adding-value system for food products. It is a complex system, whose effectiveness lies in the hands of the component parts. Although these parts are individual organizations, it is in everyone's interest for each company to appreciate its role and contribution to the wider system.

We showed earlier that it is important for retailers, restaurants and fast-food chains to send signals and demands back down the supply chain in an attempt to foster new adding-value opportunities. New opportunities can start anywhere in the chain, and possibly be introduced by those outsiders with a direct interest, such as feed suppliers and technologists. The keys to success lie in effective communications networks, receptiveness to new ideas and the perspective of mutual inter-dependency.

Conclusion

The practice of adding value in the food industry has become an integral part of business survival for the members of the industry. Critically important value can be added at any stage of the food chain, and it can be expanded as progress is made through the chain. It is only feasible, though, if each player in the chain recognizes the disparate needs and disciplines of the various sources of their raw materials, on the one hand, and the specification and demands of the subsequent customers, on the other.

The true merit of adding value, at whatever stage of the food chain chosen, can only be fully realized by a rigid senior management control programme, clearly identifying the strengths and weaknesses of the action taken and then analysing the opportunities and threats available. Total quality management provides an opportunity to take advantage of the practice and potential of an adding-value perspective, and through the very consistency of added-value measurement and presentation the appropriate customer can build up confidence in the source of supply and, in turn, generate a profitable repeat business.

Editor's note: Reinforcing points made in other chapters in this handbook, 'strategic leadership' and 'the corporate culture and values' are critically important determinants of strategic effectiveness.

Reference

Munro-Faure, L and Munro-Faure, M (1993) *Achieving Quality Standards*, Pitman, London.

Understanding strategic relationships
Nigel Campbell

Introduction

Strategic relationships, that is those of concern to current and future competitive advantage, most often exist with customers and suppliers. Indeed, the successful management of supplier relationships is one of the reasons frequently cited for the success of the Japanese automobile industry (Dyer and Ouchi, 1993). In addition, depending on the nature of the business, there may also be important relationships with research institutes, with local or central government, with joint venture or alliance partners, and with other business organizations. According to Tom Peters, the intensity, reach and breadth of these business relationships are the company's most valuable assets.

A relationship is strategic if the company is very dependent on the other organization for vital resources. A customer may take 50 per cent of the company's output; a supplier may control the availability and price of a vital raw material; a research institute may be the main source of new technology; or a strategic alliance may open access to a new market.

The strategic value of such relationships lies not just in the short-term economic consequences of cancellation. Such relationships frequently embody specialized knowledge and capabilities built up over time through formal and informal exchanges. These intangible assets can have a direct bearing on competitive advantage. How competitive would Marks & Spencer, Toyota or Benetton be without their supplier partnerships?

Of course not all a company's relationships are strategically important. Many include little information exchange and hence do not have the potential to lead to specialized knowledge and capabilities. Instead they are conducted at arm's length through the marketplace. For example, the relationship with a supplier of standard office supplies, bought on price, is of no strategic importance.

Direct relationships are not the only ones that can be of strategic significance. If customer A has direct relationships with suppliers B and C, then the nature and development of the relationship A–C may be of great significance for supplier B. In industrial markets companies are frequently embedded in a network of relationships where their strategic development is constrained by their position relative to other actors in the network. Consider, for example, the market for car tyres. General Motors, Ford, Toyota, Nissan and a dozen or more others are main customers; Goodyear, Michelin, Bridgestone and a handful of other firms are the main suppliers. What happens in the relationship between Ford and Goodyear can be of great importance to Michelin, whether it is a supplier to Ford or not. Where an industrial market, such as car tyres, has a limited number of customers and suppliers, a network of relationships links the parties together. Changes in one part of the network have important repercussions elsewhere.

In addition to the relationships that form between customers, suppliers and competitors in business markets, there are two other types of group affiliation, both prevalent in Japan. First come the federations of supplier firms centred round a single dominant manufacturing company, like those linked to Toyota or NEC. Second are the bank-centred groupings, like the Mitsui or Mitsubishi groups, the modern successors of the old *zaibatsu*. In these latter groupings presidents of member companies meet monthly, and their directors serve on the boards of other group firms. Members generally own a small fraction of each other's shares and generally rely for funds on banks and other financial institutions in their group. Where price and quality are competitive they tend to buy from and sell goods to each rather than from and to outside firms. Finally, in many cases, social ties among member firms have deep roots (Badaracco, 1991, p. 93).

So far the discussion has been about external relationships between independent organizations. Internal or intra-organizational relationships can also be strategic. In manufacturing companies the sales and production departments must cooperate fully to make the best use of production facilities and meet quality and delivery standards. To adjust to changing consumer demands and achieve an efficient production load, shared knowledge and commitment is needed, and a spirit of mutual respect. The same is true in large multinationals with geographically dispersed production and sales divisions. As Bartlett and Ghoshal (1989) have observed, the management of the multinational is much concerned with the development of effective relationships between the subsidiaries and head office and between the subsidiaries themselves.

In short, strategic relationships can be of two types – external, between independent or quasi-independent firms, or internal, between different departments, divisions or subsidiaries of one organization.

These internal and external relationships are formed between people. In each case a certain number of people from each side interact together. Their interaction occurs in the daily course of handling transactions, or they may meet more specifically as a task force or project group to sort out a particular issue. Inevitably these interactions have a social component, whose importance is well illustrated by this quote from Jack Welch of GE: 'I have dealt with Toshiba for 15 years, and it's always been a very easy relationship. When things go awry, a call to Sato-san will take care of problems in 24 hours' (Schendler, 1992, p. 45).

The importance of interpersonal relationships is also illustrated when salespersons or account executives leave a company to join a rival firm and take key customers with them. In such cases the bond between the account executive and the customer is stronger than the bond between the account executive and his/her previous employer.

The rest of this chapter is divided into three parts. The first deals with the nature of the intangible assets (the specialized knowledge and capabilities) that strategic relationships develop. We need to understand how individuals and teams acquire tacit knowledge and how this contributes to a firm's administrative heritage, core competence and organizational capability.

The next part looks at the literature on how relationships are governed or controlled. What organizational forms provide the incentives to hold the relationships together so that value is created? This section proposes that each relationship is governed by a unique mix of the same three organizational forms – market, hierarchy and network. Furthermore, the strategic ones – those that lead to important cost savings, or new technical and market initiatives – are, in large part, held together by the network form, where friendships and social obligations are sustained by commitment to shared goals and values.

The final section discusses the management of strategic relationships, which, in the conclusion, leads to the view that the management of strategy becomes the management of interactive behaviour.

Throughout the chapter a number of the illustrations and examples will be drawn from Japanese industry. This choice is deliberate. The Japanese economy provides many examples of strategic relationships. It has been described as an economy of 'alliance capitalism' in which an important aspect is

. . . the strategic forging of long-term intercorporate relationships across a broad spectrum of markets: with banks and insurance companies in the capital market, with *sogo shosha* (general trading companies) in primary goods markets, with subcontractors in component parts markets, and with competitors in new technology development (Gerlach and Lincoln, 1992, p. 493).

Relationships between *keiretsu* members, between buyers and suppliers, and even between competitors, are important in Japanese industry. Burton and Saelens (1994) and Teramoto *et al.* (1994) also report that Japanese companies are more successful in managing their strategic alliances than Western competitors. In addition, in many of these relationships friendship and a diffuse sense of personal obligation between individuals plays an important role (Dore, 1983, p. 460).

The intangible value of strategic relationships

All relationships are held together by individuals, and therefore the starting point for understanding their intangible value must be the knowledge and skills that individuals hold. There is an important distinction between two kinds of human knowledge. Tacit knowledge is personal, but subjective knowledge based on direct experience (Polanyi, 1958). Tacit knowledge is difficult to articulate and communicate. For example, it is the knowledge of how to ride a bicycle, or how to create a moving musical performance. Explicit knowledge, on the other hand, is public and can be communicated verbally and in writing.

Not surprisingly, the two kinds of knowledge are acquired differently. Explicit knowledge comes from formal study, books and lectures; tacit knowledge comes from experience, observation and action. While a copy of the blueprints will go a long way, they are far from all that is necessary to build and operate a plant efficiently.

Experts combine both types of knowledge into 'chunks' of understanding (Prietula and Simon, 1989). For example, a doctor, chess player or chief engineer builds up these chunks as he becomes familiar with the pattern of activity. He becomes expert as he learns to ignore irrelevant activities and concentrate on critical ones. In a new situation the expert activates relevant chunks of knowledge and, without seeming to examine the situation, moves rapidly to a course of action. In many vocations around 10 years of serious effort are necessary before a person becomes expert.

An important difference between medical expertise and management expertise is that the latter is usually company-specific. It grows out of an intimate, working familiarity nurtured over years of effort. Successful problem-solving in a business depends critically on the manager's personal network and his knowledge of the capabilities of his staff and colleagues.

Just as individuals have tacit knowledge, so do successful teams, small groups and departments. Knowledge resides in teams in two ways (Badaracco, 1991, p. 84). First, many tasks require too much knowledge for a single individual to grasp in its entirety. Hence, people with complementary knowledge work together. The second kind of knowledge that resides in groups is their knowledge of how to work with each other. Some of this knowledge is a kind of group know-how, a tacit understanding of how the people in the group can best work together. This knowledge is gained from the experience of working together, and it leads to mutual respect, open-mindedness and good judgement in allocating tasks.

Firms consist of many teams, groups and departments. The intangible assets they develop, like know-how and capability, are receiving increasing attention in the strategy literature, especially among those scholars who take a resource-based view of strategy, much as Itami (1982), Rumelt (1984), Wernerfelt (1984), and Barney (1986).

Nelson and Winter (1982) suggest that routine interactions between individuals, based on tacit knowledge, are an important source of a firm's capabilities. Tallman (1991) suggests that the tacit nature of some organizational knowledge helps a firm to protect its strategies from imitation. Collis (1991) has analysed developments in the global market for ball bearings and has shown how intangible assets, acquired through the operation of complex social phenomena, contribute to explaining competitive behaviour. This suggests that throughout their history firms acquire habits embedded in contact patterns, information exchanges, and regular routines (Dosi, Teece and Winter, 1990; Teece, Pisano and Shuen, 1990).

Many of these contact patterns and information exchanges are between individual company members, but they also extend to old established suppliers, customers and other business partners. In part, these relationships constrain the future strategy of the firm. Thus strategic development is grounded in what Bartlett and Ghoshal (1989) call administrative heritage, a set of tangible and intangible factors that give the firm a distinctive character and are part of the context for strategic decisions (Bower, 1970).

Preserving their distinctive character is very important for Japanese companies. In most Japanese companies an important function of top management is to preserve the company's heritage of beliefs, traditions and business contacts. For example, at Sharp, some time is devoted at every board meeting to discuss the prospects for new products. This tradition derives from the founder, Mr Hayakawa, who was an inventor. Hence Sharp is skilful at developing unique new products. Another example from Sharp is its policy of subcontracting the management of its finished product warehouses. Despite the need for the very close integration of this activity with factory production and sales receipts, Sharp uses an outside firm to manage its warehouses throughout the world. Naturally this relationship is of great strategic importance.

Strategic relationships also make a contribution to what Prahalad and Hamel (1990) call core competence – the collective learning that enables the organization to bring together technologies and production skills and thus react quickly to changing conditions. For example, in its approach to production Toyota has developed the *kanban*, or just-in-time system, into a 'core competence'. The *kanban* itself is just a small piece of paper, or a metal tag, attached to a container of parts, which indicates where and when the container should arrive. But the *kanban* system is more than just a scheduling device. Toyota executives call the system 'the essence of Toyota and its relationships'. The system requires intimate, continuous and detailed working relationships and information flows among firms. These relationships are social as well as technical and economic.

An example of a company exploiting its technological core competence was Minebea's entry into semi-conductor manufacture (Collis, 1991, p. 59) when capacity utilization was at 50 per cent, prices had fallen 30 per cent in one year, four other Japanese companies dominated the market with 76 per cent world market share, and the minimum capital investment for entry was over $150 million (Yoffie, 1988). Minebea went ahead because its top management believed that they had the necessary 'core competence' to outperform their rivals. By 1990, when Minebea was the world's largest producer of 250K Drams, their production of 50 million units was still only one-tenth of their production of precision miniature bearings. In other words, they already knew a lot about the manufacture of high tolerance, miniature products.

Technological competence does not come only from the work done by the firm's own researchers. Relationships with research institutes, university professors and innovative suppliers and customers frequently play an important role (Hakansson, 1987). Equally, strategic alliances have played a vital role in building the technological core competencces of many Japanese companies. Hitachi, Toshiba, Mitsubishi Heavy Industries and many others have used alliances to access partners' skills, and develop their own competences (Lei and Slocum, 1992). In small, compact cars GM, Ford and Chrysler have cut back production and are increasingly relying on Isuzu, Suzuki, Daewoo and Hyundai, which are moving rapidly down the learning curve and building a base for future domination of this industry.

Another concept related to core competence is organizational capability (Collis, 1991). While competence focuses on the specific technical and production skills and related assets that distinguish the firm from its competitors, organizational capability represents the ability of managers to innovate and adapt to external change. Collis (1991) suggests that, while this capability is necessary to maintain and develop any core competence, it can also be a source of competitive advantage in its own right. This is likely to arise when individuals, committed to the success of the firm, have created an effective interpersonal network. Extensive information sharing, within such a network, will help the firm avoid 'organizational inertia' (Ghemawat, 1990) and adapt itself to changed circumstances.

The development of Toshiba's laptop provides an example of an effective in-house interpersonal network formed between middle managers. Initially Toshiba developed a laptop because of its failure in the market for conventional PCs. Despite poor acceptance in Europe and America, the laptop project was kept alive by the interaction between three key individuals. These individuals, one in overseas sales, one in production, and one in planning, had all joined Toshiba at the same time, so they knew each other well. They were enthusiastic, and believed in the product's potential, and they could point to evidence from people within Toshiba who found the product very useful.

Another example is Sharp's approach to technical opportunities. Its approach is to maintain a commitment, at a low level of resources, to a wide range of technologies associated with optoelectronics. Then as soon as a promising application emerges, Sharp invests heavily to exploit the opportunity. This organizational capability has been developed over the years from the collective experience of Sharp's senior and middle managers. Sharp's leading position in liquid crystal displays emerged from this approach.

Organizational capability also extends to relationships outside the firm. Marks & Spencer has a special capability in handling relations with its textile suppliers, as does Toyota with its cascade of component suppliers. A striking example is the American company Lewis Galoob Toys, which has only 100 employees to run the entire business. Independent inventors and leisure companies come up with the product concepts, while outside specialists do most of the design and engineering. Manufacturing is subcontracted to Hong Kong and distribution is handled by manufacturers' representatives working on commission. Accounts receivable are collected by an independent credit corporation. In other words, Galoob is an intermediary that simply hooks all these independent specialists together.

To summarize, through the interactions and contact patterns of key individuals both inside and outside the company collective learning takes place, tacit knowledge is accumulated, and habits, beliefs and traditions are formed. These are the building blocks of the company's administrative heritage, core competence and organizational capability. Hence, the firm's intangible assets are created in relationships and cannot be separated from them (Hakansson and Snehota, 1989, p. 532).

How relationships are governed

The subject of governance structures cannot be reviewed in depth in this chapter. It would take too long to review all the literature on transaction costs (Coase, 1952; Williamson, 1975), as well as work on agency theory (Jensen and Meckling, 1976; Fama, 1980) and new theories of the firm (Aoki, Gustafsson and Williamson, 1990).

What is clear is that many of the relationships already described are not organized through either a market or a hierarchy (Ouchi 1980, Miles and Snow 1986, Thorelli 1986, Jarillo 1988). This has led to new explanations, of which three are presented here – those by Reve (1990), Powell (1990) and Hakansson and Snehota (1989).

Reve's (1990) approach comes from his attempt to develop a contract theory of the firm. He suggests that the firm can be conceptualized as consisting of two sets of contracts. First are internal contracts between the firm and its employees, through which the firm acquires the core skills needed to obtain a competitive position. These contracts include incentives for the employees, to ensure that the skills are kept in place. Second come external contracts, which govern bilateral relationships, such as joint ventures, licensing, franchising or other types of coalitions, or agreements, which cannot be managed through the market. Firms enter into these relationships to obtain skills and resources complementary to their own core skills. As with internal contracts, incentives, this time interorganizational incentives, are needed to sustain these bilateral relationships. Thus in Reve's formulation:

Firm = f (Core skills and organizational incentives plus complementary skills and interorganizational incentives)

Reve defines core skills and complementary skills as physical assets and investments, as well as organizational routines and culture. In other words he acknowledges the importance of intangible assets.

Reve (1990, p. 51) argues that there are two main types of control or incentive.

> In principle internal contracts rely on hierarchical controls and external contracts rely on relational controls . . . What is typically found in both cases is a mixture of hierarchical and relational elements . . .

Hierarchical controls are used when it is easy to measure and monitor results. Where performance is difficult to measure and employees have firm-specific knowledge, other relational mechanisms are relevant. These include socialization and peer pressure, where the incentive is promotion, status, participation in decision-making, etc.

When it comes to interorganizational incentives, the interacting parties seek economic self-interest. Hence the weaker partner tries to protect himself from hierarchical control by not becoming too dependent on the stronger party. Alternately, the parties rely on relational norms, resulting from social ties, trust and solidarity. The parties recognize their mutual interdependence and they seek cooperative solutions together. However, Reve (1990) also accepts that frequently both forms of governance co-exist.

The importance of relational norms in explaining the duration and stability of external relationships has been documented in empirical studies by Hakansson, 1987 (large Swedish manufacturing companies), Contractor and Lorange, 1988 (international business), and Dore, 1983 (Japanese textiles). In networks of Italian small and mid-sized textile firms, Lorenzoni and Ornati (1988, p. 55) found 'unconventional mechanisms of coordination' guiding the collaborative exchanges, including trust, reciprocity, and mutual adjustment.

Powell (1990) has proposed that these relationships are a distinct 'network' form of organization. A network exists where relationships place a heavy emphasis on cooperation, reciprocity, mutual interdependence, communication based on trust and an informal atmosphere of mutual benefit. In contrast, market governance relies mainly on price, and hierarchy depends on administrative authority. Bradach and Eccles (1985) noted that these ideal types are often combined.

A combination of governance structure seems to be characteristic of Japanese supplier–customer relationships. First, a hierarchy pertains in relationships with suppliers and customers. Suppliers are always of lower status (the Japanese say that the customer is God) and they can be ranked as first, second or third level suppliers, as in the case of the Toyota *keiretsu*. But, second, Toyota's undoubted ability to tell suppliers what to do is constrained by mutual interdependence and by social ties and obligations. Third, market forces are also at work, and suppliers must keep abreast of the latest developments, or they will find that orders for the next model go to a competitor (Asanuma, 1989).

In addition to the work of Reve (1990) and Powell (1990), another stream of research, primarily dealing with business markets, is relevant to this discussion. Originating in the University of Uppsala in the mid-1970s the research programme has included collaborators in Britain and France. The research originated from the need to find a way to describe the long-lasting close relationships frequently found between customers and suppliers in business markets. The original focus on dyadic relationships was subsequently extended to the network of relationships with suppliers, customers and competitors.

The 'interaction' approach (Hakansson, 1982) adopted to analyse the relationships treats each relationship as subject to market forces, since each party is assumed to pursue its economic self-interest. Conflict is possible as well as collaboration. A hierarchical influence can also be present if the size and power of one party is much greater than that of the other. A small supplier then becomes dependent on a large customer and must follow whatever guidelines are imposed. Social exchange, as in Powell's (1990) network form, arises to varying degrees. If both sides have a good experience of working together, it can lead to trust and mutual cooperation.

Following on from these three explanations, we propose that relationships are governed by some mix of market, hierarchy and network. The different nature of these organizational forms is summarized below:

Market   mutual independence; arms length or price-based external relationship; internal relationships have results-based remuneration (up or out) and internal competition.

Hierarchy   dependence; both parties accept that one party has legitimate authority to dominate the other as in franchising, captive distribution or captive suppliers; internal relationships based on employers' power, rules should be followed and monitoring is close.

Network   mutual interdependence; external relationships based on trust and mutual benefit as in close buyer–seller relationships and strategic alliances; internal relationships are long-term, employees are socialized and values shared.

We can now ask which of these organizational forms is most important for developing the intangible assets discussed in the previous section. Clearly these assets will not come from the market form of organization, since interaction patterns are, by definition, limited. Each party pursues its economic self-interest and looks to the relationship to provide an economic reward.

In a hierarchy interaction is more frequent, and there may be great scope for the weaker party to develop its capability, but less scope for the stronger side. For example, in a franchising arrangement the franchisee has much to learn from the franchisor. Furthermore the franchisee must normally comply with certain guidelines and instructions from the franchisor. Frequently the relationship remains fairly formal. However, some franchisors, like the Body Shop or Benetton, take steps to create a closer partnership with franchisees. They exchange ideas and develop the business together. Where this happens, contact frequency increases and the social component of the relationship becomes more prominent. In effect Benetton and the Body Shop have converted a hierarchical relationship into a network form.

Hence, since the network form thrives on regular interaction and social ties it is the most likely organizational form to lead to the development of competences and capabilities of benefit to each side of the relationship.

The special importance of the social component in the network form becomes clear when the start-up of relationships is considered. Relationships start when one party initiates a contact, triggered by its perception of the potential value of the relationship. Hakansson and Snehota (1989, p. 535) suggest that the perception of relationship potential is largely determined by social interaction.

For a relationship to go beyond the initial contact, each side must perceive the actions and reactions of the other party in a favourable light. The actions can be planned, but this can hardly be the case with reactive behaviour, as Hakansson and Snehota (1989, p. 536) point out. Like the chess player or the doctor, the manager's reactions to a new situation can only be guided by norms and values, based on past experience. To react appropriately, individuals have to internalize the organization's norms and values and have a clear sense of the structural and dynamic properties of its network of relationships and its preferred long-term position. To achieve this level of understanding of their organization and its context, individuals need extensive socialization.

In the next section we shall see what role social exchange and socialization play in the successful management of strategic relationships.

Management of strategic relationships

This chapter is mainly concerned with those relationships that play an important role in developing the intangible assets of the firm – the heritage (beliefs, reputation, traditions), core competence and organizational capability of the firm. These relationships are governed by a mixture of market, hierarchy and network. In the previous section we have suggested that social interactions in the network form are most important and that, if they are to work successfully, the key individuals handling the relationship must themselves have a deep knowledge of their own company.

To investigate this question further, we will look at three different cases. The first is the coordination of production and sales divisions in large Japanese multinationals, the second the management of close buyer–seller relationships, with examples from the Japanese automobile industry, and the third the management of strategic alliances.

Coordinating production and sales in Japanese multinationals

The divisions in many Japanese multinationals are not fully self-contained and a strong functional emphasis prevails (Japan Development Bank, 1989). In most organizations sales and production divisions are separate profit centres. The production divisions are organized around technologies and products. They control manufacturing plants, at home and overseas, and they have their own product development facilities.

Second, there are the sales divisions handling a range of products suitable for a particular customer group. For example, many Japanese electronics companies have separate sales divisions for consumer products, industrial products and components. Overseas there is usually a sales subsidiary in each major country, which is divided into consumer, industrial and component divisions.

Relationships between sales and production divisions are handled by negotiation and bargaining (market), but they are also subject to intervention by senior management (hierarchy) and to the influence of long-standing interpersonal contacts and shared commitments (network). Coordination based on each of these organizational forms is explained in more detail below:

- *Market-based coordination.* Sales and production divisions are separate profit centres. Sales divisions are not obliged to take the quantities proposed by the production divisions. They must negotiate and reach agreement on the volumes, prices and features of the products they plan to exchange. With many overseas locations and forty or more product ranges, coordination other than through an internal market would be very difficult. An open negotiation means that conflict between the needs of the market and the trajectories of the technologies are not suppressed, but rather brought into the open to stimulate innovation.
- *Hierarchical coordination.* At one time Matsushita had two divisions making cassette recorders, both of which were available through the same sales division. Eventually it became clear which was preferred by the customers. The head office then intervened to order one of the divisions to cease production. This is an example of top management controlling resource allocation. Top management also influences the relationships by controlling the domain of each division. Sometimes two production divisions are merged to realize technology synergy. At other times a production division is split up to give more autonomy to competing technologies.
- *Social coordination.* Coordination between production and sales divisions takes place in an atmosphere of trust and commitment. There are contractual elements to the relationships but they are obligational (Sake, 1990). Obligational relationships are fostered by common striving to achieve the targets set for the parent company, and by the commitments built up during discussions about product development. The sales division can hardly refuse to sell a product that has resulted from a joint development effort.

To achieve coordination with the overseas sales companies Sharp has regular six-monthly meetings. Senior managers from the overseas companies stay in Osaka for two weeks and attend a series of meetings with each of the production divisions. At these meetings shipments are agreed, transfer prices renegotiated and plans for the launch of new products updated. Since each party to the discussions is a separate profit centre, the negotiations are frequently tough, but of course all concerned share a common set of values and a common commitment to the long-term welfare of Sharp. In addition, outside the meetings there are many informal contacts between managers who have built up personal relationships over many years.

The importance of the social aspect is illustrated by the fact that non-Japanese managers almost never participate in these vital meetings. Even the Japanese trading companies that have had overseas offices for more than 100 years have found it best to keep Japanese nationals in the senior positions. A section manager in Brazil can then speak to his opposite number in London and arrange a deal, relying on a common set of values and standards for conducting business that each has internalized after many years in the same company. Each is thoroughly familiar with his own business, but also with the norms and values of the parent company.

To summarize, social interaction, based on shared understandings, plays the most important role in the coordination of sales and production in Japanese multinationals. However, these social processes are regulated by occasional interventions from top management, and they are subject to the pressures of negotiation and bargaining between profit centres.

Managing close buyer–seller relationships

For the buying company close supplier relationships reduce purchasing and production costs and improve quality and innovation (Dyer and Ouchi, 1993). Close relationships mean fewer suppliers and therefore lower purchasing costs. In 1986 General Motors needed one buyer for every 2,000 cars produced, while Toyota needed only one buyer for every 10,600 cars produced (McMillan, 1990). Actually these figures do not convey the full extent of the difference, because the buyers for General Motors were only buying 50 per cent of the car, whereas at Toyota they were buying 75 per cent.

A supplier with a close, long-term relationship with a customer can justify substantial investments in plant, equipment and personnel to serve the customer. Plants can be located near the customer to reduce inventory and transportation expenses. For instance, a survey of twenty-five Toyota suppliers found that the average distance from the plant was 17 miles (Dyer and Ouchi, 1993). Engineers can also be dedicated to working on a particular customer's requirements. They can invest in developing ideas and plans for the next model well in advance.

To achieve a close buyer–seller relationships along the lines of partnerships in Japan, the following activities are necessary (Dyer and Ouchi, 1993):

- Work together jointly to define needs, to establish priorities and to solve problems.
- Meet frequently and regularly; include courtesy visits by senior managers; share technical and cost information to improve performance.
- Make significant investments to meet the unique needs of the other party.
- Focus on total cost and quality, and work together to minimize all the costs in the value chain.
- Use flexible contracts, ones that share gains and losses as market conditions change.
- Identify and implement practices that develop trust, such as share swaps, transferring employees and starting work before the contract is signed.

The emphasis in this list is on working together, sharing information, avoiding rigid contracts and developing trust. There are many parallels between these external buyer–seller relationships and the internal coordination of production and sales departments described in the previous paragraphs. Although the suppliers are legally independent, they frequently act as in-house divisions. Suppliers frequently send engineers to work at the customer's technical centre on a regular basis. For example, Dyer and Ouchi (1993) report that Toyota had 350 engineers from suppliers working at its main technical centre in Japan.

However, it would be wrong to leave the impression that the relationship between Japanese car makers and their suppliers is a cosy one. One way in which the car companies ensure that this does not happen is to encourage competition from at least one other supplier. To do this, they are willing to give extra help to a weaker supplier. Nissan and Toyota have at least one consultant for every four to six suppliers. The free assistance the consultants supply puts pressure on the suppliers to innovate and improve to stay ahead of the competition.

Forcing suppliers to improve continuously forces them to reduce their costs continuously, and Japanese buyers then reap the benefits through lower prices. The worst mistake that a supplier can make is to take advantage of a customer's loyalty and overcharge. This can ruin a relationship, as it breaks the feeling of trust and shared objectives.

Finally, Japanese car makers are not averse to using their power to put pressure on their suppliers. In Japan the system Toyota uses is sometimes referred to as Toyota 'hell'. On the other hand, the suppliers realize that they will receive help if they get into difficulty, and only those unwilling or unable to keep up will be cut off completely.

To summarize, close buyer-seller relationships in the Japanese car industry give both sides important benefits in lower costs and more rapid innovation. Each side develops new capabilities, and the competitive advantage of the partnership is enhanced. This is achieved through intensive interactions, taking place in an atmosphere of trust and open communication. A heavy dose of social obligation, invigorated by market mechanisms and regulated by occasional hierarchical intervention, can be very effective in bringing complementary resources together to create new initiatives.

Strategic alliances

Instead of competing blindly across all segments in all markets, companies are increasingly collaborating with their competitors to gain the scale, skills or the market access they need to exploit the precise areas where they do have a durable competitive advantage.

Recently the interest of practitioners and academics in strategic alliances has reached fever pitch. The Winter 1994 issue of *Directors and Boards* is entirely devoted to this subject, and according to Rigby and Buchanan (1994) many companies in Europe and America now generate 50 to 60 per cent of their sales from alliances. Rigby and Buchanan report that the number of international strategic alliances has been growing at a rate of over 30 per cent per year, that NEC has 130 joint efforts underway, and that IBM claims to have established over 4,000 alliances.

Much of the vast literature is concerned with telling businessmen how to form and operate successful strategic alliances (Banks and Baranson, 1993; Haigh, 1992; Kelley, 1994; Bleeke and Ernest, 1994; Badaracco, 1989; Lorange and Roos, 1992; Robert, 1992; Lei and Slocum, 1992). With some oversimplification, this literature may be summarized into the following eight points:

- Have a clear view of your strategy, the capabilities you have and wish to protect, and those you want to acquire in an alliance.
- Select a partner and make sure that each understands the true motivation of the other, and where the alliance will lead to mutual benefit. Be willing to give up something to get something in return.
- Alliances are easier where partners have similar or compatible business philosophies.
- Get clarity and agreement on the initial goals, timescales, contributions, etc. However, flexibility is needed to allow the alliance to evolve as conditions change.
- Work throughout to build up mutual trust; respect cultural differences.
- Form friendships with your opposite numbers at all levels. This will help to ensure clear communication.
- Establish a commitment to learn from each other, and ensure that learning does not become one-sided.

- Transfer what you learn to in-house groups and ensure that they benefit from the alliance's success.

The guidelines above make it clear that the first requirement is for the company to know its own key strengths and to prevent them being leached out through an alliance. The ease with which this can happen is documented in a study of the semi-conductor industry by Teramoto *et al.* (1994). When the number of alliances with Western partners increased dramatically in the late 1980s, the business positions of Japanese companies improved considerably. For example, in 1989 NEC entered an agreement with MIPS Computer Systems in order to catch up in the field of reduced instruction set computer (RISC) processors. By 1992 NEC had already improved the RISC technology and was about to overhaul its technology supplier. Examples from Fujitsu, Hitachi and Toshiba could also be quoted.

To acquire knowledge from alliance partners, Japanese firms usually give managers transferred to the alliance specific responsibilities for knowledge acquisition (Pucik, 1988). They also insist that this knowledge is communicated across the organization by nominating particular persons to whom the new knowledge must be communicated. Spreading knowledge learned from an alliance is assisted at NEC and Fujitsu by the fact that all strategic alliances are managed by corporate headquarters.

Knowledge acquisition begins with an individual, but interaction with other individuals is needed to enhance the knowledge and transmit it through the organization. Hence interpersonal contact patterns and relations are vital for successful strategic alliances. Much of the literature supports this contention:

- 'Perhaps the most important element in the success of a strategic partnership is people and how well they can work together' (Kelley, 1994, p. 6).
- 'The success of alliances is shaped by people; choosing individuals for key positions is a vital step in alliance planning' (Lorange, Roos and Bronn, 1992, p. 15).

These practitioner views are supported by recent empirical research. Parkhe (1993) tested his model on data from 111 American strategic alliances that were made betweeen 1983 and 1988. He found that high behavioural transparency, long time horizons and frequent interactions promoted reciprocal cooperation. His research also leads to the view that, as time passed, the need for a formal deterrence-dominated governance gave way to a more informal, trust-dominated understanding between the parties.

Larson (1992, p. 98) in her study of seven cooperative strategic alliances of entrepreneurial firms found that, in addition to economic incentives and strategic rewards, successful alliances depended critically on a favourable history of prior personal relations and a favourable reputation. This provided a receptive context for beginning and then developing an economic exchange. Subsequently a successful trial period led to mutually reinforcing economic incentives and social processes. Moving through the trial period successfully was assisted where the alliance partners created, through an accumulation of actions, a system of social relations that transcended narrow self-interest.

To summarize, in relationships between buyers and sellers, whether internal or external, and in strategic alliances a network organizational form is beneficial. This organizational form is characterized by frequent interaction, cooperation, mutual interdependence and open communication. In these circumstances, and without giving away their core skills, the parties to the relationship can develop further capabilities and enhance their competitive advantage. This will happen most easily when the partners in the alliance understand the norms and values of their respective organizations and the goals of their evolving relationships. In internal relationships and close buyer-seller partnerships some goals and values are shared, making these relationships easier to manage. Where the same can be achieved in a strategic alliance, its prospects of success are increased.

Conclusion

Strategic alliances, buyer–seller relationships and other business partnerships are important because, through them, individuals with knowledge and skills interact to create the heritage, competence and capability of the firm. The intangible assets play an important role in strategic development.

The key to understanding relationships is to remember that they are created and held together by individuals. It is the interactive behaviour of individuals that creates intangible value in relationships. Where there is little personal contact and little exchange of information, the relationship will not be of much value. On the other hand, where contact is frequent and where information is shared, trust and mutual respect can grow and the relationship can be of value to both partners.

From this point of view the management of strategy becomes the management of interactive behaviour in an evolving set of relationships. Each relationship is a unique outcome of economic exchanges and social interactions. The organizational form governing each relationship is a mixture of market, hierarchy and network. Strategic relationships that enhance capabilities are mainly governed by the network form and its associated pattern of social obligations. But frequently market mechanisms and hierarchical regulation are also at work to help ensure that the relationship delivers strategic as well as economic and social benefits.

References

Aoki, M, Gustafsson, B, and Williamson, O E (1990) *The Firm as a Nexus of Treaties*, Sage Publications, London.

Asanuma, Banri (1990) Manufacturer–Supplier Relationships in Japan and the Concept of Relation Specific Skill, *Journal of Japanese and International Economies*, 3 (1), pp. 1-30, March.

Badaracco, Joseph L, Jr (1991) *The Knowledge Link: How Firms Compete through Strategic Alliances*, Harvard Business School Press, Boston, MA.

Banks, Philip, F and Baranson, Jack (1993) New Concepts Drive Transnational Strategic Alliances, *Planning Review*, pp. 28-31, Nov/Dec.

Barney, J B (1986) Strategic factor markets: Expectations, Luck and Business Strategy, *Management Science*, pp. 1231-41, October.

Bartlett, C A and Ghoshal, S (1989) *Managing Across Borders*, Harvard Business School Press, Cambridge, MA.

Bleeke, J and Ernst, D (1994) 'Collaborating To Compete', *Directors and Boards*, Winter.

Bower, J (1970) *Managing the Resource Allocation Process*, Harvard Business School Press, Boston, MA.

Bradach, J L and Eccles, R G (1985) Markets versus hierarchies: from ideal types to plural forms, in W Richard Scott (ed.) *Annual Review of Sociology*, 15: pp. 97-118, Annual Reviews, Palo Alto, CA.

Burton, F and Saelens, F (1994) International Alliances as a Strategic Tool of Japanese Electronic Companies, in N Campbell and F Burton (eds), *Japanese Multinationals, Strategies and Management in the Global Kaisha*, pp. 58-71, Routledge, London.

Coase, R H (1952) The Nature of the Firm, in G J Stigler and K E Boulding (eds), *Readings in Price Theory*, pp. 386-405, Richard D Irwin, Homewood, IL.

Collis, D J (1991) A Resource-Based Analysis of Global Competition: The Case of the Bearings Industry, *Strategic Management Journal*, 12, pp. 49-68.

Contractor, Farok J and Lorange, Peter (1988) *Cooperative Strategies in International Business*, Lexington Books, Lexington, MA.

Dore, R (1983) Goodwill and the Spirit of Market Capitalism, *British Journal of Sociology*, 34, pp. 459-82.

Dosi, G, Teece, D J and Winter, S (1990) Toward a Theory of Corporate Coherence: Preliminary Remarks, Working Paper, University of California, Berkeley, March.

Dyer, J H and Ouchi, W (1993) Japanese-Style Partnerships: Giving Companies a Competitive Edge, *Sloan Management Review*, Fall.

Fama, E F (1980) Agency Problems and the Theory of the Firm, *American Economic Review*, 76, pp. 971-83.

Gerlach, M L, and Lincoln, J R (1992) The Organization of Business Networks in the United States and Japan, pp. 491-520.

Ghemawat, Panjak (1991) *Strategy, Commitment and Choice*, Free Press, New York, 1991.

Hakansson, H (ed.) (1982) *International Marketing and Purchasing of Industrial Goods*, Wiley, New York.

Hakansson, H (1987) *Industrial Technological Development: A Network Approach*, Croom Helm, London.

Hakansson, H and Snehota I, (1989) No Business is an Island: The Network Concept of Business Strategy, *Scandinvian Journal of Management*, 4, 3, pp. 187-200.

Itami, H and Roehl, T W (1987) *Mobilizing Invisible Assets*, Harvard University Press, Cambridge, MA.

Japan Development Bank (1989) *Organisation Structures of Japanese Companies*, Japan Development Bank, Tokyo.

Jarillo, J C (1988) On Strategic Networks, *Strategic Management Journal*, 9, pp. 31-4.

Jensen, M C and Meckling, W H (1976) The Theory of the Firm: Managerial Behaviour, Agency Costs, and Ownership Structure, *Journal of Financial Economics*, 3, pp. 305-60.

Kagono, T and Campbell, N (1994) Organizational Perestroika: Intra-Company Markets in Japanese Multinational Corporations, in N Campbell and F Burton (eds), *Japanese Multinationals, Strategies and Management in the Global Kaisha*, pp. 113-25, Routledge, London.

Kelley, G N (1994) The Age of Strategic Partnerships, *Directors and Boards*, pp. 4-6, Winter.

Larson, A (1992) Network Dyads in Entrepreneural Settings: A Study of the Governance of Exchange Relationships, *Administrative Science Quarterly*, 37, pp. 76-104.

Lei, D and Slocum, J W (1992), 'Global Strategy, Competence-Building and Strategic Alliances, *California Management Review*, pp. 81-97, Fall.

Lorange, P and Roos, J (1992) *Strategic Alliances: Formation, Implementation and Evolution*, Blackwell, Oxford.

Lorange, P, Roos, J and Bronn, P S (1992) Building Successful Strategic Alliances, *Long Range Planning*, Vol. 25, No. 6, pp. 10-17.

Lorenzoni, G and Ornati, O (1988) Constellations of Firms and New Ventures, *Journal of Business Venturing*, 3, pp. 41-57.

McMillan, J (1990) Managing Suppliers: Incentive Systems in the Japanese and U.S. Industry, *California Management Review*, p. 51, Summer.

Miles, R E and Snow, C C (1986) Organizations: New Concepts for New Forms, *California Management Review*, 28, pp. 62-73.

Nelson, R R and Winter, S G (1982) *An Evolutionary Theory of Economic Change*, Belknap Press of Harvard University Press, Cambridge, MA.

Ouchi, W (1980) Markets, Bureaucracies & Clans, *Administrative Science Quarterly*, Vol. 25, pp. 129-41, March.

Parkhe, A (1993) Strategic Alliance Structuring: A Game Theoretic and Transaction Cost Examination of Interfirm Cooperation, *Academy of Management Journal*, Vol. 36, No. 4, pp. 794-829.

Polanyi, M (1958) *Personal Knowledge*, Routledge, Kegan Paul Ltd, London.

Powell, W W (1990) Neither Market nor Hierarchy: Network Forms of Organization, in Barry M Staw and L L Cummings (eds), *Research in Organizational Behaviour*, 12, pp. 295-336, JAI Press, Greenwich, CT.

Prietula, M J and Simon, H A (1989) The Experts in Your Midst, *Harvard Business Review*, Vol. 67, Iss. 1, pp. 120-4, Jan/Feb.

Reve, T (1990) The Firm as a Nexus of Internal and External Contracts, in M. Aoki, B. Gustafsson and O E Williamson (eds), *The Firm as a Nexus of Treaties*, Sage Publications, London.

Rigby, D K and Buchanan, R W T (1994) Putting More Strategy Into Strategic Alliances, *Directors and Boards*, Winter.

Robert, M (1992) The Do's and Don'ts of Strategic Alliances, *The Journal of Business Strategy*, pp. 50-3, March/April.

Rumelt, R P (1984) Towards a Strategic Theory of the Firm, in R B Lamb (ed), *Competitive Strategic Management*, pp. 556-70, Prentice-Hall, Englewood Cliffs, NJ.

Sako, M (1991) The Role of Trust in Japanese Buyer-Supplier Relationships', in M Aoki, and G Brunello, (eds), *Ricerche Economiche*, April-Sept., pp. 449-74.

Schendler, B R (1993) How Toshiba Makes Alliances Work, *Fortune*, pp. 42-7, October.

Tallman, S B (1991) Strategic Management Models and Resource-Based Strategies among MNCs in a Host Market', *Strategic Management Journal*, 12, pp. 69-82.

Teece, D J, Pisano, G, and Shuen, A (1990) *Firm Capabilities, Resources, and the Concept of Strategy: Four Paradigms of Strategic Management*, University of California at Berkeley, Harvard University, University of California at Berkeley respectively, December 1990.

Teramoto, Y, *et al* (1994) Global Strategy in the Japanese Semi-conductor Industry: Knowledge Creation Through Strategic Alliances, in N Campbell and F Burton (eds), *Japanese Multinationals, Strategies and Management in the Global Kaisha*, pp. 71-85, Routledge, London.

Thorelli, H B (1986) Networks: Between Markets and Hierarchies, *Strategic Management Journal*, Vol. 7, pp. 37-51.

Wernerfelt, B (1984) A Resource-Bases View of the Firm, S*trategic Management Journal*, 5, pp. 171-80.

Williamson, O (1975) *Markets and Hierarchies: Analysis and Antitrust Implications*, Free Press, New York.

Part Two STRATEGY DEVELOPMENT

Chapter 4 The processes of strategy development

Too much planning may lead us to chaos, but so too would too little, and more directly.

(Henry Mintzberg (1993) *The Rise and Fall of Strategic Planning*, Prentice-Hall)

For many years during the 1960s and 1970s strategic planning was seen as the most appropriate and robust means of creating strategies. The relevant school of thought implied that strategies could be designed and then implemented. Strategic analysis, forecasting and creative positioning in respect of competition were stressed. The important contribution of these ideas has never been in question, but later schools of thought have proposed that there are other, equally valuable, explanations of how strategies are created in reality in organizations. These views in general tend to be descriptive rather than prescriptive in nature.

Chapter 4 by Andy Bailey and Gerry Johnson summarizes the findings (so far) from an investigation into strategy creation in UK organizations. The authors conclude that a number of strands are in evidence, in a complex mix. The mix differs for different organizations, and the complexity is enhanced by different managers in the same organization having a different view of the reality.

The important strands are as follows. Planning clearly has a contribution to make; the strategies are often changed incrementally as planned strategies are implemented and it is realized that the competitive environment is fluid. On occasions strategies can be forced on an organization by a powerful external stakeholder; in other circumstances a powerful strategic leader can dictate strategic direction. Culture and politics invariably have vital roles to play, where again we can see power and influence at work.

In the end we have to decide on the appropriate role and contribution of planning in strategic management. Mintzberg emphasizes that, however strategies and strategic ideas might be conceived, it is important to plan their implementation. He refers to this as strategic programming as distinct from strategic planning.

The processes of strategy development

Andy Bailey and Gerry Johnson

Introduction

This chapter is concerned with the processes by which strategy is developed within organizations. It builds on research into the nature of strategy development being undertaken within the Centre for Strategic Management and Organisational Change at Cranfield School of Management. Initially the process of strategy development is discussed, a number of explanations of the process are presented and an integrated framework is developed. This framework is subsequently used to illustrate the strategy development process operating in a number of organizations. The implications for the strategic management process are discussed.

Research in the field of strategic management has typically been divided between the investigation of 'content' or 'process'. Much of the research in the field, though, has concentrated on issues relating to the content of strategy (see, for example, Porter, 1980; Hamel & Prahalad, 1989). While strategy content research is important for the investigation of strategic management, the process by which strategy is developed is of equal importance. Indeed, if the process of strategy development is to be effectively managed, e.g. to effect strategic change, then the processual aspects of strategic management are especially important. This chapter concentrates on the process of strategic management with the intention of providing a broader, more realistic picture of the way in which strategy is developed in organizations.

The early works of writers such as Ansoff (1965) and Andrews (1980) and the books of the 1970s, in particular on corporate planning, emphasized the importance of strategy, and have guided thinking in the area, thinking which has been dominated by the view that strategies are developed through a particularly analytical and intentional process. The basic framework which this 'rational' planned view offers suggests that through the application of appropriate analytical and systematic techniques and checklists, organizations are able to secure their own success. Moreover, such an approach allows assumptions to be made about the future, assists in the reduction of uncertainty and facilitates the systematic development of strategy. This view and its associated frameworks have become deeply entrenched within strategic thinking, while the prescriptive and normative modes so generated have significantly influenced the approach to strategy formulation in practice, in education, and in research.

To view strategy development in this logical and rational manner is appealing, and it is not surprising that this view has enjoyed such prominence. In management education, strategic texts have traditionally emphasized the rationality of analysis, planning, and implementation as a step by step process. Within organizations this school of thought suggests that formal strategic planning processes and mechanisms can operate in a rational and objective manner to allow the comprehensive analysis of the internal and external environments, the development of alternative strategies, the selection of an optimum strategy, and the production of objectives, goals, budgets, and targets to guide implementation. In short, this rational planning approach is often what is regarded as 'good practice'.

However, the processes of strategy development that exist in organizations cannot typically be explained in such ways. Organizations are open to an array of influences both from inside and outside when developing strategy. Consequently, the strategy development process of an organization is likely to reflect the mix of influences which come together to direct how strategy emerges. The seminal work of Allison (1971), in the context of policy studies, demonstrated that the process of strategy development could be accounted for not only in terms of a rational framework of understanding but also in terms of both political and organizational frameworks. The strategy development process of an organization may then result from, and be influenced by, the broad social, political, and cultural aspects of the organization or by external pressures as well as from a planned approach of the organization to its environment.

The emergence of strategies

A natural assumption of the rational planned view of strategy development is that strategies are formulated and implemented in a linear manner and that an organization's *intended* strategy will be implemented in its entirety to become *realized* as actual strategy. Here strategy is conceived of as being formulated, perhaps through some planning process, and resulting in a clear expression of strategic direction, the implementation of which is also planned in terms of resource allocation, structure and so on (route 1 in Figure 4.1). However, this may not always be the case. Unexpected shifts in the environment, unforeseen problems in implementation or limitations in the process can operate to restrict the efficiency of strategy development and its realization. The result of this may mean that an organization's intended strategy is not realized as actual strategy (Mintzberg, 1978; Mintzberg and Waters, 1985). In effect much of what is intended follows route 2 in Figure 4.1 and becomes *unrealized*. There may be all sorts of reasons for this, and the rest of the chapter helps explain some of these.

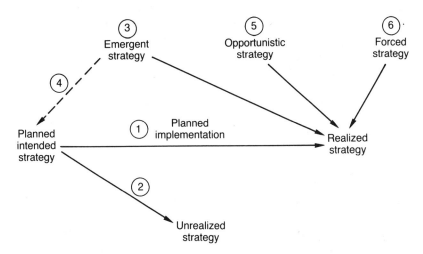

Figure 4.1   *Strategic development routes*

The fact that a planned, intended strategy is not realized does not mean that an organization has no strategy. Strategy can be seen as the direction an organization actually pursues over time, intended or not. As such, strategy development can be conceived of as an *emergent* process (route 3 in Figure 4.1).

The distinction between what is intended and what is realized may not be so defined and the two may interact. A strategy that starts as intended may alter and become more emergent as it is implemented, while an emergent strategy may become formalized and more deliberate as it enters the accepted wisdom of the organization and is encapsulated within its longer-term strategy. Indeed, an intended strategy that appears to have come about through a planning mechanism may still be of an emergent nature. For example, the planning process may perform the role of monitoring the progress or efficiency of an emerging strategy. On the other hand, it may do little more than pull together the views and 'wisdom' of management or of industry experts which has been built up over time. As such a planning system may merely operate to support and justify the received wisdom within, and general direction of, an organization (route 4 in Figure 4.1). This route has inherent dangers, given that the firm appears to be taking a proactive, systematic, approach to strategy development, and this may mask a somewhat complacent view of the situation the organization is in.

Strategies may also come about in opportunistic ways (route 5 in Figure 4.1). There may be changes in the operating environment that may be taken advantage of in an opportunistic manner and, as such, lead to changes in the realized strategy of an organization. Finally, strategy may be imposed (route 6 in Figure 4.1). For example, government legislation may force an organization to alter its operations, whether because of the need to comply with new environmental regulations or the privatization of public utilities. Similarly, a down-turn in the economy may force an organization to follow a strategy of retrenchment, with divestments and the cutting of costs. Such pressure may be dealt with through planning mechanisms within the organization; or through some other mechanism, such as individual decision-making by senior executives. In any event, such imposed strategy development can result in significant long-term changes for an organization.

Explanations of strategy development

This next section reviews in more detail the different explanations of how strategies may develop. While these explanations are not novel or indeed definitive, they do represent meaningful classifications of the process that make intuitive sense to managers and are understandable. It is important to stress it is most unlikely that any one of the explanations given accounts entirely for the processes at work in an organization: strategy development needs to be understood in terms of a mix of processes.

The planning dimension

Strategic planning is perhaps the most traditional view of how strategy is developed in organizations. The dimension indicates that strategy development is a distinctly intentional process, with a logical, rational, planned approach to the organization and its environment. Further, it implies that through the application of appropriate analytical and systematic techniques the 'right' decision can be taken.

The strategies that develop are the outcome of sequential, planned and deliberate procedures and are often the responsibility of specialized departments. Clear and well-defined strategic goals and objectives are set by the senior members of an organization. These goals may reflect the desires of the shareholders or potential threats and opportunities that the organization becomes aware of through its constant monitoring of the business environment. As a goal or strategic issue is defined, the organization and its environment (both internal and external to the organization) are systematically analysed in terms of, for example, strategic position, the position of competitors, organizational strengths, weaknesses, and resource availability. The information collected is assessed and strategic options capable of attaining the goal or resolving the strategic issue are generated.

These strategic options, or courses of action, are systematically assessed against the criteria of the strategic goals and objectives to be achieved. This evaluation incorporates an assessment of both the estimated consequences of the alternative courses of action, e.g. in terms of risk versus return, and the value of these consequences. Similarly the long-term potential of the options is estimated. The option judged to maximize the value of outcomes, best fits the selection criterion, and presents competitive advantage, is chosen. The selected option is subsequently detailed in the form of precise plans and programmes and is passed from the top downwards within the organization. Throughout this process strategies are determined and guided by those decision-makers in senior management positions, and are implemented by those below, who act on but are unlikely to decide on strategy.

In line with the systematic development of strategy, the resources required for implementation are determined and appropriately allocated, and similarly the systems for monitoring and controlling the new strategy are determined. A strategy developed through this planned, sequential routine should then be implemented fully and in a 'surprise-free' manner.

While this planned intentional notion of strategy development is appealing, it is not without its problems and inherent dangers. In particular it lacks consideration of the less 'objective' aspects of the organization and their critical influence on strategy development. Indeed, this dimension of strategy development could be seen as devoid of personal emotion or political activity (Etzioni, 1989). Consequently, the strategy developed will not reflect the interests of any particular group or be restricted by the organization's traditions.

However, regardless of the problems, the discipline and techniques of planning approaches can be useful because they may provide a framework for strategic thinking. The elements of the planning process represent a useful means of analysing and thinking about complex strategic problems, and if managers also address the problems of managing strategy within the social, cultural and political world of organizations, then such thinking can be very helpful.

The incremental dimension

In the late 1950s Lindblom (1959) suggested that managing strategies through logical, sequential, planning mechanisms was unrealistic. He argued that, given the complexity of organizations and the environments in which they operate, managers cannot consider all possible options in terms of all possible futures and evaluate these against pre-set, unambiguous objectives. This is particularly so in an organizational context in which there are likely to be conflicting views, values, and power bases. Rather, strategic choice takes place by comparing options against each other and considering which would give the best outcome and be possible to implement. Lindblom called this strategy building through 'successive limited comparisons', but argued that it took place in the everyday world of managing, not through planning systems.

Strategy development as characterized by this incremental dimension involves an adaptive response to the environment. Strategy is therefore seen to be worked through in action, and does not follow the neat sequential model of analysis, choice and implementation. Unlike the planning dimension, this model of strategy development does not operate to identify *a priori* the best or optimal solution (Mintzberg *et al.*, 1976). Rather managers can be thought of as having a view of where they want the organization to be in the future and try to move towards this position in an evolutionary way (Quinn, 1980).

Managers accept the uncertainty of their environment because they realize that they cannot do away with this uncertainty by trying to know factually about how the environment will change. Instead they seek to become highly sensitive to environmental signals through constant environmental scanning.

Strategy development is therefore an iterative process, encompassing feedback loops to previous phases where problem and solution may be redefined or redeveloped (Lyles, 1981), following exposure to the business environment. Commitment to a strategy is therefore kept tentative and subject to review during the early stages of its development. There is also a reluctance to specify precise objectives too early, as this might stifle ideas and prevent the sort of experimentation that is desired. Objectives are therefore likely to be fairly general in nature. Over time those strategies that are successful are retained by the organization while those that are inappropriate are eliminated. This ensures that the strengths of an organization are maintained, as changes in the environment are matched with changes in procedure, without excessive risk to the organization.

In comparison to the planning dimension, this adaptive approach removes from top management and the corporate centre the sole responsibility for the task of strategy development, those in the lower levels of the organization becoming active participants. Indeed it is the organization's sub-systems, each of which is concerned with different strategic issues (for example, acquisitions or major reorganizations), which raise the awareness of potential strategic problems.

Further different strategic decisions should not be seen as entirely separate (Quinn, 1980). Because of the interplay between an organization's sub-systems, each manager will know what his colleagues are doing, and will be able to interpret their actions and requirements. The managers are, in effect, learning from each other about the feasibility of a course of action in terms of resource management and its internal political acceptability. Together with the constant readjustment and limited commitment, this knowledge and understanding allows the long-term direction of the organization to be monitored, and the organizational mix of resources and skills to be altered in reaction to environmental changes. The process thus broadens the information base available, builds organizational awareness and increases the active search for opportunities and threats not previously defined.

Such a process is seen by managers to have benefits. Continual testing and gradual strategy implementation provides improved quality of information for decision-making and enables the better sequencing of the elements of major decisions. It also encourages managerial flexibility and creativity and increases the possibility of creating and developing commitment to change throughout the organization. Smaller changes, developed by managers throughout the organization, are less likely to face the same level of resistance as that faced by major changes, imposed by the organization's executives.

The political dimension

This dimension reflects strategy development, which is dependent on power and influence. Organizations are political entities, and powerful stakeholders or interest groups can influence the inputs into decisions and the strategies followed. These stakeholders, ('any group or individual who can affect or is affected by the achievement of the organization's objectives' (Freeman, 1984)), which could include customers, banks, shareholders, government, trade unions and organizational members, each have different concerns. These concerns may be in conflict; there may be differences between groups or managers, between managers and shareholders, or between powerful individuals. These differences are likely to be resolved through the processes of bargaining, negotiation, or dictate. The result is that goals and objectives, strategic issues and even strategies are derived from this political process and not from an analytical neutral assessment and choice. For example, the decision to adopt a strategy will not be solely based on merit; rather it will be shaped by the power of the group proposing and sponsoring the strategic option.

The level of influence or power these stakeholders are able to exercise differs (Heller *et al.*, 1988) and is often conditional upon the organization's dependency upon these groups for a resource (Pfeffer and Salancik, 1978) and the potential difficulty in replacing the present stakeholder as the source of that resource (Hinings, *et al.*, 1974). Similarly, the influence of a stakeholder is not constant from decision to decision. The decision situation determines the level of stakeholder involvement and both their level of influence and the dynamics of that influence throughout the process. For example, the influence of top level decision-makers decreases as a strategy enters the implementation stage, while the influence of lower level managers increases.

Influence over decisions may also be gained through the provision of information. Information is not politically neutral, but rather a source of power, particularly for those who control that which is seen to be important. Information can be distorted, intentionally or not, to advance the interests of particular groups. These distortions may result from the provision of information that reflects the interests of the provider or through the provider operating to restrict the flow of information, both of which can legitimize the desires of the interest groups (Pfeffer and Salancik, 1978).

It would be wrong therefore to assume that the identification of key issues and even the strategy eventually selected emerge in a politically neutral environment. Strategic options and strategies will be championed, not only on the basis of the extent to which they offer benefit to the organization, but because they have implications for the status, influence, and vested interests of particular groups. Only through a political process of compromise and mutual adjustment will a generally acceptable strategy emerge (Mintzberg and Waters, 1985). Final adoption will be dependent on the strategy's acceptability to both the stakeholders influencing the decision-making process and those who must implement the strategy, and not solely because it fulfils objective criteria.

The cultural dimension

The cultural dimension represents a 'way of doing things in the organization' that impacts on the strategy followed. Organizations faced with similar environments will not necessarily respond in the same way. The strategy they choose to pursue will not result from a precise planned response to their environment, but from the attitudes, values, and perceptions held in common among the members and stakeholders of that organization. Further, management cannot be conceived of simply in terms of the manipulation of techniques or tools of analysis. Management is also about the application of managerial experience built up over many years; and often within the same organization or industry. Their experience is not only rooted in individual experience, but on group and organizational experience built up over time, for rarely do managers work in isolation. It is important therefore to recognize the significance of cultural aspects of management in the development of strategy. Indeed, strategy may be seen to result from a learned response to a particular strategic stimuli based on what the organization holds as taken-for-granted (Schein, 1985).

Strategy development as explained by the cultural dimension is very much about the past, about managerial experience and expectations, and about the assumptions and beliefs of an organization. As such, managerial action, within the strategic process, is likely to be based on taken-for-granted frames of reference which are brought to bear by a manager, or group of managers, and which will affect how a given situation is perceived and how it is responded to. Indeed, the search for strategic solutions and the development of strategy will be directed by past experience, similar situations and the organization's history.

Given that future strategy is driven to a large extent by a way of doing things in the organization, then the associated taken-for-grantedness is likely to be handed on or inherited over time within a group. That group might be, for example, a managerial function such as marketing or finance; a professional grouping, such as accountants; an organization as a whole; and more widely an industry sector, or even a national culture. Just as these frames exist at the organizational and sub-unit level, they also exist on an industry-wide basis (Spender, 1989), or indeed at a national level. Managers, then, are influenced by many frames of reference when developing strategy. However, especially important for the strategic management of most organizations is the organizational frame of reference – its specific set of assumptions – or the organizational paradigm (Johnson, 1992).

The paradigm comprises the deep rooted beliefs and tacit assumptions of the organization and relates to the way things are done and what is done. These assumptions and beliefs are rarely talked about, and are unlikely to be made consciously explicit by managers. Examples might include the deep-rooted assumption that banks are about secure lending; local newspapers are about purveying local news (i.e. as more their *raison d'être* than advertising); that universities are about doing research; and so on. As such, these deep-rooted assumptions can play an important part in strategy development.

The paradigm, then, represents a collective experience without which managers would have to re-invent their world afresh for circumstances they face or decisions they need to take; it enables new situations to be perceived in a way that is not unique (Schon, 1983) and provides a shared framework through which the world the organization operates within can be interpreted (Schwenk, 1988). In this way it allows the experience gathered over years to be applied to a situation so that managers can identify strategic issues, direct the search for strategic solutions, decide upon relevant information, assess the strategic solution or course of action as to the likelihood of success and so develop the 'appropriate' course of action. In short, it provides a mechanism through which managers can respond to a situation in the 'right' way and develop the 'right' strategy, as defined by the other managers in the organization.

An organization's paradigm is, then, built up from different influences, such as history and past experience (both personal and organizational), industry sector, and professional ethos. The strength of these influences will depend on a number of factors. For example, an organization with a relatively stable management and a long-term momentum of strategy is likely to have a more homogeneous paradigm than one in which there has been rapid turnover of management and significant change forced upon it. Organizations with a dominant professional influence, perhaps an accountancy firm, are likely to demonstrate a homogeneous paradigm. Industry influences may be particularly strong if the transfer of staff between firms is limited to that industry, as it often is in engineering or banking, for example, or the environmental constraints are very dominant and commonly experienced, as they are, for example, in public-sector organizations.

Thus an organization's strategy will develop in accord with and within the confines of its culture and dominant paradigm. The cultural influence operates to orientate the definition and solution of a strategic problem internally, ensuring a strategic response is based within the domain of the organization (Schwenk, 1988) and the history of its members (Nutt, 1984). Strategies outside the frame of reference of the organization that are novel and new are likely to be resisted. As such, strategic decision-making reflects a future and shared direction that perpetuates an organization's history and routines.

The command dimension

Here a particular individual is seen to have a high degree of control over the strategy followed. The organization's strategy is primarily associated with a central powerful figure (for example, the chief executive or a similar figure with institutionalized authority). Perhaps less commonly it may relate to the power of a small group of individuals at the top of the organization.

The determinants of the strategic aspirations and the strategy followed may emerge from a vision that represents the desired future state of the organization. As such, a vision may result from the intuition and innovation of its orginator and be developed from both intuition and a rational understanding of the organization's strategic problems, an understanding that enables innovation to be made. The vision may be based on radical ideas and may challenge accepted norms, contradict established principles and paradigms, and go beyond familiar experience and knowledge (Trice and Beyer, 1986).

A more mundane explanation is that strategic aspirations may simply be the result of a strategy transferred from one organization and context to another. This may come about because a new executive applies his or her existing frame of reference from another context to the new organization to which they have been appointed. For example, some of the new chief executives appointed to the newly privatized UK industries in the 1980s came from private sector companies. They brought with them frames of reference from competitive environments in which profit motivation was taken as given. What was normal and obvious to them was often seen as new and visionary in the organizations they moved into.

However these strategic aspirations are determined, they are associated with an individual to the extent that the individual becomes the representation of strategy. It is the individual who becomes the tangible link to strategy and the perceived source of that strategy for the organizational members. The individual is perceived to determine strategy. While an individual's vision may represent the organization's strategic direction, it does not need to be commonly shared throughout the organization. Rather the strategy and future strategic direction are characterized and determined by the 'commanding' individual.

Whether the power of the central figure is achieved through the generation of an idea and 'vision', through the organization's history, or by virtue of position, it inevitably places enormous strategic control and power in the hands of the individual who gains the capacity to translate intention into a sustainable reality (Bennis and Nanus, 1985).

The influence of the command mode of strategy development is likely to relate to a particular time phase, e.g. a crisis situation, and may overwhelm objective analysis of the organization's position. The history of organizations reveals that the command capacity has been an important influence on strategy development, and there are examples of organizations in which influential leaders have been effective in turning their organization around. However, these influences have been continued at times when a cooler examination of the business situation would have suggested that their influence and future aspirations for the organization were becoming inappropriate.

The enforced choice dimension

This dimension suggests a process of strategy development in which an organization's external environment operates to limit strategic direction and choice. Indeed, this fits well with the view of some writers on management, who argue that organizations have little or no control over the choice of strategies they follow. Factors in the environment impinge on the organization in such a way as to encourge – even determine – the adoption of organizational structures and activities suited to that environment (Hannan and Freeman, 1989). These external constraints operate to prescribe strategies and limit the role organizational members play in their selection (Aldrich, 1979). Equally the strategies an organization can follow tend to be common to all organizations within an industrial sector or market. In short, the success of an organization is due to fit between strategy, structure and environment directed by external pressure rather than any rational and intentional choice.

Barriers in the environment operate to restrict the strategies that can be followed and reduce the level of intentional strategic choice. Indeed, any strategic change that does occur is likely to be instigated from outside the organization. This is a responsive rather than a proactive move resulting from external pressure, e.g. within public sector organizations from pressure brought to bear by the government. These limitations are such that influence over the environment is likely to be very low; rather the organizations in this instance may have to buffer themselves from the environment.

A number of allied assumptions are associated with this dimension. These centre around the notion of fit between an organization and its environment. If fit occurs, an organization will survive. If the organization becomes mismatched with its environment, then it must adapt or else die. However, the ability intentionally to change is exceptionally limited. It has been suggested that changes occur within an organization through variations in its processes, structures, and systems. While the process of organizational innovation and variation may occur as a rational intentional response to the environment, they may occur equally unintentionally through conflict over control of resources, ambiguity of organizational reality, accident, errors, tactical moves, or luck. It is these variations, however they occur, that produce the potentially advantageous or dangerous innovations for an organization. Those variations that fit the changes in the environment and that are appropriate and beneficial to the organization produce advantage and so contribute to the chance of an organization's or sub-unit's survival (Aldrich and Mueller, 1982). These successful variations are retained and subsequently disseminated throughout the organization and across its generations through culture, symbols, socialization, administration and training.

The view taken in this chapter is that for some organizations the impact of the environment is, indeed, very large; and that degrees of managerial latitude are severely reduced. However, this is not so in all environments; and even where those pressures are severe, it is the job of managers to develop the skills and strategies to cope with the situation.

Integrating views of strategy development

Each of the above dimensions, described in their singular and archetypal forms, is capable of explaining some aspects of the strategy development process. However, given the complexity of both the strategy development process and of the organization in general, it is unlikely that one dimension would adequately describe the process operating in all organizations, in every situation, and at any point in time. Rather, it is probable that the dimensions and the processes they describe are not mutually exclusive but occur in combination. Indeed, in most organizations managers see strategies developing through a mix of such processes.

This chapter does not therefore aim to identify the dimension that 'best' describes strategy development across all organizations or prescribe the mode of strategy development that should be utilized. Rather it aims to demonstrate that organizations differ in their process of strategy development. Research has indicated that different processes of stategy development or strategic decision-making occur across organizations (Mintzberg, 1973; Shrivastava and Grant, 1985) and even within the same organization (Johnson, 1987) and that the process operating can and does change. Indeed, given the complexity of strategic decisions, it is unlikely that strategy development can be explained from a unitary viewpoint; the strategy development process is likely to be multifaceted (Fredrickson, 1983). Consequently, although valuable in explaining components of the strategy process, narrowly focused or unitary frameworks may simplify the process and not take sufficient account of managerial understanding. The complexity of the process is therefore more likely to be conveyed by a comprehensive framework of explanation than through the application of a narrowly focused framework (Derkinderen and Crum, 1988).

The research on which this chapter is based has thus adopted an approach combining all the above mentioned dimensions of strategy development into an integrated and comprehensive framework. It is an approach which we suggest can facilitate a clearer understanding of the strategy development process and its complexity. This understanding is aided through the use of strategy development profiles, the construction of which is described below.

The strategy development profile

The alternative explanations or views of strategy development identified above were operationalized to identify characteristics singularly attributable to each of the dimensions. Based on these characteristics, statements were developed for use in a self-completion questionnaire, which was administered to senior managers, from a cross-section of industries. They were required to indicate the degree to which the statements were characteristic of their organization. Through the analysis of their responses, managerial perceptions of the organization's process of strategy development were revealed. The numerical representation of these perceptions were subsequently plotted to develop strategy development profiles of the separate organizations. It is important to note that these profiles represent how managers see the process of strategy development within their organizations.

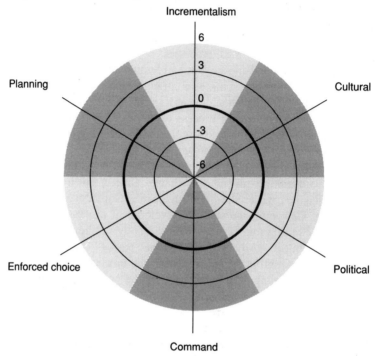

Figure 4.2 *Strategy development profile*

Interpretation of the strategy development profile is based on distance from the mid-point ring (highlighed in bold (Figure 4.2)). This mid-point represents the standardized mean of all those individuals we have sampled, so points moving away from this ring towards the outside of the profile (accompanied by a positive score) represent the degree to which the dimension is seen to be characteristic of the strategy development process of the organization. Points moving inwards towards the centre (accompanied by a negative score) represent the degree to which the dimension is seen to be uncharacteristic of the process. Points at zero, or low positive or negative scores, indicate that the attributes associated with that view are not particularly characteristic or uncharacteristic of the organization.

Strategy development process in action

Using the integrated framework and strategy development profile discussed above, the following cases explore the different patterns of strategy development that exist in organizations. The potential advantages and problems these combinations present are discussed. In addition, an example of differences in the perceived process from within the same organization will be explored to show the potential conflicts that may surface and the impact these may have on the acceptance of strategic change.

Case A – The planning commander

The strategy development profile for this engineering organization indicates that while strategy is seen to develop through an intentional planned response to the environment, it is under influence from an individual with centralized power. As discussed above, only in very rare circumstances will a single explanation for strategy development exist.

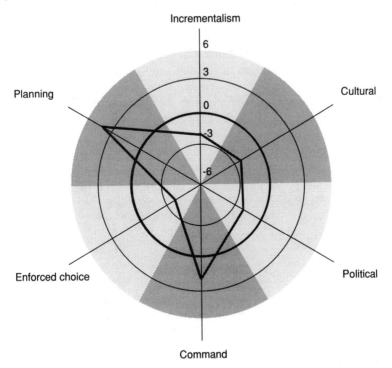

Figure 4.3   *Case A – The planning commander*

The organization is seen to have definite and precise strategic objectives (Figure 4.3) and to be developing a number of strategic options capable of attaining these objectives. The options are assessed against the objectives to be achieved before the 'best' option is selected. Precise procedures are subsequently developed for the attainment of the objectives, with the strategy being made explicit in the form of precise plans used to communicate the strategy throughout the organization. Strategy development, then, is seen to be based on a systematic analysis of the business environment.

However, while this process is characterized by the planning dimension, it is not the sole influence over strategy development. Rather influence is also seen to emerge from a senior figure as characterized by the command dimension. Here strategy is seen to be associated with powerful groups taking strategic decisions, though within the confines of both the planning process and a shared 'vision' of the organization's future. Indeed, while this vision is particularly associated with the chief executive, it is also seen to be commonly shared across the organization. As such, it represents a commonly shared view about the strategic direction that should be pursued.

The relationship between the notion of command and vision with the existence of a defined planning process raises a number of questions. These centre around the extent to which one influence moderates the other or the extent to which they actually operate in conjunction. Is the planning process driving the definition and communication of the strategic direction of the organization, with the vision or mission simply supporting this commonly shared view of the future? Conversely, is the chief executive's vision the driving force behind the strategy, with the planning process operating to justify and validate this vision, by providing the numbers and specific actions needed for its achievement.

In any event, the processes at work appear to have led to the development of a strategy that is commonly agreed upon. The low political influence confirms that there is little need for bargaining and negotiation between groups in order to secure acceptance of the strategy. Also barriers in the environment are not seen to restrict the strategies that can be followed; nor is the strategy imposed by those external to the organization.

This low level of environmental influence suggests one of three scenarios. Firstly, it may indicate that an organization's planning processes are such that they enable the organization to keep ahead of the business environment, and so instigate any changes before being forced to. Alternatively, the process depicted may represent an external business environment that has little impact on the organization, and thus requires little attention. This latter scenario is potentially dangerous, for if the operating environment were to change and become more influential, the organization would be caught unprepared. Also of potential danger is the third explanation, which is that the powerful executives who influence strategy have failed to recognize the impact of their business environment.

Case B – The logical incrementalist

The strategy development process seen to be in operation in this major leisure service organization is characterized by an incremental approach to the operating environment though under influence both from the formal process of planning and from the impact of the organization's culture.

The strategy the organization develops, emerges gradually as the organization responds to the need to change. It is a highly adaptive process, with small changes being made to strategy in order to match changes occurring within the operating environment and the marketplace. Indeed, there would seem to be some level of experimentation, with the consequences of various strategic options being tested out through exposure to the business environment. Here, then, strategic change is likely to build from, and on, the strategy the organization is currently following. It is unlikely that major, radical changes will occur. See Figure 4.4.

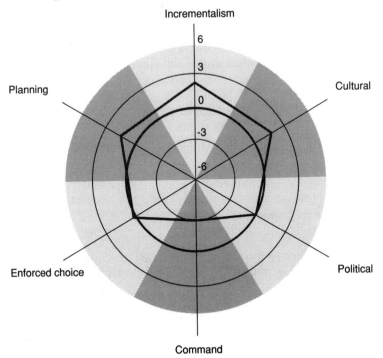

Figure 4.4   *Case B – The logical incrementalist*

The process is seen to be adaptive in nature, driven by both planning and cultural elements. The organization has defined strategic objectives, which are pursued and made explicit through precise strategic plans. A well-developed procedure for the assessment of potential strategic options exists – a procedure likely to combine the processes of 'rational' and incremental assessment through the constant testing of these options in the environment. There are defined procedures for the development of the organization's strategy, which is undertaken in a systematic manner.

Cultural influences are also an important dimension. These are seen to relate to a way of doing things in the organization that has developed over the years, impacting on the strategies developed and pursued. As such, the search for strategic issues and their solution is directed by what has occurred previously within the organization. There also exists across the organization a strong sense of shared beliefs and assumptions based around what the organization is about, what the future direction should be, and what constitutes threats or opportunities. While these shared beliefs are anchored in the organization's past, they are also changeable, and do not just represent a perpetuation of the way things were.

Given that strategy development is adaptive in nature, it is interesting to question what is the interplay between the cultural and the planning dimensions? To what extent is the planning process operating to challenge the assumptions and influence of culture? Is it merely operating to provide data to support strategy development within the confines of the current culture? Alternatively, is the planning process operating to reorientate the organization away from a reliance on the taken-for-granted? In this scenario the strategy changes required may still be filtered through the organization's existing culture to reduce the potential for resistance and non-implementation. Indeed, the shared assumptions and beliefs may even form a readily accessible and effective means through which required change can be communicated and achieved.

Case C – The professional service firm

In comparison to the above case, the process of strategy development in this professional service partnership is seen to be primarily driven by its political and cultural processes and an adaptive or incremental response to an influential environment.

Unlike in many corporations where an individual's involvement in decision-making at an operational level may be strongly influenced by role and function, partnerships operate much less rigidly. Decision outcomes are more likely to reflect the level of power and influence held by various individuals and interest groups, the strength of which may change given different issues. It is interesting to find that such decision-making forces are also reflected at a strategic level.

Within this organization the firm's strategies, which are strongly related to the desires of interest groups, are likely to be developed by powerful individuals and groups through negotiation, debate and compromise. In this manner strategic problems are defined, and strategies that accommodate conflicting interests are developed. Participation by interest groups in the process is determined according to the issue; the same individuals or groups may not be involved in each decision. The strategy developed, then, reflects the interests of groups within the organization. See Figure 4.5.

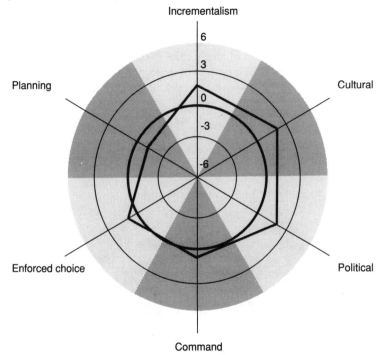

Figure 4.5   *Case C – The professional service firm (T1)*

Equally the firm's long professional history and associated culture are likely to influence the identification of issues and options, and mediate the choice of strategies. Further, the cultural beliefs and assumptions are likely to allow the various power groups to relate to each other within routines that are taken for granted. Within this culture, the strategies pursued emerge in an adaptive manner through a series of continual small changes and steps that those in the organization believe enable the firm to keep in line with the business environment.

In addition, the firm, which does not generally seem to be in a position to influence the environment in which it operates, appears to respond to environmental influences rather than making strategic decisions unprompted by external forces. Indeed, strategies are not seen to develop in any systematic planned manner; little in the way of set procedures for the development of strategy exist.

The danger is that this lack of planning may prevent the partnership looking forward in a proactive manner; there may be too much reliance being placed on reactive responses to changes in the environment. Ultimately this may lead to difficulties for the partnership, for while the prevailing strategic direction may reflect past successes, it may not entirely fit the requirements for sustained success in the future, The root cause of, this problem is that there may be little to challenge, and no questioning of, the taken for granted.

However, the appointment of a new chief executive changed this situation, as illustrated in Figure 4.6. The process of strategy development was no longer characterized by a logical adaptive approach. Rather strategy is seen to relate primarily to the power of the 'big man'. It is his aspirations for the future of the organization that is seen to provide the focus for strategic direction.

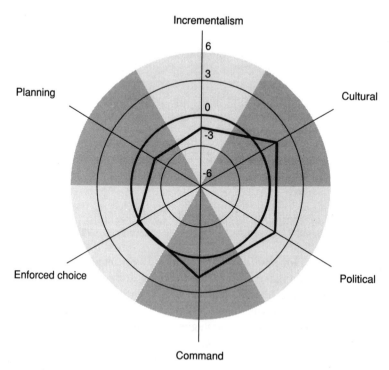

Figure 4.6   *The professional service firm (T2)*

Although influence over strategy development here is still seen to be closely related to political processes, particularly those associated with the possession and utilization of power, the importance of this dimension has diminished. Similarly, the influence of the organization's culture on strategy development has also been subdued by the power of the managing partner.

However, the relationship that exists between these three influences is of great significance. The professional ethos permeating the organization and its members provides a common understanding and an established power structure through which political activity can be exercised. Indeed, the command figure has emerged from this structure. Thus, even though the managing partner is seen to have ultimate control, his power is moderated. In addition, as this individual has developed and progressed through the same professional and organizational structure as his colleagues, so he is likely to hold a similar view of the world and the strategic issues faced. This in turn is likely to reduce the level of conflict within the organization, particularly at a senior level.

Looking to the future, it is interesting to consider whether the authority of the new senior figure will prevail, or whether in fact the cultural and political dimensions will once again dominate the strategy development process.

Case D – The archetypal public sector organization

This example is a common configuration of processes seen within the public sector. It is a process of strategy development that is characterized by the dominant external influence of the environment and by the internal influence from cultural and political forces. This local government division sees its freedom of strategic movement to be severely limited by central government legislation, expectations and financial control. Indeed, the external environment is such that strategy is imposed by those outside, with internal power bases having little influence in this.

However, political activity in the form of negotiation and bargaining within the organization are important factors in issues concerning the implementation of the strategy, e.g. in the prioritization of strategic tasks, and/or in the allocation of financial resources. In fact in this part of the process the highly influential and deterministic external environment directly impacts on the internal power structure of the organization. It is those groups who deal with the external environment and who operate as boundary spanners (Jemison, 1981) who attain greatest influence over the operational aspects of the strategy. Controlling externally derived resources and information, much of which is likely to relate to the external environment, these groups could ultimately restrict or delay the implementation of the preset strategy. See Figure 4.7.

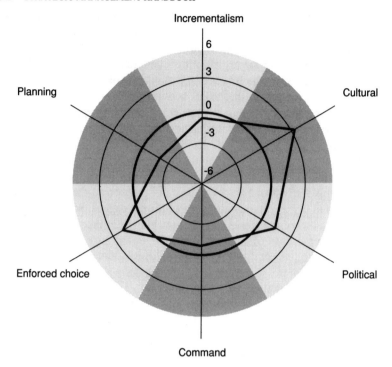

Figure 4.7   *Case D – The archetypal public sector organization*

The process of strategy development in this organization could present substantial problems for change. It appears that what strategic change there is, is dictated by forces outside the organization and through internal power struggles or political negotiation. Such a combination does not bode well for repositioning strategy if the operating environment were to change rapidly, e.g. by becoming more competitively oriented. There are however, organizations that have faced such circumstances and have appeared to change the processes that drive the strategy within themselves.

Figure 4.8, showing the profile of an organization in transition between the public and private sector, is an illustration of this. Under these conditions the strategy development process is perceived to be related to the planning and incremental dimensions though still under influence of the external environment, as depicted by the enforced choice dimension.

In particular, planning is perceived by the organization's members to be a major influence over the process of strategy development. This is seen to relate particularly to the existence of definite and precise strategic objectives and the assessment of potential strategic options against the explicit objectives to be achieved. However, planning in this instance is seen to be moderated by an adaptive approach to strategy development. New strategies deliberately build on existing strategies, with small continual changes to strategy ensuring that the organization keeps in line with its business or operating environment. Indeed strategy is seen to emerge gradually as the organization responds to the need to change and adjusts its strategy to match the changes that occur in its marketplace.

Such contrasting patterns from two organizations operating in a similar environment pose interesting questions. Do the forces shown to be dominant in the transitional organization represent what the members feel are the forces

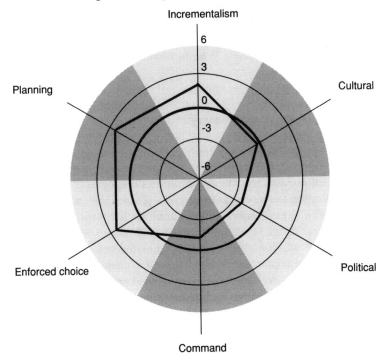

Figure 4.8   *Case D – The transitional public sector organization*

that will facilitate a smooth transition into the private sector, rather than a reflection of the processes actually at work? Do the organization's members perceive that with an archetypal planning process in place any potential problems associated with transition can effectively be planned out: for example, that planning processes somehow diminish the political forces so typical of public sector organizations? Unfortunately, however appealing and traditionally acceptable the implementation of a planning system may be, this approach may well prove inappropriate if strategy development is driven by alternative forces, e.g. by the organization's culture or its political processes.

Alternatively, executives may have been brought in from a different environment to effect the change, and they may not appreciate the strengths of the cultural and polical dimensions. If this is the case, it is likely that problems emanating from the long-established ways of doing things will be encountered upon the implementation of a new strategy.

Example of differences in process

While the above examples of the strategy development process occurring within organizations presents the process as commonly agreed upon, differences between organizational groups have been identified. In Case E differences in terms of the process will be highlighted between board and senior level managers.

Case E – Executive and senior manager

Within this international manufacturing organization there are two distinct groups, which consist of those based in the organization's executive and those who are its senior managers. The organization's executive see the process of strategy development to be characterized by a planned intentional response to the organization's environment but within an adaptive or incremental approach. Indeed, defined strategic objectives are seen to be developed based on a systematic analysis of the business environment. These executives believe that specific procedures are followed both in the analysis of the environment and the development of potential solutions. However, this assessment is not solely captured within the planning procedures; rather strategies are modified through implementation. The resulting exposure to the business environment is not unintentional or haphazard, but deliberate. There is also seen to be a clear view of the future the organization is progressing towards and which provides both the executive and other decision-makers with a self-contained criteria against which potential actions can be assessed. See Figure 4.9.

This is not a view of strategy development shared by the organization's senior managers. While both groups see strategy developing in an adaptive manner, what constitutes the driving force of the process differs. Here strategy is seen to develop from the internal political activities of the organization. Indeed, strategy is seen to be defined within the organization by those groups with power. As such, the strategies pursued are seen to reflect the interest of particular groups as opposed to the organization as a whole.

The idea of the organization following defined and systematic procedures in defining its strategic direction is not seen by the senior managers. Neither are

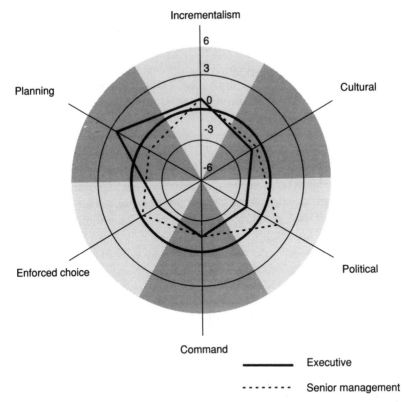

Figure 4.9   *Case E – Executive and senior managers*

plans that communicate the strategy and the mechanisms for its achievement seen to exist. Rather influence over the process is attained through the control of critical resources and information.

While there is disagreement on the major influences of strategy development, the two groups do agree on the relatively low influence of the external environment, the absence of any senior figure setting the strategic direction, and the minimal influence of the organization's culture over the process, a factor not surprising, given that the organization has recently been through major change, including its acquisition by another corporation. Indeed this latter point may account for some of the differences. The process as perceived by the executive may reflect a new process which is being developed, even imposed, as a result of the acquisition but which has not yet permeated to those at the level below. However, regardless of the mechanisms through which the differences have emerged, they require careful management in terms of increasing the participation of all relevant parties in the strategy development process.

Conclusion and implications

The cases in this chapter have indicated that strategy is not developed in an identical manner in all organizations. Rather the process is seen to differ. Indeed, numerous configurations of strategy development have been identified between managers across industry sectors and between different organizations within the same sector. Furthermore, the cases have also shown that the configurations of strategy development do not necessarily, or even usually, encompass the archetypal planning process, where strategy evolves as a result of a rational analytical approach.

The consequence of this is that a unitary dimension to understanding strategy development is ineffective in conveying the complexity of the processes seen to exist. However, the approach discussed in this chapter overcomes this problem through an integrated framework, combining six explanations of the strategy development process.

In dealing with these six processes, as they are to be found in organizations, this chapter has been descriptive and not prescriptive. There is no suggestion here that because such processes exist, this is how strategy should be managed. However, it is important to understand the reality of strategy-making in organizations, not least because those who seek to influence the strategy of organizations do so within that reality. There is little point in formulating strategies that may be elegant analytically without having an understanding of the processes actually at work. Although there has been no suggestion within this chapter that any one mix of strategy development processes is superior to another, this would be an interesting area to be addressed by research. Could a number of optimum process configurations be found to exist in given competitive conditions? Indeed this type of question is becoming of increasing interest among researchers (Meyer, Tsui and Hinings, 1993).

In the meantime, there are many practical benefits to managers in this work. Through the use of this integrated framework a clearer understanding of the strategy development process can be achieved and the process occurring within organizations can be brought to the surface. This understanding in turn acts to stimulate discussion and exploration by senior executives of the strategic development process in operation.

This is of vital importance when an organization faces a change in strategy, for if a change is to be successfully achieved, it is essential that the processes that are driving strategies are understood and managed. Moreover, within an organization it is possible that different perceptions will exist as to what these driving processes are: to ensure that strategy is implemented effectively managers need to understand the strategy development process as seen by their colleagues. The level of conflict typically encountered in strategy development may, then, be reduced and the efficiency of the process improved.

References

Aldrich, H E (1979) *Organizations and Environments*, Prentice-Hall, Englewood Cliffs, NJ.

Aldrich, H E and Mueller, S (1982) The evolution of organizational form: Technology coordination and control, in Staw, B M and Cummings, L L (Eds) *Research in Organizational Behavior*, Vol. 4, pp. 33- 89.

Allison, G T (1971) *Essence of Decision – Explaining the Cuban Missile Crisis*, Little Brown and Company, Boston.

Andrews, K R (1980) *The Concept of Corporate Strategy*, Revised edition, R D Irwin, Georgetown, Ontario.

Ansoff, H I (1965) *Corporate Strategy*, McGraw-Hill, New York.

Bennis, W and Nanus, B (1985) *Leaders: The Strategies for Taking Charge*, Harper & Row, New York.

Derkinderen, F G J and Crum, R L (1988) The development and empirical validation of strategic decision models, *International Studies of Management and Organization*, 18, 2, pp. 29-55.

Etzioni, A (1989) Humble decision making, *Harvard Business Review*, pp, 122-6, July-August.

Fredrickson, J W (1983) Strategic process research: Questions and recommendations, *Academy of Management Review*, 8, 4, pp. 565-75.

Freeman, R (1984) *Strategic Management: A Stakeholder Approach*, Pitman, Boston.

Hamel, G and Prahalad, C K (1989) Strategic Intent, *Harvard Business Review*, 67, 3, 63-76.

Hannan, M T and Freeman, J H (1989) *Organizational Ecology*, Harvard University Press, Cambridge, Mass.

Heller, F, Drenth, P, Koopman, P and Rus, V (1988) *Decisions in Organizations: A Three Country Comparative Study*, Sage Publications, London.

Hinings, C R, Hickson D J, Pennings, J M and Schneck, R E (1974) Structural conditions of intraorganisational power, *Administrative Science Quarterly*, 19, 1, pp. 22-44.

Jemison, D B (1981) Organisational versus environmental sources of influence in strategic decision-making, *Strategic Management Journal*, 2, 1, pp. 77-89.

Johnson, G (1987) *Strategic Change and the Management Process,* Basil Blackwell, Oxford.

Johnson, G (1992) Managing, Strategic Change – Strategy, Culture and Action, *Long Range Planning*, 25, 1, pp. 28-36.

Lindblom, C E (1959) The science of 'muddling through', *Public Administration Review*, 19, pp. 79-88, Spring.

Lyles, M A (1981) Formulating strategic problems: Empirical analysis and model development, *Strategic Management Journal*, 2, pp. 61-75.

Meyer, A D, Tsui, A and Hinings, C R (1993) Configurational approaches to organizational analysis, *Academy of Management Journal*, 36, 6, pp. 1175-95.

Mintzberg, H (1973) Strategy making in three modes, *California Management Review*, 16, 2, pp. 44-53.

Mintzberg, H (1978) Patterns of strategy formation, *Management Science*, 24, 9, pp. 934-48.

Mintzberg, H and Waters, J A (1985) Of strategies, deliberate and emergent, *Strategic Management Journal*, 6, pp. 257-72.

Mintzberg, H, Raisinghani, D and Theoret, A (1976) The structure of 'unstructured' decision processes, *Administrative Science Quarterly*, 21, pp. 246-75.

Nutt, P (1984) Types of organizational decision processes, *Administrative Science Quarterly*, 29, 3, pp. 414-50.

Pfeffer, J and Salancik, G R (1978) *The External Control of Organizations*, Harper and Row, New York.

Porter, M (1980) *Competitive Strategy*, Free Press, New York.

Quinn, J B (1980) *Strategies for Change – Logical Incrementalism*, R D Irwin, Georgetown, Ontario.

Schein, E H (1985) *Organizational Culture and Leadership*, Jossey-Bass, San Francisco.

Schon, D A (1983) *The Reflective Practioner: How Professionals Think in Action*, Temple Smith, London.

Schwenk, C R (1988) *The Essence of Strategic Decision Making*, D C Heath & Co., Lexington, Mass.

Shrivastava, P and Grant, J H (1985) Empirically derived models of strategic decision making processes, *Strategic Management Journal*, 6, pp. 97-113.

Spender, J-C (1989) *Industry Recipes: The Nature and Source of Managerial Judgement*, Blackwell Ltd, Oxford.

Trice, H M and Beyer, J M (1986) The concept of charisma, *Research in Organizational Behavior*, Vol. 8, JAI Press, pp. 118-64.

Part Three STRATEGIC ISSUES AND CHALLENGES

Figure 1 in the Introduction to this handbook shows how leadership and culture are at the heart of strategy. It has been acknowledged for many years that key roles for the strategic leader are the provision of direction for the organization, the structure and the communications system. The culture – the 'way things happen inside organizations' – is inevitably tied in with structure and communications. Chapter 11, strategy **evaluation**, takes this further and argues that the strategic leader should seek to ensure the organization has a range of strategically important competencies.

Different leaders offer different personal strengths, styles, skills and competencies. A particular leader may be ideal in certain circumstances, inappropriate in others; leaders may need to change as strategies and organizations change and develop. Some leaders, however, are flexible and able to adapt more than others. Sir Graham Day's chapter provides a number of interesting and thought-provoking reflections based on several years experience as a strategic leader of a number of large UK corporations.

Leaders and organizations increasingly have to deal with the challenges, opportunities and threats of industries that are becoming more and more global in nature. Trade barriers are reduced; the Asia Pacific region has the fastest growing economies in the world; and many companies in the UK must see Europe, if not the world, as a single market and look for critical mass on an international scale. In turn, the growth and the developing strategies of multinational organizations present challenges for governments. This is the theme of Peter J Buckley's chapter.

Peter Buckley's chapter, like the contribution from Denis Smith later in this section, is academic in origin; both chapters address critical strategic issues but they require careful study.

There already exists a considerable base of published research concerning the growth and success of multinational corporations. Single country companies – partly because of government interference – have not been able to obtain the potential benefits from international specialization and trade; multinational businesses create internal markets which span frontiers and thus overcome some of these barriers.

The challenge now for individual multinationals is one of developing a global strategy, together with a structure capable of implementing the strategy, which harnesses the assumed potential synergies. These strategies and structures encompass strategic alliances and joint ventures, discussed earlier in Chapter 3, in an attempt to exercise greater control of resources and the supply chain and thereby sharpen competitiveness. Buckley outlines a number of models for examining these issues.

This chapter then looks at the wider implications for the international economy of the power of multinational corporations and the impact on the companies of an increasingly turbulent international environment. Buckley demonstrates that capital markets are now international; goods and services markets are regionalized through both common interests and economic groupings like the EU; individual countries and governments – with their distinctive cultures – inevitably remain concerned with domestic employment, inflation and other macro-economic indicators. Another dilemma of the 1990s is the fact that both economically (resource efficiency) and competitively (market access) it can make sense for UK-based multinationals to locate more and more production overseas. The UK is not alone in this, and the exodus of manufacturing to lower labour cost countries highlights a conflict between the objectives of the businesses and those of their home governments.

Buckley argues that intra-company movements comprise the basis for much of the world's trade in goods and services and consequently nations must now see themselves as competitors of other nations for inward investment and economic development – witness the relative success of the UK *within Europe* in attracting Japanese investment in selected industries such as motor vehicle assembly. The chapter thus highlights how attempts to deal with these tensions form a major challenge for both corporations and governments in the 1990s.

Internationalization also gives ethical and social responsibility issues an added sharpness, with the case for corporate ethics increasingly accepted. In July 1994 a new international code of ethics was launched in Caux, Switzerland, stressing the need for moral values in business decisions. The code affirms the responsibilities of organizations to a wide range of stakeholders and to the countries in which they operate. Businesses are expected to act honestly and fairly, with behaviour governed by a spirit of trust that goes beyond the letter of the law. Both domestic and international rules should be accepted.

Linda Bennett's chapter, **Ethics and strategy**, first examines the origins of the now accepted links between ethics, social responsibility and strategy, and, second, shows how ethics impacts on strategic decision making in a variety of ways.

Earlier chapters have illustrated how an important strategic challenge for organizations is the ability to deal with uncertainty and discontinuity; successful companies can suddenly be faced by a crisis in today's dynamic and competitive environment. Denis Smith argues that the role of excellence within companies (a key facet of the culture) has long been espoused by management gurus as the way to ensure organizations achieve their full capabilities. Reality, however, indicates that many organizations are actually frail, and, consequently, it is essential that managers accept the propensity for failure in organizations and develop their strategies accordingly. Managers in successful companies often delude themselves into believing they understand (and control) the reasons behind the success.

Smith's chapter therefore studies crises, disasters and catastrophes, using corporate, natural and socio-technical examples, to give us greater insight into how companies might seek to manage the increasing turbulence and chaos in their environments. Companies should develop strategies for avoiding crises (as far as is possible) and for dealing with crises when they do occur. To achieve this they need to appreciate a number of underlying issues, in particular that culture and behaviour patterns in some organizations create what have been termed 'resident pathogens' which are basically crises waiting to happen.

All major organizations are complex systems; ideally the parts (the subsystems) will coordinate to create synergy or positive emergent properties. On occasions the parts will conflict, sometimes inevitably, sometimes unexpectedly, to create a more catastrophic and undesirable down-side. Everyday events such as a crowd coming together for a football match (Hillsborough) or technical, engineered creations such as roll-on/roll-off ferries (Herald of Free Enterprise, Estonia) are similarly complex systems which occasionally fail. Denis Smith uses the example of the Titanic to bring out a number of lessons which can be transferred to an organizational setting. The quality of communications and an understanding of events are always critical.

Smith uses a number of complex diagrams to illustrate and develop his arguments. A detailed study is required to grasp all the points, but the underlying principles are important and straightforward.

The chapter demonstrates three levels of crisis. First, a crisis of management, implying a failure to learn from events (successes and potential failure signals) and communicate effectively. Second, a crisis of operations, the actual failure event. Third, a crisis of legitimation, where blame is directed and there is a further inability to learn and communicate about what really happened. Seven Cs are identified which can be used to investigate any crisis situation. Three of these are 'warm' (people related), namely *culture, communications* and *configuration* (power and influence issues); the other four are 'cold' (technocratic), namely *control, coupling and complexity* (the nature of the event itself), *cost* and *contingency planning*. Smith argues that a major reason for our failure to learn – such that we perpetuate the potential for crises and disasters – is that we focus on the four cold issues and ignore the criticality of the three warm factors.

The chapter is really supporting the case for learning organizations – highlighted in the introduction to this book (p. 10) and discussed further in Chapter 12 – by talking about more open, flexible organizations. Smith also makes a case for using different and more qualitative measures and indicators of performance, which itself is the subject of Chapter 11.

Smith concludes that the lessons from the theory are clear – we must learn more about success and failure and respond to these lessons in different ways. However, considerable work remains to be done before this theoretical underpinning is translated into practical guidance to allow us to identify and hopefully eradicate the crisis-prone organization.

5

Reflections on leadership
Sir Graham Day

Introduction: the importance of leadership

In my view four attributes characterize those companies that are successful over time, namely:

- leadership,
- having a clear direction,
- good communications within and without the company, and
- fast, comprehensive and continuing learning.

Of these four, the most important to my mind is leadership, and I rank leadership first because without it a company is unlikely to possess or develop the other three important attributes.

My academic and business experience over four decades tells me that relatively few essentials determine the success of most business organizations. I am not brushing aside the basics of day-to-day management activity, nor the need to provide excellent products and services and to have adequate financing, but, with these as givens, I have come to believe that it is the leadership required to determine first, the direction in which a business must go, and, second, provide the drive required to get it there, that are the dimensions ultimately distinguishing the corporate winners, on the one hand, from the also-rans and losers, on the other.

My comments in this chapter, incidentally, refer primarily to organizations in Western countries rather than those in the fast-growing and successful countries of Asia Pacific. By contrast, for example, leadership in Japan is

---

This chapter is an edited version of a lecture given by Sir Graham Day in Leeds in 1994 to an audience invited by Yorkshire Water plc.

institutionalized and sometimes entrepreneurial. One excellent example of where leadership is institutionalized rather than personalized is their choice of prime minister, where it has become a question of 'Who can we agree upon?' Over a period of time successful entrepreneurial leaders like Matsushita, who started by manufacturing light-bulb fixtures in a garage after the Second World War, become institutionalized. Why is this?

The modern Japanese culture is relatively new. The Meiji was restored to the throne in 1868 after thirteen generations of Tokugawa Shoguns: at this time Japan was economically a long way behind the West. The economic revolution that followed gave rise to the present-day society. Feudalism was abolished, education was Westernized and many of today's corporate giants were established. Clearly there has been a second dramatic industrial revolution since the end of the Second World War. Bureaucratic government systems and regulations have been established, and they dominate the economic structures; hence the institutionalization. As a result, the Japanese concept of leadership continues to flow from a position-based respect.

The influence of the Japanese on industries in the UK has largely been through fear rather than leadership. Fear for what was happening in the marketplace, and the fear of the competition. I suppose what we have seen happening reflects an attitude of 'If you cannot beat them, you join them, or you bring them within the walls of your tent'. I think personally this is a good thing.

The leadership challenge of the 1990s

Importantly, effective leadership in a company operates to counter tendencies towards structure- and process-induced rigidity. Indeed, effective leadership will not permit these impediments to be created in the first instance, and in this respect business organization owes much to the military. The military, and in particular the Army, was the organization that first had to contend with size – in particular, masses of men and materials. To achieve victory, armies had to have well-defined objectives that were communicated effectively and understood as appropriate by surbordinates; but above all they had to be led to achieve victory. Consequently, much of what has been written about leadership includes references to military leaders, the aspects they share in common and those idiosyncrasies that distinguish them individually.

Leadership in the military is not merely functional, it must be visible. The military leader who is functionally adequate but insufficiently visible or, when visible, is perceptionally inadequate, will fail. He or she will fail the leadership challenges. In considering the requirement to have *observable leadership*, the military have coined the phrase 'command presence'. It has been suggested by some cynics that in the military how one appears may be more important than how one performs, with visions of the single-dimensional cardboard figure frequently appearing on cinema and television screens. However, while presence is an important element of leadership, it is only the outward manifestation of a myriad of attributes that go to comprise the effective leader.

The challenge for those who must identify and select leaders in all walks of life is to discover whether there exists in an individual that combination of functional abilities and nature of personality that, when combined, will beneficially comprise the elixir of leadership. Neither the functional skills nor the personality characteristics in isolation will individually do the trick.

I observed through the 1970s and 1980s that many in business were prone to conclude that functional skills, backed up with intellectual prowess, were all that was required for effective management. Subordinates would follow simply on the basis of the correctness of the decisions reached by these presumed managerial elite.

Today we know that that is not enough. We have discovered that persuasion, encouragement, precept, example and ultimately the express or implied 'Follow me' are what is required to secure both commitment and results. Thus, the appeal is not simply to the mind but also to the emotions. Positive outcomes, by and large, are not the result of managerial correctness on the part of persons in organizationally superior positions. Most agree that leadership in the true sense has nothing to do with rank and everything to do with effectiveness.

The identification of leadership attributes is difficult; even a comprehensive description of leadership itself is elusive. Required attributes can be identified and specified, but if these qualities are all present, do they in aggregate equate to leadership? I would argue they do not. There is always an elusive 'something else' that is either present or absent. Field Marshal the Viscount Wavell, soldier and writer, said of leadership that 'You know when it is there, and you know when it is not'.

If leadership is not merely the aggregation of individually desirable or required characteristics, then how do we begin to understand its complexities? Carl Jung, the psychologist, concluded that some individuals are predisposed to be more effective. This conclusion suggests that *ab initio* each of us in personality terms is likely to be more or less successful in a leadership role. The quest for leadership – and an understanding of it – is not just an intellectual exercise for academics, it is a critical task for those charged with establishing appropriate corporate governance for a wide variety of undertakings, including business management. If leadership is absent in a company, that company will atrophy and all its vital signs will weaken. The word *leader-*

ship, used by the media in a power position sense, is reserved for rank and position rather than to explain effectiveness; but, of course, the two aspects cannot be mutually exclusive.

Qualities for effective leadership

With leadership increasingly recognized as a critical element in the commercial and industrial world, we can easily see that, in addition to an acknowledged need for presence, there are many other, sometimes subtle, elements. Professor Abraham Zaleznik (1977) of the Harvard Business School argues that 'Leadership is made of substance, humanity and morality . . . We are painfully short of all three qualities in our collective lives'. It is significant that Zaleznik does not talk of attributes but of **qualities**, referring not to skills or abilities but to dimensions of character.

I suggested earlier that a leader is not a one-dimensional cardboard figure. Zaleznik is also saying that a leader must have substance, for if one is to relate to others, then clearly the human touch becomes imperative. Leadership is about hearts and minds. Zaleznik further argues that leadership requires other qualities of humanity. Above all, leaders should be moral persons. If anyone doubts the need for leaders to have high moral standards, consider Hitler. Despite his early electoral rigging and his policing techniques, Hitler was a leader who, for a considerable time, enjoyed massive support and adulation from the German people, satisfying many of the requirements on any leadership checklist. However, among others, he failed the moral requirement.

On the subject of ethics Sir Adrian Cadbury used to say 'If you have to ask, the answer is "No"'. If you have to go to the point of saying 'Well, is it acceptable if I do this?' the answer is 'No' because it obviously suggests you are too close to the line. In many instances, particularly in extreme circumstances, managers become tempted to place just a toe, rather than the whole foot, over the line. But it is enough, and on a slippery slope a lot will be caught out.

I believe there are three key **objectives** of leadership. The first is to change compelled performers into contributing participants. The second is to lever the strengths of individuals and the group, and the third is to create a climate for achievement. Putting these leadership objectives another way, leadership is about achievement, and achievement is obtained through deploying the strengths of others in a way in which the result is greater than the sum of the parts. To deploy these strengths effectively, they must be offered freely rather than have to be compelled.

What, then, is needed for leadership? In addition to those three main qualities identified by Zaleznik, I would suggest that leaders need:

- vision; a strategic ability, including anticipation and direction;
- a willingness to commit;
- the staying power to see something through;
- the requisite skills;
- and enough charisma – call it command presence if you will – to persuade others that they should follow.

Napoleon reputedly asked whether officers proposed for promotion to senior command were lucky. It may well be that luck is a further element; however, I prefer to conclude that luck is present when there is genuine leadership and a clear direction.

Ambition or aspiration?

'Brutus hath said that Caesar was ambitious.'

Nye Bevan once said in the House of Commons: 'There is poverty in this nation, poverty of aspiration'. While I personally like to see ambition, in the form of aspiration, on the part of people with whom I am working, I am less happy with ambition that is so naked one senses that almost everything is or could be subordinated to that ambition. I regard such naked ambition as very worrying; but, at the same time, if someone does not aspire at all as a manager, then I would personally mark that person down in an evaluation. It is, however, perfectly legitimate for someone to say to you in an annual review: 'I really don't aspire to go any further. (Possibly) I am not prepared to live with the travelling, not prepared to live wherever . . . I have other personal priorities'. If that person is a consistently solid performer, then I think you have to respect his or her personal judgement and attempt to plan their career within the limits he or she has chosen to apply. It is the same with a very good employee who, say, has a heart problem, or something similar. You are going to sit down with that employee and determine what can be done in organizational terms to obtain the benefit of his or her skills and expertise, and at the same time ensure that he or she lives to enjoy a pension and beyond.

Changing the leader

A good leader can usually move from business to business and remain an adequate performer with very solid functional skills. This is something that most of us hope we will be able to achieve consistently, but in difficult situations making such transitions can be hard. Experience and a track record expression when thinking about change. In sporting terms, the message is 'Don't drop the ball!'

I think, though, that if one has been engaged in a very fundamental and necessary root and branch shake-up in an organization, there comes a point in time when it is preferable to leave and hand over to someone who will consolidate the gains. Ideally this will be someone who is not going to let everybody sit back, become complacent again and return to the old ways.

I genuinely believe that leadership comes in all sizes and shapes, and that you very seldom get good leaders who are exactly the same. They might have some fundamental characteristics, typically operational characteristics, in common but there are numerous examples of great British companies that have performed well under Leader A and then 'got blown away' under Leader B, who had performed very well as a subordinate before being promoted to the top spot. The issue of whether a good Number 2 can move up to be an equally successful Number 1 is a major challenge for many organizations.

The outcome of poor leadership

Many people who read this chapter will have observed management, and I speak in the collective sense, where true leadership was not present and where management amounted only to control. I believe that such control produces three negatives:

- the negative of pressure without motivation,
- the negative of process over substance, and finally,
- the negative of organization without improvement.

When these three negatives are present, one will also be able to observe debilitating company rigidity, a lack of initiative, and no competitive advantage.

The importance of delegation

Leadership and control, then, may well be the antithesis of each other. A good leader has a declared direction and the ability to galvanize others in support of moving in this selected direction. The mere issuing of orders will not elicit the quality of support needed for success; the good leader will also have sense enough to delegate details. Theodore Roosevelt, a former President of the United States, said 'The best executive is one who has sense enough to pick good men to do what he wants done and self-restraint to keep from meddling

United States, said 'The best executive is one who has sense enough to pick good men to do what he wants done and self-restraint to keep from meddling with them while they do it'. I believe that remains as true today as when Roosevelt said it, although I suspect that if he were to reconsider his words today he might not be so gender-specific.

If one is working in an organization where the semantic of delegation is used but the practice is not within the dictionary meaning – in other words, delegation means 'You get on and do it' – it will be very hard to change the culture. Delegation requires a coaching approach: 'Let me tell you what we are trying to do, and what I would like you to do is – this is your contribution'. It is an attempt to communicate everything which will enable persons to understand their role and contribution and then allowing them to do it in their own preferred way.

Changing to this from the first culture is extraordinarily difficult. Early in the process the delegator has to learn to follow the forbearance which Roosevelt suggests.

It is important for people not to make a tragic or a fatal mistake but preferable, if it so happens, for them to move down a route towards a mistake, hopefully discover it and then backtrack. This is necessary for organizational learning. It is equally important to allow subordinates to do something in a way you or I might not have chosen, but, if you are *en route* to securing the objective, then leaving them alone to have a go. Defining when one can encourage and support in the delegation process, and not interfere, is a prime management task and, again, it is difficult.

It becomes much easier, though, as the culture in an organization changes in the way described above. If one is in an organization where such empowerment is not part of the culture, effective delegation is very difficult, because people are fundamentally conditioned to being told what to do and then pressurized until they comply. Now the leader's approach is 'If it is wrong it is their fault and if it is right it is to *my* credit'.

Exceptional leaders

I read recently a summary of a private study to which I had earlier contributed. The study had been undertaken for the Boeing Aircraft Company and it examined the characteristics of world-class firms. Among the conclusions was the recognition that world-class firms possessed what was described as exceptional leadership. This exceptional leadership was defined as 'The chief executive officer's ability to inspire confidence, communicate and implement his vision to all levels of corporate hierarchy and the community at large'.

For me the interesting dimension in this definition is not simply the aspects of inspiration and communication, but the clear statement that these attributes should extend to the community at large. Of course, in the case of the Boeing Aircraft Company, that community is the world. Early in my time at Canadian Pacific, working for a remarkable man named Les Smith, it was impressed upon me that if you were responsible for others you had to be visible. In the largest country in the world, with thousands of miles of rail track extending over four and a half time zones, and with local bosses who are distant from headquarters, being seen was essential. Les Smith called it 'walking the property'. In Les Smith's practice it also meant getting to know your people and providing help when help was needed, both personally and corporately. Today in popular business books one reads about 'walk round management'. It is not a new concept – Les Smith was there first. My experience tells me that you do not need size and distance to justify walking the property. Being seen and, in consequence, becoming available and approachable, is obviously easier in a single-site organization.

I have found that precept and example are compelling. Included are simple evidences of personal adherence to working hours when on site; clear control of expense accounts, distinguishing between the company's money and one's own; and always, unfailingly, maintaining a high standard of politeness to everyone.

Teaching leadership

I believe that people can be taught, and should be taught, those elements of leadership that are functional and can be learned. In addition, I believe that they can, through leadership simulations within a peer group, become increasingly sensitized. With an enhanced sensitivity and some of the techniques they may become more effective leaders within their scope.

I do think, though, that there is an additional 'something else' some people have. This extra quality may hardly ever be visible, or it will only emerge in particular circumstances. I have found more than one example in my life – not a dozen but more than one – where I wrongly assessed someone I was working with. I perceived them to be very run of the mill managers, nice and safe, suitably effective but not really of leadership material. I subsequently learned that in their private life these people had very important leadership roles in the larger community.

Succession issues

When I worked for Canadian Pacific I also remember being sent to Toronto. I was 33 years old at the time and my Number 1 was 58. I hired a relatively inexperienced graduate of 23. My superior knew he had plateaued in the organization but he still came to my office one day and said 'Graham, you know if you are not careful Peter Mills is going to have your job'. I replied: 'George, if that is what happens, that is okay. It is what I am paid to do. I am actually paid to try and find and hire the best people I can, and if I can't cope if they are better than I am, that is simply the way it is'. And he thought I was absolutely mad – absolutely mad.

I am afraid that some chief executives who are generally good and effective have some emotional difficulty with planning for succession. They cannot come to terms with the realization that this is a critical role for a board of directors. I think they find a search for a successor to themselves can be very threatening but, unfortunately, fear can become a self-fulfilling prophesy and speed up the change-over.

The outcome of effective leadership

In the introduction to this chapter I suggested that three other attributes of successful companies flowed from leadership:

- clear direction,
- good communications, and
- learning.

The preparation and (appropriate) dissemination of a corporate plan provides, in my experience, an ideal leadership opportunity. The leadership should not necessarily be driving the process, but using it to encourage broad-based participation and commitment. In good companies even the lowliest employee should have a clear concept of what the business is about, what outcomes are being sought, and his or her role as a contributor. When all the stakeholders – employees, investors, bankers and the community, as well as customers – understand the direction a company is taking, achieving objectives is very much easier.

I realize that determining the **direction** in the first place may not be straight-forward. In functional terms of course that is what the corporate planning process is all about. In leadership terms the *responsibility* for the plan and its delivery lies solely with the chief executive. Elements of preparing the plan can and should be delegated, and should be participatory, but never the ultimate responsibility. Leadership includes accepting and discharging responsibility.

It should always be remembered that **communication** is at least 50 per cent listening – not merely out of courtesy, although that in itself is important, but listening to hear views and opinions we may not always welcome. This aspect of communication also reveals whether information offered is being received and understood, and whether it is accepted or rejected.

Communication requires consistency, time and effort. A few well thought through, well-delivered messages, consistent over several years, are (usually) the most effective. A series of flavour of the week utterances from management is not only useless, it can be damaging.

Let me emphasize consistency with a well-known and well-used expression from the British Army. The old instruction handbook puts it this way: 'Tell them what you are going to tell them, tell them, then tell them what you told them'. It remains a good and realistic method of communication today. Never forget that the British Army has produced many excellent leaders. While some of them were called Montgomery and Slim, others were called Smith and Brown, of much more lowly rank. Most organizations are the same in principle.

External communications requires essentially the same treatment but with a different emphasis. While 'more is good' internally – which, after all, is a primary leadership focus – 'less is better' externally. An effective leader uses external communications to talk about the immediate past, emphasizing accomplishments, and the present. Although a leader may have to give public notice of a future event, the effective leader never talks about future specific goals or intended accomplishments. Such talk is usually mere puffery. My experience suggests that those leaders who live by PR die by PR. An effective leader will ensure that all external communications are, first, required; second, factual; and, third, short and comprehensive. It is all too easy to finesse the first, be tempted to embroider the second, and spend too little time on achieving the third. Remember, the leader should communicate effectively with the community, and this is a qualitative requirement, not a quantitative one.

Finally, but very importantly, **learning**. Fast learning on the part of a company may be that company's only competitive advantage. In the final analysis few companies have such a dominant market share, such clearly differentiated products or services, and such a price advantage, that speedy and continuing learning is of lower importance. Learning at the corporate level is the aggregation of learning throughout the business, learning that is directed, focused and made relevant through leadership. Learning by an individual, frequently not directed towards a company's specific business objectives, lifts the individual and his or her self-worth. The result is an employee with a much more significant contribution to make. Learning, particularly in today's world, is of primary importance to all businesses. The aware leader will use learning both as an essential tool and as an effective motivator.

In conclusion, leaders in business, and I hope elsewhere in our society, are not to be and should not be found only at the apex of the pyramid. In a good organization leaders emerge at all levels, and, may I remind you, leaders come in all sizes and shapes, all colours and creeds, and in two sexes.

Reference

Zaleznik, A (1977) Managers and Leaders: Are they different? Harvard Business Review, May–June.

6

The global environment
Peter J. Buckley

Introduction

This chapter seeks to place strategic management decisions in the context of a rapidly changing global economy. Section 2 introduces some fundamental concepts for the explanation of the role of multinational firms in the world economy. Section 3 examines decision-making in the multinational enterprise and the particular factors that drive firms' foreign market servicing strategies. Section 4 examines the international competitiveness of firms and nations and heads to the view that a 'conflict of management' exists in the globalizing economy (Section 5). Section 6 looks at the role of government policy in relation to attracting inward investment. Section 7 concludes.

Theory: The role of multinational firms in the world economy

As the internalization theory of the multinational firm plays a central role in international business theory, it is worth reprising its major premises. Put simply, this approach hypotheses that firms grow by replacing imperfect (or non-existent) external markets by internal ones. When combined with locational variance in the prices of spatially fixed inputs (non-tradeables), the theory can predict the pattern and direction of growth of multinational enterprises (Buckley and Casson, 1976 and 1985; Casson, 1987; Buckley, 1988). This approach needs to be combined with market power considerations deriving from Hymer (1968) to give a satisfying picture of the rate and direction of growth of multinational firms (Buckley, 1990).

There is, of course, a large literature and a rich empirical tradition examining the relationship between market power and multinational firms.

The literature up to 1982 is summarized by Caves (1982). The view that market power and internalization approaches are substitutes is put in Cantwell (1991) and elsewhere in Pitelis and Sugden (1991). Buckley (1988) is an attempt to show that the two approaches are not only *not* substitutes, they are actually complementary. After all, a crucial premise (perhaps *the* crucial premise) of the internalization approach is that firms internalize *imperfect* external markets up to the point where the costs of further internalization outweigh the benefits (Buckley and Casson, 1976, p. 37). Authors writing in a vein that contrasts the two misconceive the original message of Stephen Hymer (1968 and 1976).

In order to appreciate the bearing of the internalization approach on the role of multinationals in the world economy, it is essential to keep in mind the premises of the approach's purview:

1   The firm performs other functions than routine production. The coordination of these functions requires management decision-making and intermediate markets in knowledge and expertise. These alternatives (management and the market) may in certain circumstances be complementary means of solving allocation problems. Communication costs within and outwith the firm are crucial in coordination and may be operated upon by cultural differences.

2   Most multinational firms are also multi-product firms, giving rise to economies of scope as well as economies of scale. Coordination across product groups yields significant returns to effective management of joint inputs and joint products.

3   Multinational firms are, by definition, multi-plant (or multi-unit) enterprises. The minimization of transaction costs between plants owned and controlled by the same entity presents a major answer to the dilemma posed by the ability of below optimal scale multi-plant units being able to out-perform unitary firms (Scherer, 1975). Again, the management role in reducing such costs is vital.

4   It is possible, by using financial markets and markets for factor services, to achieve a separation of functions within the firm (Casson, 1985). Thus, for example, the funding, ownership and utilization of foreign assets can be carried out by different bodies. There is no necessity for these to be combined in a single multinational firm. Management judgement on the scope of functional separation in international capital markets is like any other internalization decision – a question of betting on beating the market outcome. This provides a direct link between the internalization approach and one based on internal competences.

5   The internalization approach is not identical to a view of the multinational enterprise that is always and everywhere market-perfecting. The firm can,

and will, invest in erecting barriers to entry and other forms of rent-seeking behaviour. It will further use its external influence to have others erect protective devices (notably governments). These points are developed below.

6   Crucially, the orthodox approach is rooted in a view of the world that incorporates limited information. Management decision-taking in this context is perforce plagued with errors (ex-post) and unintended consequences.

However, this might give the impression that firms are driven entirely by external circumstances. Firms, even the most powerful and dominant, could be perceived as merely responding to changes in their environment.

In the simple approach the role of management is confined to three key areas. First, managers make internalization decisions about the scale and scope of the firm. These 'buy' or 'build' decisions determine the interface between the firm and the market and the degree to which horizontal and vertical integration proceeds (Casson, 1987). Second, managers, in making internalization decisions, choose the direction of growth of the firm by identifying market imperfections and seeking opportunities to profit by appropriating rent. Third, managers can play a proactive role in contriving market imperfections in order to maximize opportunities for growth. The role of management as conventionally portrayed thus is the sequential identification, exploitation and creation of profitable market imperfections as opportunities for growth.

It is, however, possible to go further than these basic propositions and to suggest a fourth management strategy lying within the conventional purview. This strategy is to seek to raise the transaction costs of competitors. In this context, internalization is a strategic weapon. Two types of this strategy can be identified. The first is to achieve exclusive access to key inputs. One example is to achieve a 'corner' in key resources. Another is to secure key factor inputs by the design of exclusive contracts whose purpose is to keep managers and other key personnel tied into particular firms for long periods of time. Such contracts (enhancing pensions, loyalty bonuses, provision of complementary resources, penalties for contract breaking) are observed not only for managers but also for key R & D workers, salespeople, designers and production engineers. The second strategy is to achieve competitive advantage in the market for final goods by tying in customers. This covers strategies from building brand loyalty and awareness to the provision of a full range of products so that customers are not obliged to seek a product outside the firm's range. Such strategies raise the cost to the consumer of a product switch and increase the transaction costs of competitors.

Decision-making in the multinational firm – foreign market servicing strategies

The foreign market servicing strategy of multinationals is the set of choices firms make on which production plants (including service facilities) should be linked to which final markets and the channels through which this is carried out. Conceptually simple distinctions between exporting (X), licensing (L) and production through foreign subsidiaries (I) can be made by contrasting the location of value added, which separates X from the other two, and the internalization effect, which separates external licensing L from internally controlled X and I.

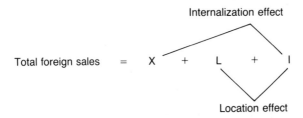

Figure 6.1   *Contrast between location of value added and the internalization effect*

In practice of course these distinctions are far from simple. A straightforward planning model can be derived by splitting the cost of each method of market servicing into a set up cost, which increases with deeper modes of market servicing (X→L→I), and a variable cost of operating the function, which decreases with the number of transactions managed (X→L→I). Consequently, at a given level of market penetration, the lower variable costs of a high cost set-up mode (I) make it the cheapest form of operation (Figure 6.2).

Examining point-of-time costs is one way of examining this choice. A complementary approach is to take a long view of developments in a particular market in terms of changes of state. Figure 6.3 represents alternative routes to a foreign direct investment.

It is possible to take the above argument rather further by examining linkages within sub-activities and sub-functions of the firm. Figure 6.4 examines flows between sub-activities of marketing – here listed as stockholding, distribution control, promotion, the agency function (generating customers) and retailing. The multinational firm faces two crucial decisions on each of these activities: (1) where the activity should be located and (2) how the activity should be controlled. If we take two simple oppositions – home and abroad, internal and market – as the choices, the decision set is still

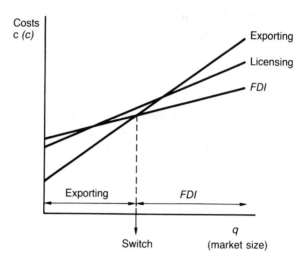

NB   In this example, licensing is never
the preferred alternative.

Reproduced from Buckley and Casson (1981), p. 80.

Figure 6.2   *The timing of a foreign direct investment*

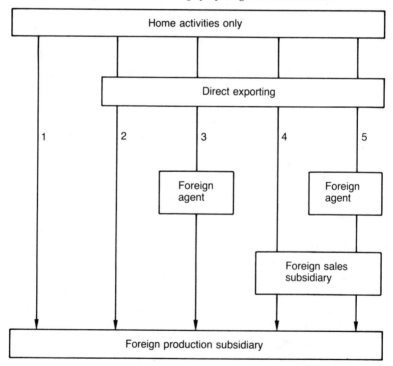

Figure 6.3   *Routes to a foreign production subsidiary*

formidably complicated. Coordination of the marketing function within a single market requires management of all the flows in Figure 6.4. When multi-market firms are operating, flows between all these different markets (of product as well as information) must be managed.

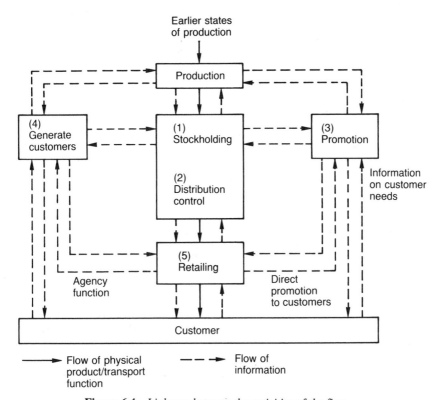

Figure 6.4 *Linkages between the activities of the firm*

Contemporary theories of international business shed a great deal of light on the optimal form of business organization in individual markets. It is possible to take a simple view of 'deepening involvement', from exporting forms, to licensing, to direct foreign investment. Table 6.1, however, goes further in differentiating modes of international cooperation according to five criteria. These are (1) equity versus non-equity ventures, (2) the nature of time limits on the cooperation, (3) space limitations, (4) the range of transfer of resources and rights, and (5) the mode of transfer – internal to the firm or through the market. Some of the entries in the table are controversial, but they enable managers to construct a check-list based on the company's objectives, optimal degree of exposure and previous experience of individual markets.

Table 6.1   A typology of international cooperation modes

Form of cooperation	Equity or non-equity	Time limited or unlimited	Space limited	Transfer of resources and rights	Mode of transfer
Wholly-owned foreign subsidiaries	Equity	Unlimited	At discretion of MNE	Whole range	Internal
Joint ventures	Equity	Unlimited	Agreed	Whole range?	Internal
Foreign minority holdings	Equity	Unlimited	Limited	Whole range?	Internal
'Fade out' agreements	Equity	Limited	Nature of agreement	Whole range? For limited period	Internal, changing to market
Licensing	Non-equity	Limited by contract	May include limitation in contract	Limited range	Market
(Franchising)	Non-equity	Limited by contract	Yes	Limited+ support	Market
Management contracts	Non-equity	Limited by contract	May be specified	Limited	Market
'Turnkey ventures'	Non-equity	Limited	Not usually	Limited in time	Market
'Contractual joint ventures'	Non-equity	Limited	May be agreed	Specified by contract	Mixed
International sub-contracting	Non-equity	Limited	Yes	Small	Market
Alliances	Usually	Limited	Yes	Variable	Non-market

International competitiveness

Figure 6.5 shows a model of competitiveness that includes three key elements: performance, potential and (management) process (3Ps) (Buckley, Pass and Prescott, 1992). It envisages competitiveness not as a state but as a *process*, relying on the interaction of the three key elements. The model can be utilized at the national level or the firm level (indeed, also at the intra-firm, division or product levels). Thus we can envisage 'virtuous circles' in which good performance leads to resources being invested in future potential (training, R & D, etc.) and an efficient management process leading to improved performance. We can also envisage a 'vicious circle' in which declining performance, badly managed, leads to lack of investment in future potential.

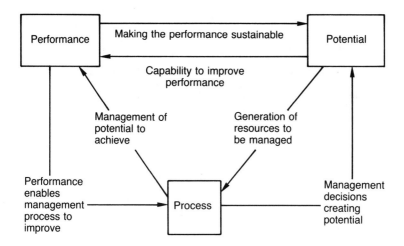

Figure 6.5   *Aspects of competitiveness*

Several issues of importance emerge. First, competitiveness is a wider concept than efficiency. Efficiency is the optimal allocation of resources to achieve the desired objectives. Competitiveness includes the choice of the most important objectives. In summary, competitiveness includes both efficiency (reaching goals at the least possible cost) and effectiveness (having the right goal). Second, competitiveness is a relative concept. It must be defined relative to some other state of the world. The possibilities are (1) relative to a different point of historical time (thus leading to the notion of a loss of competitiveness, (2) relative to a different economic space (nations compared with other nations, firms with their closest (foreign) competitors) or (3) relative to a well-defined counterfactual position – what would have happened if some action had not been taken?

One issue of crucial importance for the global economy emerges from this analysis. That is the dissonance between the competitiveness of the firm and the nation. Figure 6.6 shows that in measuring the competitiveness of an international firm, *all* its elements must be considered in performance, potential and process. As some of its assets will be located abroad, maximizing the competitiveness of an individual firm may conflict with the competitiveness of its parent country. For instance, appropriate advice to a European pharmaceutical company might be 'invest in R & D in Japan'. This might well conflict with improving the competitiveness of its parent country and of the EU as a whole. This radical impact of this dissonance is only just beginning to be felt.

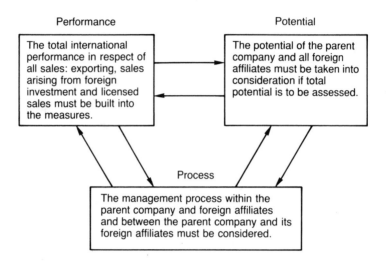

Figure 6.6   *Measuring competitiveness in a global marketplace*

This view of the dissonance between the competitiveness of firms and that of their parent countries leads to issues of 'Who is us?' (Reich, 1991). For whom should government policies in a more integrated global economy be designed? For *all* firms within the country (including foreign owned ones)? For all firms of the parent country's ownership wherever they are located? Policies targeted on these two groups would be very different indeed. This analysis is continued in the following section, where a 'crisis of management' of the global economy is identified, arising from the existence of national labour markets coexisting with regional goods and services markets and global capital markets.

Regional issues: Europe and its competitors

Ostensibly the integration of Europe post-Maastricht continues apace. The completion of the 'Single European Market' and the integration of non-European-Union countries in the European Economic Area (EEA) is testimony to the creation of a huge regional market. It is possible that this region will consist of a 'core' of the EU countries and a 'periphery' of East and Central Europe, Mediterranean rim states and parts of the former Soviet Union. Harmonization of policies on the free movement of goods and services, regulations and the external tariff will continue to cement integration.

However, there are also contrary pressures within this integrated Europe. Competitive policies between states based on different cultural perceptions and on the protection of national labour markets will ensure that integration does not mean homogenization. Company strategies will still need to recognize the (largely cultural) differences even between members of the EU. Currency differences still remain and still present an extra dimension of risk, which does not exist within federal single currency states such as the USA.

Europe, as a region, also faces regional competition from North America, where integration moves centre round the North American Free Trade Association (NAFTA), which may well grow to encompass more of central America and eventually South America, where separate regional integration moves are advancing. In Asia too economic integration is on the agenda, not least because of the expansionist foreign direct investment of Japanese firms within the region. The Newly Industrializing Economies (NIEs) such as Korea, Singapore and Taiwan have made a huge impact on global trading patterns, and they are being emulated by the 'emerging NIEs', including Thailand and Indonesia, with a third wave of 'transition economies' (such as Vietnam) to follow. This region, with the newly dynamized China at its head, represents a powerful challenge based on cheap labour and internationally mobile capital and know-how. The region is not solely dependent on inflows of capital – the internal regional circulation of capital is also a formidable engine of growth (Buckley and Mirza, 1988).

We can thus envisage a regional 'struggle for the world product' grafted on to national competitiveness. The issue of the combination of factors that makes a region dynamic and successful is a central question.

Internationalization of firms and the conflict of markets

Figure 6.7 is a simple attempt to examine the current state of the world economy in a very broad-brush fashion. It suggests that world markets can be characterized by international markets in capital, regional markets in goods and services, but national labour markets. Multinational enterprises thus play a major role in creating and sustaining global capital markets, in consolidating regional harmonization in product markets, and in exploiting differences (in wage rates) in fragmented labour markets. Multinational firm strategies and national government policies thus at times conflict, at times they coalesce and at times they are complementary.

National governments are put in the position of attempting to manage largely national labour market policies (on employment, wage rates and their implications for inflation, training, fiscal policies) in a context where firms are servicing largely regional goods and service markets usually based on free-trade areas or political units (NAFTA, EU) in which barriers to trade, investment and physical goods movements are unrestricted (or at least in which the barriers are declining). Overlaying all this, we observe an approximation to an international capital market, where governments have very restricted power to manipulate domestic interest rates because of the abilities of individuals and corporate bodies to move mobile capital ('hot money') across the exchanges.

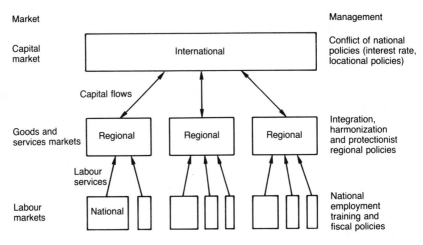

Figure 6.7 *Internationalization of firms – conflict of markets*

We may therefore regard the current world economy to be in a 'crisis of management'. Attempts by governments to manage independent fiscal policies, social and employment policies and interest rate policies, are frustrated by the regionalization of product markets and the internationalization of capital markets.

In both these areas, multinational firms are the most important players. They have been instrumental in campaigning for the removal of barriers to trade and the free movement of goods and services, so as to exploit economies of scale and scope, and they have largely created the international market in capital. In response, governments have (forlornly) tried to regulate labour markets, and fiscal and monetary policies in conditions that work against independence. This was realized in the debate on the 'Social Chapter' of the Maastrict agreement, when Britain's 'opt out' could usher in an era of competitive social policies to match competitive policies on interest rates and fiscal policy. The gainers from competitive macro-policies are multinational firms. As nation states attempt to outbid each other in order to attract or retain inward investment through cheap loans, subsidies or tax concessions, multinational firms reap the rewards. The more mobile the investment, the more scope there is for 'grantsmanship' (shopping around for the best package of incentives) on the part of multinationals.

Cooperative policies between governments may be at least part of the answer in attempting to harmonize policies and reduce the ability of firms to play off one country against another. In a common market, where barriers to trade and investment are removed, it is inevitable that firms will locate where immobile factors are the cheapest. This will mainly mean labour costs, but if social overhead costs and taxes differ between different parts of the common market, they will become a key location factor in themselves. Hence the necessity to harmonize social overhead costs and taxation across common markets. It is worth pointing out that a general increase in social overheads and taxes will have the effect of deterring multinationals completely, but this effect will be reduced by the attractions of large markets. It must be of some current concern, for instance, that cost levels in the EU are escalating relative to East Asia. Consequently the 'crisis of management' is at two levels – *within* trade blocs and *between* trade blocs.

The role of government policy intervention in multinational firms' location strategies

It is important for government policy-makers to recognize the strategic decision-making process of multinational firms if they are to be effective in attracting inward investment. Figure 6.6 is an attempt to crystallize a large body of theory into a narrow straightjacket. There is a large body of literature on the internationalization process (Buckley and Ghauri, 1993) which examines the evolution of direct investment over time. The points made in this literature translate into a decision process into which governments can intervene – with greater or lesser degrees of success. In terms of Figure 6.8, governments often attempt to attract inward investment almost when the die is

PHASE 1	*Initial impulse* Protectionism or threat of protectionism/dumping External approach From sales office	
PHASE 2	*Discussion phase* Internal dialogue	*Up to 3 years* (Sales office/International dept, Product Division/middle management)
	Definition of project:	Market size (as defined by sales office) Agglomeration, role models, Visibility of country/region
PHASE 3	*Decision phase* Project team (3–10 people). Sometimes target country settled.	*1–2 years* Detailed examination.
Source:	Literature of International Business, especially Aharoni (1966); Buckley *et al.* (1988, 1983); Hood and Truijens (1992).	

Figure 6.8 *The process of investment decision-making*

cast, i.e. in 'phase 3'. They attempt to get their location on to the short list of sites to be visited by the project team. This is often too late. The phase before this ('phase 2') where the entrant firm, via its sales office, has defined its market and often its objectives, may be more appropriate. Indeed, there is no substitute for being in on the first phase – the initial impulse.

It is thus contended that government promotional efforts would be more successful if governments better understood the decision processes of multinational firms.

Conclusion

This chapter has introduced some basic theoretical concepts that serve to highlight the role of the multinational firm in the current global environment. It suggested that multinational firms have a key role to play in determining the development of the global economy, in particular by their foreign market servicing decisions, which determine, in large part, the location of economic activity. The dissonance between the competitiveness of *firms* as against *nations* was seen to be an outcome of multinational firm's strategic decisions raising questions of *for whom* government policies are intended. This was widened by a consideration of the extent to which the strategies of multinational firms pose a crisis of management for the global economy. Governments are attempting to manage national labour markets in conditions where goods and services markets have become largely regional and capital markets international. The role of government policy is one aspect of multinationals' decision-making – locational choices are also examined in the context of the strategic decision-making process observed in firms. The interaction between the strategic decisions of firms and the global environment is a crucial element in the future of the world economy.

References

Aharoni, Yair (1966) *The Foreign Investment Decision Process*, Harvard University Press, Cambridge, Mass.

Buckley, Peter J (1988) The limits of explanation: Testing the internalisation theory of the multinational enterprise, *Journal of International Business Studies*, Summer, 2, pp. 181–93.

Buckley, Peter J (1990) Problems of developments in the core theory of international business, *Journal of International Business Studies*, Vol. No. 4, Winter, pp. 657–65.

Buckley, Peter J and Casson, Mark (1976) *The future of the multinational enterprise*, Macmillan, London.

Buckley, Peter J and Casson, Mark (1985) *The economic theory of the multinational enterprise*, Macmillan, London.

Buckley, Peter J and Hafiz Mirza (1988) The Strategy of Pacific Asia Multinationals, *The Pacific Review*, Vol. 1, No. 1, pp. 50–62.

Buckley, Peter J and Pervez N Ghauri (eds) (1993) *The Internationalization of the Firm: A Reader*, Academic Press, London.

Buckley, Peter J, Berkova, Zdenka and Newbould, Gerald D (1983) *Direct Investment in the UK by Smaller European Firms*, Macmillan, London.

Buckley, Peter J, Newbould, Gerald D and Thurwell, Jane (1988) *Foreign Direct Investment by Smaller UK Firms*, Macmillan, London.

Buckley, Peter J, Pass, C L and Prescott, Kate (1992) *Servicing International Markets: Competitive Strategies of Firms*, Blackwell, Oxford.

Cantwell, John (1991) A survey of theories of international production, in Christopher N Pitelis and Roger Sugden (eds) *The Nature of the Transnational Firm*, Routledge, London.

Casson, Mark (1985) The theory of foreign direct investment in P J Buckley and M Casson, *The economic theory of the multinational enterprise*, Macmillan, London.

Casson, Mark (1987) *The firm and the market*, Basil Blackwell, Oxford.

Caves, Richard E (1982) *Multinational Enterprise and Economic Analysis*, Cambridge University Press, Cambridge.

Hood, Neil and Trijens, Thorsten (1993) European locational decisions of Japanese manufacturers: Survey evidence on the case of the UK, *International Business Review*, Vol. 2, No. 1, pp 39–63.

Hymer, Stephen (1968) The large multinational 'corporation'. An analysis of some motives for the international integration of business, *Revue Economique*, Vol. 19, No. 6, pp. 949–73. English version in Mark Casson (ed) *Multinational Corporations*, Edward Elgar, Cheltenham.

Hymer, Stephen H (1976) *The international operations of national firms: a study of direct foreign investment*, MIT Press, Cambridge, Mass. (Original PhD written 1960).

Pitelis and Sugden (1991) See Cantwell.

Reich, Robert B (1990) Who is us?, *Harvard Business Review*, Vol. 68, No. 1, January-February, pp. 53–65.

Reich, Robert B (1991) Who is Them?, *Harvard Business Review*, Vol. 69, No. 2, March-April, pp. 77–88.

Scherer, F M *et al.* (1975) *The economics of multi-plant operation: an international comparisons study*, Harvard University Press, Cambridge, Mass.

7

Ethics and strategy
Linda Bennett

Ethics and observing the law: similarities and differences

In 1982 Agha Hasan Abedi said to an interviewer that the philosophy behind the banking empire he had set up was 'the age old philosophy of banking: there is nothing new about it. Our greatest concern, and our greatest desire, is to protect the interests of our clients, the depositors'. There were, he added, other objectives: to serve a useful purpose for clients and staff (emotively called 'the family'); and to observe at all times what he called the 'moral dimension' – 'no material end can be achieved without a moral aspect behind it'. Above all, it was his ambition to create the first Third World bank of international standing, and thus to compete with the most powerful of the western banking houses.

The rest is history. The spectacular collapse of the Bank of Credit and Commerce International (BCCI) in 1991 has been well documented, and is still the subject of litigation in many countries, and of intense debate. Abedi has been dismissed as a crook and a confidence trickster who used his personal charisma and the influence of his wealthy friends to hoodwink shareholders, clients and staff, and to deceive the regulatory authorities. There now seems to be little doubt that BCCI was involved in the worst types of crime, including investment fraud, terrorism, drugs and illegal arms trafficking. Perhaps even more serious, from the ethical viewpoint, was the fact that throughout the world BCCI's ready ability to corrupt public officials seemed to help undermine institutions that have been set up to protect the public, including law enforcement agencies, central banks and auditors. Some of these have claimed, or have proved, that they were not corrupt, but negligent – raising yet thornier questions. The saddest irony of all is that the victims who suffered most were investors from Third World countries – the vulnerable would-be entrepreneurs whom the bank was ostensibly set up to help.

It could be argued that the story of BCCI bears only a tangential relationship to a discussion of the role that ethics plays in strategy, because the banking empire was developed on a foundation of extreme anti-ethical practices whose exposure cannot offer useful lessons to 'ordinary' businessmen. The latter, it may be assumed, are concerned with establishing more refined ethical norms than the avoidance of outright and deliberate law-breaking. Paradoxically, however, and not least because the avowed mission of BCCI took a strong ethical line, the story of BCCI does highlight many of the issues that are relevant to the debate on strategy and ethics:

- The question of the **leadership** of the organization. How much power should the strategic leader and key executives have? How can this be controlled without undermining their creativity? In the last analysis, does personal integrity have to be relied upon, and if this is the case, can either the individual's role or the culture of the organization be a corrupting influence?

- Following on from the above, the question of ethics and the **mission** of the organization. Is the notion of ethics often merely used to build 'image'? What are the true objectives of the organization, how do they match up to ethical standards, and whose are the ethical standards? How should they be monitored within the organization?

- The question of what value should be placed by **stakeholders** on a strategic thrust that is based on a strong ethical stance. Who are the stakeholders, and what are their rights and safeguards? Can the company build up a strategically useful 'architecture' by employing ethics to gain the commitment, support and loyalty of the stakeholders?

- The question of ethics and the **product**. Should the mere letter of the law be followed, or does the company owe more than this to its customers? To be seen to give customers more than their legal due may be strategically useful or even essential. Does the self-interest leading to such a strategy undermine its intrinsic ethical value, and does this matter? How far should the organization bow to pressure groups, and how can it protect itself from them?

- The question of **monitoring** the activities of the organization from the outside. How should this be achieved – and who regulates the regulators? When does 'negligence' become criminal? What is the dividing line between anti-ethical behaviour and breaking the law? Can an organization be successful or be said to be making a useful contribution to society in any circumstances if it is employing 'negative ethics'? Can the organization itself be culpable, without blame attaching to any of the individuals within it?

- The question of ethics and the **Third World**. What is the strategic significance of dealing with countries that are less economically well-developed? How can the ethically-aware company come to terms with cultural differences that have an impact on its company/national ethical beliefs?

As the range of this list indicates, every major activity or task undertaken, decision made, and strategy developed by an organization is attended by the need to address ethical considerations. Organizations – and their leaders – differ in the stances which they adopt. Moreover, ethical approaches may be varied according to the different circumstances in which the organization is placed, and the different countries in which it operates. There is no worldwide 'norm' of accepted ethically correct behaviour; therefore it may sometimes be necessary to follow certain questionably ethical (from one's own or one's national perspective) methods in order to succeed and to compete. Nevertheless, it may be possible to suggest that there is some universal 'boundary' beyond which neither the individual nor the organization may pass.

The whole question of ethics is therefore complex and full of tensions; both despite of and because of this, it is vital for the organization and its leaders to think through the issues and come to some clear conclusion or expressed standpoint. To be successful in the 1990s, it is necessary to acknowledge that ethics matter – but ethical issues, influenced by national, organizational or individual bias, may still be addressed with a selectivity born of expediency.

Hence it is the purpose of this chapter to address the question of how ethics make an impact on strategic decision-making, by examining a connected series of key issues. Its objective is to stimulate and help to structure thought on the subject. Better to enable this, it will draw particularly on the work of John Kay and his model of 'strategic architecture' as a route to competitive advantage. (The concept of 'architecture', as expressed by Prahalad and Hamel (1990) and developed by Kay (1993), examines the organization in terms of its key linkages and relationships, both internal and external. These ideas will be explained in more detail later.)

Ethics and strategic leadership

In order to consider the role of the strategic leader meaningfully within the context of ethics, it is useful to look briefly at how the notion of ethics evolved within western organizations (the western bias derives from the fact that the West has a longer and better documented corporate business history, and also because Anglo-Saxon organizations, in particular, have become sensitive to ethical issues in recent years), and to examine some modern definitions of ethics.

Solomon (1991) points out that business ethics as such is a very youthful addition to the field of 'applied' ethics. Nevertheless, some codes of business behaviour have existed, either tacitly or written down, since ancient times. In the Middle Ages these were bedevilled with conflicting religious ideals, which led to such practices as the social ostracism of 'userers' (often conveniently non-Christian Jews). The concept of making a profit 'without working' was frowned upon – illustrating the important point that the fundamental nature of business ethics is that 'the rules of the game change as society's values alter' (Sturdivant, 1981). By the nineteenth century the religious conundrum had been solved quite neatly, at least in Protestant business circles, by the amalgamation of the Protestant ethic with the so-called 'work ethic'. The key notion was that a person's occupation was regarded as a 'calling' from God, and personal morality was measured by how excellently this calling was fulfilled; the nature of the occupation itself was relatively unimportant, and therefore might include 'usury' and other financial services that did not comprise obvious toil. Each person was expected to lead a humble, even ascetic existence, but this was not to be confused with finding any inherent evil in wealth, or with the belief that there was a predestination separating the 'elect' from the 'damned'. (Therefore it was not his affair if his neighbour was less wealthy and 'fortunate' than he, though this did lead to the transformation into public benefactors of such super-rich magnates as J D Rockefeller and Andrew Carnegie.)

Such ideas fitted well with the teachings of Adam Smith and the early economists, who taught the virtues of thrift and enterprise, but also the essential selfishness of economic activity. The basic tenets of classical economic theory were that economic progress, materialism and the right of the owner to do what he liked with his property were all desirable, and that in order to achieve these ends it was necessary to make the maximum profit possible, to defer to the wishes of shareholders, to acknowledge that the individual was free within the law, and to deplore undue legislative interference. Unions and any kind of collective-bargaining activities were disliked.

The effects of this spiritual and ideological conditioning on the strategic leader's attitude towards running his business were profound. Not only employees, but also consumers, were considered to be of relatively little account. The axiom *caveat emptor* ('let the buyer beware') prevailed. A curious feature of the resulting ethical norms was the industrial leader with a 'split personality', who could be civilized and caring within his domestic environment and local community, but totally ruthless and 'corrupt' (in modern terms) in his business dealings. Such people, while apparently not experiencing any difficulty with this dual role, epitomized by their actions the dilemma of business ethics, which have been defined as 'the study of decisions made by individuals within organizational roles under conditions of conflicting objectives and values' (Sturdivant, 1981). There is to my knowledge no all-encompassing definition of business ethics, but other helpful approaches towards defining it include '(Business Ethics are) not issues of right versus wrong, but conflicts of right versus right' (Joseph L. Badaracco Jr, quoted by Solomon) and, perhaps the most succinct and relevant to this paper 'What you are as determined by what you do' (Grant, 1993).

British and American companies differed from their European counterparts by generally effecting the split between owners and management at a much earlier period. By the beginning of the twentieth century most Anglo-Saxon organizations of any size were not managed by their owners. A net result of this was that it led to an early questioning of the profit motive as the be-all and end-all of a business's *raison d'être*. There was a gradual acceptance of the idea that the interests of shareholders should become only part of a wider perspective of managerial goals, which took into account the needs of all 'stakeholders'. In the 1950s Peter Drucker's very influential work on Management by Objectives suggested that profit should be only one of eight key objectives considered when formulating strategy. In his ardent desire to gain acceptance for the business career as being as serious and as socially acceptable as careers in the traditional 'professions', Drucker made one of his key objectives that of acting with social responsibility. Following this, more work began to appear on business ethics, and business leaders began to realize that it would be increasingly difficult to dodge or ignore ethical issues.

That people running businesses do not necessarily make the maximization of shareholder wealth a priority does not automatically make them more ethically sound, however. The work of Cyert and March (1963), and others, suggests that senior managers may be motivated by personal ambitions such as the quest for power, empire-building, and self-aggrandizement, which have little to do with the 'good' of the organization, its customers or employees. Powerful and acquisitive leaders in America and Britain during the past decade (a period of government deregulation in both countries) have come under attack for the following practices:

- Paying themselves too highly in relation to their employees and to the profits their organization is making.
- Radical 'restructuring' of their organizations, which often means the (sometimes panic-inspired) laying-off of many hundreds of employees.
- Excessive borrowing undertaken to acquire other companies (known as 'leveraged buyouts' and often hostile in nature) with the intention of making their empires grow more quickly, ultimately often leading to the issuing of so-called 'junk bonds'.

- Blatant law-breaking. This, of course, may take many forms. Some of those recently publicized include 'insider trading' on the stock exchange, i.e. using internal knowledge of the company's activities to buy and sell its shares at propitious moments; bribery; and the appropriation of funds that do not, either technically or actually, belong to the company in order to bolster its share price (most famously illustrated by Robert Maxwell's seizure of the Mirror News Group pension funds to pay the interest on debts acquired in setting up the Maxwell Communications Corporation).

With the exception of the last point, the key people concerned have defended such behaviour, saying that senior staff deserve to be rewarded for undertaking massive workloads and responsibilities; that growth is an inescapable imperative in western economies; and that 'restructuring' becomes inevitable in times of recession and therefore hard choices have to be made if the organization is to survive at all. This is Sturdivant's 'dilemma' demonstrated. Clearly, the issues are not cut and dried. The question is, who can – or should – monitor and control the activities of the strategic leader? Who has the information and the power to undertake the task adequately, and at the same time the sensitivity not to undermine the flair and insight that (presumably) enabled him or her to get the job in the first place?

As with other issues concerning corporate ethics, America and Britain have been first to address this problem in a systematized way. (Vogel, 1993, claims that America is the leader.) In America the Securities and Exchange Commission has sought to regulate corporate governance more closely, particularly by making it mandatory to disclose the process by which executive pay is determined. In Britain the Cadbury Committee was set up to consider how companies could be governed more ethically, particularly with regard to safeguarding shareholder interests, and therefore how executives could be made more accountable. When the Committee's recommendations were made public in 1992, they were widely praised for their moderation, good sense, and the flexibility of their approach. The main recommendations were that companies should disclose the extent of compliance with the Cadbury Code to maintain a stock exchange listing; that board authority should be divided between the chairman and the chief executive; that the pay packages of the chairman and the highest paid UK director should be disclosed in the annual accounts, and split into salary and performance-related pay; and that each board should have an audit committee composed wholly of non-executives.

Many top companies have since embraced these recommendations or declared an intention to put them into practice. However, the Cadbury Code has received some criticism. At present, it is not legally compelling. It has been said that it is not strict enough (the rigour versus flexibility dilemma); and that it places too much emphasis on non-executives, who are, by definition, not stakeholders in the company. In the attempt to achieve impartiality, could key interests of the company therefore be sacrificed to incomplete understanding or even indifference? It is also heavily weighted towards financial measures, which are easier to quantify and therefore to regulate. Finally, it is biased towards safeguarding shareholders, and shows less concern for other stakeholders.

What emerges, from both the philosophical and the practical controversy, is the desirability or otherwise of having an acknowledged set of 'rules' to work from. This warrants attention, not just within the context of the Cadbury Report, but in order to understand how a specific organization fundamentally sees itself, what it believes itself to be about, how this is presented, and therefore on what strategic course it is set. Traditionally, the chief executive occupies the main role here – establishing, explaining, defending and implementing the strategy is the core of his or her job – and although the decisions he or she makes will be fundamental to the future well-being of the organization, it is much less feasible for them to be monitored from the outside. How enlightened an attitude towards the other stakeholders is demonstrated may be the most useful ethical yardstick, as we shall discuss further.

Ethics and the mission of the organization

Since the Second World War, most organizations of any size have tried to encapsulate what they are about in a 'mission statement'. Working in the 1990s means working in an age obsessed with exhaustive documentation. The mission statement is now no longer deemed sufficient. In the new, caring, sharing, socially conscious (or perhaps simply chastened by the experiences of the 1980s) society that has been self-consciously promoted, citizens' charters, written promises to maintain standards higher than those prescribed by the law, and codes of corporate practice have proliferated. A professed commitment to high ethical values has become a powerful source of competitive advantage. As a consequence, organizations have begun to publish, and to publicize, not just the 'mission statement', which forms the Chief Executive's preface to the glossy annual report, but the set of values underpinning the way the company operates.

Obviously such action can be a great force for good. Channels of communication are opened, and, if the job is done well, shareholders, customers and employees are able to establish exactly where they stand. The National Westminster bank provides an example. In 1993 it distributed a ten-page document to more than 90,000 employees, stating that its priorities were integrity in its dealings, delivering customer satisfaction, and creating opportunities for staff. It touched on conflicts of interest, criminal activities, and accepting entertainment. The document received publicity in the press.

A significant feature of this document was that it was a participative effort. More than 600 people had been consulted at all levels within the company in 1991 in order to compile it. It was therefore markedly different from its predecessor, a top-down 'set of principles', which appeared in 1986. While the earlier version had been noticeably more intimidating, it had placed much less emphasis on accountability. Perhaps therefore it had been more of an exercise in image building than the 'real thing'. To its credit, NatWest had apparently moved from paying lip-service to the idea of a charter, to establishing a genuine working model that 'belonged' to the people who would observe and enforce it.

Lip-service is one of several problems attaching to the current corporate craze for devising codes of conduct. To publish a code is one thing: actually to observe it, except in situations where it is necessary to be seen to observe it (as, for example, when challenged by a customer), is another. How meaningful is a particular code in any case? It may be couched in such general terms that it amounts to no more than an expansive affirmation of the company's duties in law. The problem of the company using ethics merely to project a positive image keeps rearing its head. As we have seen in the extreme case of BCCI, to have an appropriate ethical image was essential to the expansionist strategy, based on securing the trust of those whose help he required, of Abedi; but the 'moral dimension' to which he referred was a sham, thinly papered over with some vague expressions of idealism.

We come therefore to another difficulty with using codes of practice, including the Cadbury Code: that of reductionism. However well-meaning the code itself may be, the existence of it may encourage people to observe the minimum that it requires: in other words, to obey it in letter rather than in spirit. This blurs the distinction between doing what is right and what is legally correct that forms the main difference between ethical behaviour and obeying the law. If codes of behaviour ultimately just set up another layer of rules to be ostentatiously stuck to, their ethical usefulness is limited; though it could be argued that they do perform a function even so, since it is the nature of ethical values to shift with time. Thus, assuming that it is more refined and sensitive than what the law demands, today's code of conduct, although it may be imperfectly observed in practice, can help to reform tomorrow's law. Some contribution to civilization is being made.

If we accept that codes are helpful but of limited value and influence, we are faced again with the issue of the personal integrity and set of values of the strategic leader in establishing a strategy. Ludwig and Longenecker (1993) have argued persuasively that a leader's personal values may be corrupted by either his status or the expectations that the organization itself places on him when he reaches the top (calling this the 'Bathsheba Syndrome'); and they add that many organizations do not prepare their leaders for the role that they are about to assume, nor make the leader aware that the privileges that he or she receives are not a personal accolade, but held in trust by him or her so that he or she can run the organization better. If this is accepted, then a chicken-and-egg situation of the right organizational climate producing the right leader, and vice versa, exists.

How to break out of the latter syndrome poses interesting questions (one logical solution, that of 'headhunting' a suitable leader, engages one in a further ethical conundrum, described by Welch, 1992); but clearly what is being discussed is the impact of the organization's **culture**. How the culture contributes towards ethical values that can then enable the development of a strategy not easily emulated is what the leader as strategist needs to fathom; in so doing, he gains an understanding of his own motives and whether his personal values 'fit' with those of the organization. It may be that it is not until he reaches the top that he makes such a profound reflection, and the ensuing stringent test of his own integrity. His influence on how the organization's values are then expressed and made manifest is of critical importance.

What value should stakeholders place on professed ethics, and how can their ownership of a common ethical code contribute to strategy?

The foregoing argument suggests that the strategic leader will need a powerful reason for adopting a 'genuine' ethical stance as part of his or her strategy. No reason can be more powerful from the executive's viewpoint than that it will enable and maintain competitive advantage. Much has been written on competitive advantage, and this is not the place to attempt an exhaustive review of the subject. Kay (1993) offers one approach to an understanding of competitive advantage by using the term 'distinctive capability'. He identifies only three types of distinctive capability:

- Innovation, which he characterizes as difficult to maintain, because it invites imitation.
- Reputation, which is easier to maintain than create, but meets the essential conditions for sustainability, i.e. that it persists over time, and that it is not readily appropriable by others.
- Architecture, which is a system of relationships within the firm, or between the firm and its customers, or both.

It is upon the concept of architecture that we will focus in order to consider the contribution that ethics may make to competitive advantage.

According to Kay, architecture consists of a network of relational contracts within or around the firm, viz., with and among employers (internal architecture); with suppliers and customers (external architecture); and among a group of firms engaged in related activities (networking). It will be seen immediately that, despite the pronouncements of latter-day classical economists such as Milton Friedman, who was still declaring in the 1980s that 'the social responsibility of business is to increase its profits', thinking about for whom the corporation exists and upon whose behalf it acts has moved a long way since the proprietor–magnates of the Protestant work ethic believed that the interests of the shareholder were paramount. It will also be apparent that, in order for a company to build a successful architecture, it has to become an open system, since the purpose and value of architecture is that it creates knowledge and routines through the open exchange of information, and is therefore able to respond flexibly and imaginatively to continually changing circumstances in a manner that is unique to itself. The 'owners' of such an open system, each adding value to contribute to this unique quality, are no longer shareholders but stakeholders, (of whom the shareholders form one group). Openness implies, not just the free interchange of knowledge, but the ready sharing of values, and an absence of duplicity.

External architecture and ethics

Ethics and the customer

How does the way in which the company addresses its ethical position in relation to each of the stakeholders help to build the architecture? We will begin with what Kay designates the 'external architecture', since there are few organizations today that would not think first of their customers when considering this question. Although the power of the consumer varies according to such other factors as the degree of industry concentration and the extent of the company's technological prowess, customers have become of paramount importance, not only in times of recession and over-capacity, but because they are now well-educated and sophisticated. This does not simply mean that they 'know their rights', are aware of the law, and only too willing to embrace the idea of 'caveat emptor' (or, in the terms used in this paper, that they oblige the company to adopt the lowest feasible ethical stance of obeying the law); it also means that, as well as needing the support of their purses in order to survive, the company needs to be able to tap into their knowledge and perspicacity in order to develop its products successfully for the future.

The company therefore has to build channels of communication with its customers to make use of their viewpoint, and to establish bonds of trust. The post-war rise of the art of 'marketing', as opposed to 'selling', is one manifestation of this. Marketing is a two-way street; it heightens consumer awareness by conveying information, and at the same time tries to find out exactly what consumers want. The position sounds simple, but it bristles with ethical considerations. To take the first of these proposed functions of marketing: the way in which information is conveyed to potential customers is bound to be affected by the biases of the seller. At a certain point they may pass beyond the boundary of the law: hence the existence of such bodies as the Advertising Standards Authority. Advertising provides the advertiser with tempting opportunities to distort information, either by withholding key facts, or by what Riley (1993) calls 'implicature' – implying with non-sequiturs rather than addressing factual matters. This is not to allege that advertising *per se* is an undesirable practice; indeed Gray (1992) has made a good case for its importance to any free society. Despite the growing sophistication of consumers, there is also a need for them to be on the same 'wavelength' as the vendor when buying products that need to be accompanied with information from the seller in order to be used safely. That sellers should address these issues positively is a basic ethical point, but one that again approaches the borderline territory of ethics and the law.

For ethics to become part of an 'architectural' relationship with its customers, the company has to do much more than just satisfy the minimum legal requirements. The genuinely open, two-way flow of information should make possible the second function of marketing, i.e. it should establish what the customer wants – and not only do this, but follow it up with continuous new developments based on the continuing information flow. The more sophisticated and high-tech the industry, the more strategically vital the information. Building up such relationships, however, may present the company with some hard choices. For example, at what point does a drug manufacturer reveal that there may be harmful side-effects to one of its most lucrative products? At the first stirrings of suspicion, caused by anecdotal evidence, or after exhaustive research has been undertaken? If it chooses the latter, and the tests prove positive, many lives will have been put at risk, there may be large claims for compensation, and the company's reputation will be tarnished; but if it chooses the former, and the tests prove negative, the company will have lost a great deal of revenue and perhaps still have suffered (needless) damage to its reputation. The situation gains in complexity when the product passes through several 'customers' before it reaches the end-user.

Is it therefore possible to be too ethical? Young (1993), in a detailed case study about the ethical desirability of a NASA contractor insuring against unsuccessful rocket launches, claims that it isn't, because the company will benefit strategically in the long term from adopting the ethical high ground. Young's reasoning is that it will gain more customers eventually because it has been seen to act fairly; but the issue is surely also whether it is able to survive in the short term. Singer (1993) presents a balanced argument that puts the points of view of both those who believe it is and those who say it isn't; in the process he also offers a useful (though not definitive) distinction between ethics and social responsibility:

> Strictly speaking, ethics is a discipline for dealing with questions of good or bad, right or wrong – but there is also a broader definition, at least in the minds of many executives and ethicists, that embraces issues of so-called social responsibility . . . Issues of bribe-taking, the stealing of competitive information and sexual harassment clearly accord with most people's notion of ethics, but others, such as affirmative action . . . investing in South Africa, empowering workers and hiring the hard core unemployed can be addressed only if one accepts an expanded concept (of social responsibility).

Not all writers make this distinction, and it is important not to get sidetracked by the semantics; but it reinforces the idea that building an effective relational architecture calls for more than just observing the law.

Ethics and pressure groups

There is a group of stakeholders (which may be described as para-customers) that also has to be considered when companies are acting as open systems and facilitating the flow of information – the pressure-group. Consumer watchdog groups have become a rising power in the last decade; it is probably not coincidental that they have proliferated as governments have sought to lessen their regulatory role. On the face of it therefore pressure groups seem to be beneficial to the consumer, because they are safeguarding interests that might otherwise be overlooked; and they certainly derive their power from the public at large, which perceives them as acting from altruistic motives. Pattakos (1989) suggests that there are other forces at work within pressure groups, pointing out that frequently two or more groups will form coalitions, and that once a group has achieved its objectives, it is likely to take up another cause rather than 'disband': therefore the members of such groups gain something from the dynamics of the situations they create, as well as acting from pure disinterestedness.

The long-term tenacity that they are likely to manifest, therefore, makes them very dangerous adversaries, and in some cases of dubious ethical pedigree. Making information freely available to them is one way of reducing the damage that they are able to do to the company's reputation; when considering how to disclose information, however, the company needs to achieve a balance between effective dissemination and the cost that will be incurred.

From the perspective of the satisfied customer, this should not be too high, since it is ultimately he or she who pays – an instance of business ethics requiring sensitive trade-off and balance, rather than to be pursued with unrelenting zeal.

Ethics and hospitality

A particularly difficult issue (ethically speaking) which needs to be addressed when relations with customers are being built is the one of gift-giving and corporate hospitality. Bribery is clearly regarded as corrupt and illegal in the western world (though not, for example, in the Middle East) but whether or not it is defensible for companies to offer gifts and hospitality to thank clients, or to attract new ones, is less clear cut. For many companies this is a question of policy rather than strategy (though carrying potentially significant positive or negative effects on the strategic aim); but there are organizations, e.g. financial advice companies and some direct selling agencies, which base their strategy upon using hospitality to meet, advise, listen to and do business with customers. A study by Barry (1992) shows that corporate hospitality achieves a high 'hit rate', and is many times more cost-effective than advertising; but is it ethical? Organizations truly trying to build 'relational architecture' may be able to cut the Gordian knot of this dilemma, since the free and sincere relationships they develop with customers and suppliers will enable all parties to clarify the rationale behind the giving. Giving and accepting gifts and hospitality only becomes unethical when there is an intent to coerce, or a perception that one is being coerced. Openness can dispel feelings of shadiness; it can also make refusal without offending possible where there is any question of doubt or embarrassment.

Ethics and suppliers

Suppliers form the second strand of Kay's 'external architecture'. That they and the company and the company's customers form links in a value chain of activities means that many of the issues we have considered relative to customers are relevant also to suppliers. There are two major further considerations in relation to suppliers: that of reciprocal loyalty, and that of quality. Embracing the idea of architecture almost inevitably links these two concepts, since unless its operations are exceptionally simple, any company seriously pursuing a quality programme will build links with suppliers that cannot be broken at whim. The relationship therefore only becomes threatened by serious issues – effectively, not delivering the required quality (where 'quality' is understood to include issues of integrity) for whatever reason – when the ethical course of action may be to discontinue the arrangement, since loyalty to the customer is paramount.

Ethics and the consumer of tomorrow

There is a third stakeholder belonging to the 'external architecture': the consumer of tomorrow. It is because there is widespread fear of what organizational activity is doing to the planet, and its impact upon our descendants (consumer awareness of this has been increased by the campaigning of determined pressure groups), that during the past two decades there has been an accelerating interest in the contribution of 'environmental friendliness' and 'environmentally ethical behaviour' to company strategy. Today few companies can afford to ignore environmental issues, or omit to state their environmental policy. Some companies have built the whole of their strategy upon being environmentally responsible, with huge success.

The Body Shop offers an example. When Anita Roddick was asked how environmental issues affected her strategic approach, she replied:

> Well, it's neither the first nor the last, it just is. It's like breathing. Every decision is made, every new act or every new movement or whatever we do has an environmental consciousness. The most important thing is environmental management. On the company's board, we have a member who is absolutely responsible for the environmental education and management for the company. Then we have an environmental department manned by very strong environmental scientists and workers who have come out of the environmental movement. Then each department within our company has a representative for the environment who is responsible for an environmental audit every six months.

There are an increasing number of shareholders looking for 'green' portfolios, and companies intentionally or inadvertently, breaking international environmental laws, e.g. Exxon, in the *Exxon Valdez* oil-spill catastrophe, both incur large fines and suffer immense damage to their reputations. There is therefore a pressing imperative to address the environmental issues relevant to the organization.

As with broader ethical issues, paying attention to the environment means addressing a moving target. Companies that are going to benefit most strategically from a positive environmental approach need to anticipate what consumer views will be on the subject 5 or 10 years hence, and develop new products accordingly. Royal Dutch Shell developed 'green' (lead-free) petrol well before its competitors, and gained not from being able to charge a premium price for the product (since customers were initially unwilling to switch from leaded petrol if unleaded petrol cost more, and subsequently, as competitors brought out rival products, the petrol quickly acquired a commodity status), but from being perceived to be an environmentally aware organization. The perception of course could not be sustained if the company did not go on to develop its environmental awareness in other ways, particularly in the case of unleaded petrol, where the product is more accurately described as less harmful than harmless.

Ethics and environmental responsibility

The strategy of keeping just ahead of the public on environmental issues, or, in the case of some organizations, merely appearing to do so, belonged particularly to the 1980s, and underestimated consumer perspicacity. In the late 1980s consumers became disillusioned with companies that made large unsubstantiated 'environmentally friendly' claims for their products. In the 1990s, in order to arrange its interaction with the environment with strategic effectiveness, the company needs to address the fundamental issues; it cannot get away with tinkering with its appearance by applying socially acceptable cosmetics. Again, difficult decisions will have to be made, since current thinking on environmentally responsible behaviour has become both stringent and far-reaching. Bebbington and Gray (1993) suggest that the 'capital' available to humanity can be divided into three categories:

● Critical natural capital (those elements of the biosphere that are essential for life, and must remain inviolable), e.g. the ozone layer, a critical mass of trees.
● Other (sustainable, substitutable or renewable) natural capital (those elements of the biosphere that are renewable), e.g., non-extinct species, woodlands, or products for which substitutes can be found.
● Man-made capital (elements created from the biosphere that are no longer part of the natural ecology), e.g. machines, buildings, roads, products, wastes, etc.

The point that they make is that man-made capital is generally increased at the expense of the other two types of capital, and it is this capital that is almost universally measured by humanity to establish success and profitability. (Accountants are the conventional measuring agents of profitability, and it is interesting that evaluating environmental 'profit and loss' has come to be regarded as their role. We shall return to this later.) Organizations of the future will have to find ways of creating 'profit' without undermining the supply of natural capital. In the long term this implies a social revolution, not just the Royal Dutch Shell stratagem of taking incremental measures to pre-empt public opinion; in the short term it will make corporate survival increasingly difficult – and already some measures are becoming compulsory. America now has a range of laws that protect the environment and encourage companies to police each other. The only way that companies can succeed in relating their environmental performance to conventional profitability – a future condition of survival – is to build environmentally responsible action into the fabric of their architecture.

McDonald's have undertaken to do this by developing a programme of Environmental Quality Management (EQM), a parallel concept to Total Quality Management (TQM). Prince and Denison (1992) point out the similarities between EQM and TQM: both emphasize continuous improvement, paradigm and culture shifts, innovative solutions, systems analysis, and use the same tools – brainstorming, data-gathering, checklists, measuring and monitoring, etc. As with the environmentally sensitive strategy described by Anita Roddick, McDonald's relies above all on employee participation at all levels to make the system work. It is necessary now to consider what this means in ethical terms.

Internal architecture and ethics

Ethics and employees

The internal architecture of the organization is built up through its employees. (It will later be argued that there are others who also have an impact upon it.) This paper considers the internal architecture after the external architecture, taking the premise that every belief, relationship and activity pertaining to the organization only gains legitimacy by keeping the customer continually in view.

When the issues of leadership and ethics were discussed earlier, it was suggested that the culture of the organization plays a large part in determining the ethical standards of the strategic leader, and that his or her communication of these standards helps to establish the way in which the organization behaves. Consequently, he or she reinforces, or sometimes modifies, the culture. The culture of the organization is therefore likely to have a significant influence on the ethical values of the employees. Clinard and Yeager (1980) point out that cultural norms within an organization might 'encourage or discourage deviant behaviour'. Cochran and Nigh (1990) developed and tested seven hypotheses of the cause of corporate crime, the four proving positive being (1) that the more profitable a company is, the less likely it is to engage in criminal activity; (2) that rapidly growing companies often engage in illegal corporate behaviour; (3) that diversification is likely to lead to law-breaking; and (4) the larger the company, the more likely it is to be engaged in some kind of corporate law-breaking. This leads Cochran and Nigh to speculate about whether the company itself can be regarded as an 'artificial individual', and be guilty of a crime even if no individual is guilty.

Two categories of white-collar crime have been identified: that which is committed by businessmen or professionals to increase individual, as opposed to organizational, wealth; and that which is committed on behalf of the organization, with the prime purpose of increasing organizational wealth (although there may be personal spin-offs). Ernest Saunders' role in the Guinness-Distillers takeover bid, for which he was imprisoned, may be said to fall into this latter category. Staw and Szwajkowski (1975) add that in companies whose culture pays close attention to financial performance, tremendous pressure may be put on managers to achieve 'results'. As the examples suggest, most of the extant research addresses criminal behaviour within organizations, for the obvious reason that statistics on it are easier to obtain; but it is worth affirming again that 'ethical' implies more than not breaking the law.

Whether or not the organization itself can exist as an entity and therefore assume guilt that belongs to no specific individual is a question of legal and semantic casuistry that can have little place in the current debate on ethics and corporate architecture. To embrace the idea that the organization can only exist as an entity can only be described as buck-passing, but there is a starting point common to the two alternatives: the notion of culture. Schein (1985) says that companies with 'thin' cultures are less likely to survive in times of adversity, whereas companies with 'thick' or strong cultures pull together and win through. A problem occurs when the culture is 'thick' and wrong. This is particularly true of culture as a manifestation of the company's ethics. How can the company make sure of getting it right? Ewin (1993) offers an answer: to base the core of the company's culture on the concept of loyalty to the consumer rather than loyalty to the corporation:

> If the consumer is taken as the ultimate object of loyalty, so that loyalty to the corporation is loyalty to the corporation-as-serving-the-consumer, then the loyalty will be one directed towards excellence in the corporation's products, and will not be likely to lead to the hiding of corruption or inefficiency in the corporation ... excellence of this sort is very likely to be in the long-term interests of the corporation, even if not in the interests of those who want to make a quick killing and then get out of business.

This is an eloquent endorsement of the strategic and ethical value of 'architecture'. In fact, it takes Kay's idea one step further: for instead of 'belonging' to the employees, with the associated potential dangers of being 'thick' and wrong, the culture is, as it were, held in trust for the consumer. (It should be noted that a safeguard needs building in for not supporting the customer if he wishes to engage in unethical behaviour. Bequan, and others, have written entertainingly on all types of business fraud, including those perpetrated by consumers.) The idea is, however, valueless unless there is a supporting structure for committed employee participation (putting the onus for making it work back with the strategic leader and senior management). As Young (1993) points out, 'employees invariably know where to tap to make the system work'. By the same token, employees know when the company's strategies or policies are ethically questionable. But does the culture really empower them to say so? 'Whistleblowers' have rarely been rewarded for their revelations, and many have been ostracized, sacked, made redundant or even committed suicide after they pointed out some unethical practice within their company. If Ewin's argument is accepted, then whistleblowing not only ceases to be a disloyal act, but should be perceived as advantageous to the company.

The practical truth of this might be illustrated by an employee's pointing out to his superiors that the company's production processes are polluting a local river. The news may be unwelcome, but if it is heeded, it may prevent the company from incurring a large fine or having to shut down its activities altogether – neither of which can be of benefit to the consumer, who may also be put at risk by the pollution itself. (The example also raises the issue of responsible behaviour towards the consumer of tomorrow by caring for the environment, which has already been discussed.) But the senior management of the company may take the view that stopping the pollution is not worth the sacrifice of short-term profit, and hope that the company won't be found out; they may then take steps to silence the employee, or to make his revelations ineffective. The employee will very probably know in advance what their response is likely to be, because he understands the culture of the organization. Therefore, only an ethically enabling culture is likely to produce employee ethical participation.

Employee empowerment forms the basis for effective relational architecture. Singer (1993) quotes Henderson (1992), who says, basing his theory on a case study of People Express Airlines, a company that went into liquidation partly because it 'tried so hard to impart dignity to individual workers and managers that it led to attitudes that were not viable over the long term', that it is possible to take the practice of 'empowering' too far. This mistakes the point of empowerment, which is not to abnegate senior management responsibility, nor to make the interests of employees paramount, but to create an enabling architecture within the organization to serve the customer better.

Kay illustrates the concept by citing the case of Marks & Spencer, a company somewhat paternalistic in its approach, but which has developed relational architectures between customers, employees and suppliers. He says the key to its successful internal architecture is to empower each employee to the degree necessary to do his or her job and make a creative contribution to the company, but not to the extent that any one person gains a total information overview that would give them power over the organization. In other words, the whole is worth more than the sum of its parts; the system is open, but it is not unprotected. This is evidently another instance of the need to strike an ethical balance: that of not exploiting the employees, whilst safeguarding against the creation of the 'wrong' culture. Achieving such a balance is still not without its problems: for it may not be easy to identify who is best qualified to decide which level of knowledge is appropriate in each case.

The internal – external interface: auditors and regulators

We have now said much about openness and ethics, and openness and architecture. Financial disclosure and control is one of the most sensitive areas of corporate openness, for a number of reasons:

- Product-line reporting, if published in too much detail, can give valuable information to competitors; on the other hand, an insufficiently detailed breakdown of sales and earnings, especially in conglomerates, can perpetrate inefficiencies and lead to taxation anomalies.
- Conservative forecasts, based on financial information alone, can lead to a drop in share prices at times when the support of shareholders is critical.
- 'Creative', or alternative, accounting methods (addressing such matters as inventory valuation, asset depreciation, recording of revenues, and the capitalization of expenses) can, conversely, give an unjustifiably bright picture of the company's circumstances.

The position of the company's own accountants is a delicate one. They need to be sufficiently 'empowered' to have a clear overview of the financial situation (and this is indeed a legal requirement; some of Robert Maxwell's former accountants have not avoided prosecution by being able to make the claim that they 'did not know'), and 'loyal' in Ewin's sense – in other words, to adopt a position of unimpeachable moral integrity. If the ethical climate within the organization does not permit the latter, then in order to perform their function they may not 'fit' with the culture. The position of the company's auditors is yet more sensitive. They do not form part of the internal architecture of the company – in fact, they should choose strenuously to dissociate themselves from it – yet they do have an influence on that architecture, both in their capacity as advisers and as legal appraisers of how the company has presented its financial affairs. In short, they constitute a very special type of stakeholder. A way of describing them would be to say that they stand at the interface of relational architecture.

Heaston *et al.* (1993) conducted a survey of internal auditors in 1993 which concluded that, although there were pressures placed on internal auditors as a group, these were connected to time constraints rather than overt attempts to compromise their ethical standards. This is not to say that budget/time constraints, which constituted a particular cause of concern, are not without ethical significance; it is interesting also that these worried internal auditors as a group more than they worried audit directors and managers. Clearly, from the architectural point of view, if insufficient resources (of finance, personnel, and time) are allocated to the internal audit, then the company is only imperfectly fulfilling its duty to stakeholders, since the way it presents itself may be based on errors that have gone undetected, and may have been perpetrated and added to over a number of years, and it cannot claim to be operating as efficiently and effectively as possible.

Connected with this is the difficulty (which was expressed in Heaston's survey) of having to rely on information gathered in previous years, and an inability, through lack of resources, to plan and supervise carefully the audit activity. As a result, deliberate abuses as well as inadvertent mistakes, e.g. the misuse of expense accounts, theft, bribery and conflicts of interest, may remained hidden. The external auditors are unlikely to pick up all of these. When asked how their problems could be resolved, the internal auditors that Heaston interviewed said that they looked first to their personal moral values; second, to the corporate business environment, particularly to their superiors; and third, to their professional resources. A company management philosophy emphasizing ethical conduct, a company code of ethics, clear communication of appropriate ethical behaviour by management, and help from co-workers in resolving ethical problems were all regarded as important. McCuddy *et al.* endorsed Heaston's findings in a separate survey undertaken in 1993, which concluded:

Pressures to behave unethically may be related more to attributes of the business firm itself than they are to employees of those firms. This suggests that if the pressures to engage in unethical behaviour are to be lessened, change efforts should focus on the organization and its culture rather than on the individual members of the organization.

What is being discussed in both cases is the creation of a viable and intelligent internal architecture. Embracing the internal auditor within this, so that he is not regarded as nuisance or a cause for suspicion, may be very difficult for some organizations. In Britain and America accountants have their own professional code of ethics (CIMA published a Code of Ethical Guidelines in 1993, and the Institute of Management Accountants in the USA also has a code), but it is significant that even between these two broadly similar business cultures there are differences, and the prospect of creating a unified world code is distant – a matter of relevance when the largest companies operate in many countries and deal with customers worldwide.

A difficulty with professional codes in architectural terms is that they tend to separate the professional and his or her activities from those of the rest of the organization, thus creating a fresh obstacle to integrating him or her into the architecture – even though it could be argued that if the architecture is ethically sound, there should be no conflict. Making accountants responsible for measuring and documenting the company's activities in the wider environmental context (a growing practice, the idea of which was introduced earlier in this paper) may help either to erode or to exacerbate their sense of apartness, depending on the fundamental strategic precepts upon which the company is run. In many companies this function, if conscientiously carried out, could prove to be a poisoned chalice. For most organizations at present, the information put together by the accountants in the annual report, which is heavily biased towards short-term financial achievements, acts as their most significant declaration of what they are about.

That the bias needs to change becomes immediately evident if Drucker's (1993) view that the 'social ecology' of the twenty-first century will consist of a vast network of organizations that will supersede governments, nationalism and race – in short, will take care of the future of the world itself – gains credence. A narrow focus on financial profit would then provide a hugely inadequate operational basis. In enlightened companies the role of the accountant could become even more pivotal, provided that accountants themselves have the vision and necessary support to undertake the task – 'even more pivotal' because accountants already occupy a pivotal role in terms of strategic architecture, i.e. that of providing information about the company to the shareholders. The task is a delicate one. Can shareholder perceptions of what the company should be about be altered, or have shareholders already begun to alter their views? Is it sometimes the company itself that needs to catch up?

How to regulate the regulators remains a difficult problem. From time to time some big event or scandal promotes a major change in or review of how professional bodies are controlled, e.g. Robert Maxwell's alleged misappropriation of many millions of pounds of pension funds in 1991 resulted in the far-reaching changes recommended by the Goode Report in 1993. That such reviews take place is ethically 'healthy'; but they are still subject to the perennial problem, already discussed in the section on the Cadbury Report, of combining appropriate safeguards with sufficient flexibility to accommodate the needs of others – in the case of Goode, contributing employers. Therefore they not only lose some of their 'bite', but leave scope for the regulator, though probably motivated by a different set of priorities, to be as unethical as those whom he or she seeks to regulate.

Shareholders, ethics and architecture

Within the context of this paper, accountants have been described separately from the other builders of internal architecture because of their unique 'pivotal' or 'interfacing' role. Their nearness to the shareholder, and their importance as a channel of information to shareholders both for the present and the future, have been considered. Shareholders are not, strictly speaking, contributors to the internal architecture at all, because, although their capital is being used, they do not (unless they additionally fulfil some other function within the company) contribute to the networks and relationships the company is creating to establish its unique identity. It might be reflected that this represents a total shift in attitude from the position that prevailed 100 years ago, when shareholders were **all** that was considered of importance in the organization, and all other factors, including the customer, were believed to be expendable. Yet it would be absurd to deny that shareholders are still crucial stakeholders. To use a systems metaphor, shareholders 'own' the organization as a system in the sense that they are able to put a stop to its activities – by withdrawing their capital.

Therefore, in building its architecture, the organization has not to seek to include shareholders, but to gain the positive endorsement of shareholders. Getting the architecture right is the key, but this of itself does not necessarily mean that the relationship with the shareholders will be secure. The time when both come under the most intense threat is when the company is being targeted for a takeover bid. This is also a time when the desire of all stakeholders to behave scrupulously towards each other, even if it is there, may be complicated by intense pressure from conflicts of interest.

The most fundamental source of conflict stems from the split of management and ownership, represented by what we have characterized as the internal/external stakeholder relationship. The existing senior management of a company, which makes the decision whether or not to try to repudiate a takeover bid on behalf of the shareholders, usually stands to lose the most if the bid is successful. Hanly (1992), basing his work on stakeholder theory, argues that it is only ethical for management to take steps to repudiate takeover if it is in the interests of all stakeholders. How to determine this is difficult: research generally suggests that few takeovers are successful in the long term. Nevertheless, however imperfect its powers of forecasting, it is necessary not only for management to believe that it is acting in the interests of the shareholders, but to be able to justify such a belief.

Management may fight its case on 'presumption of justifiable defence', and has the advantage of being able to address the shareholders direct; the 'raider', or prospective buyer, bases its case on 'presumption of takeover agency'. Raiders have the disadvantage of not being able to address shareholders direct, but only through the agency of open letters, public announcements, etc. In the colourful literature that has grown up around takeovers, 'shark repellent' is the blanket term used to describe attempts to repudiate unsolicited attempted takeovers. The emotive terminology is not accidental. Common shark repellents include offering a 'poison pill' – sometimes known as a 'flip-in pill' – which allows shareholders to purchase common or preferred stock at a substantial discount. The shareholder may then sell the stock at a much higher price, making it more expensive for the would-be raider to acquire a critical mass of shares, or retain the newly acquired shares to lower the percentage of total shares held by the raider.

'Greenmail' is another stratagem, this time comprising the buying back of a raider's shares at a higher market price in order to block a hostile takeover. The 'greenmailer' is the raider, who is thus threatening to engage in a hostile takeover of the company unless the management agrees to buy back its stock at a premium. Or the management might encourage a 'white knight', or company more congenial to its ideas, to put in a better bid for the company and 'rescue' it from the raider. The management might itself outwit the raider, and engage in a leveraged buyout, i.e. with the help of outside financiers, purchase the shares of the company and 'take it private'. This both removes the threat of takeover, and the need to be accountable to the shareholders; but servicing the debt can mean selling off assets, incurring huge redundancies, or taking on dangerously high gearing, in turn resulting in the issue of junk bonds. Furthermore, managers engaged in buyouts often prove not to have the long-term interests of the company at heart so much as their own secure leisured futures, and sell again within 5 years.

Finally, the managers may choose not to repudiate the raider, even though they do not believe that takeover is in the interests of the company, because they have been offered key positions in the new order, or 'golden parachutes' – large exit remuneration packages – for their cooperation. In this last situation, it is often the case that, while a leader who has proved ineffective gains a substantial payout, ordinary employees are faced with redundancy, and the resulting meagre statutory payments.

The potential for unethical behaviour by senior managers, shareholders and raiders is easy enough to detect in this list; sometimes the courses of action may well be ethically justifiable between the three groups, but even then the interests of customers, employees, suppliers and other stakeholders in the network of the organization's activities are still unlikely to be given much consideration. How therefore can the issue of takeovers be effectively **and** ethically addressed? The decisions made will inevitably reflect the power of the participants. If the true power of the organization is reflected in its architecture, then the interests of these other stakeholders will carry weight, since it has then to be acknowledged that the company itself is worth less (may in fact be worth very little) if it is tugged and chopped so that the architecture is no longer complete. This does, however, bring us back to the original point: that the shareholders must appreciate the architecture, either as it is, or as managers envisage it developing. An illustrative example is offered by ICI's successful repudiation of Hanson's (presumed) takeover bid in 1992. The company already had a strategy in place to split its two mains activities, without destroying the synergy of the group; in other words, it had remodelled its architecture, without destroying any of the networking benefits of existing arrangements. Shareholders were convinced, and Hanson failed.

Networking and ethics

The third strand identified by Kay to be woven into the firm's architecture is that of 'networking' with other companies engaged in related activities. Exactly what this idea should include depends on the nature of the business, what industry it is in, and how one defines the concept of 'an industry'. Whether one accepts Michael Porter's original (1985) definition of an industry as a group of firms engaged in the same activity, or prefers his later (1990) view of it as a 'cluster' of strategic rivals whose very rivalry creates competitive advantage, this is clearly the place within Kay's framework to discuss ethics and competition.

Once again, it is not our main purpose to consider downright law-breaking within the competitive environment. It is possible to think of many sensational examples, covering topics as diverse as industrial espionage, libel, and sabotage. However instructive (and entertaining!) it may be to investigate these, they can play no part in the company's avowed strategy. Within the vast field of ethics and competition, this paper will confine itself to two areas that are of particular relevance to current strategic thinking – that of ethics, joint ventures and strategic alliances; and that of ethics and foreign direct investment.

Networking: joint ventures and strategic alliances

In his earlier work Porter is suspicious of joint ventures, because he says that one partner always has more to gain than another, and that there are therefore always winners and losers, with the 'winner' possibly terminating the relationship at a point when its continuation has become vital to the loser. Later, he expresses a qualified acceptance of the practice, but he is still of the opinion that the 'networking' relationship, whose importance he acknowledges, gains more from direct rivalry than from cooperation, arguing that an industry kept on its mettle by fierce competition continually pushes back the frontiers of adding value and innovation. Kay, on the other hand, is an advocate of joint ventures and strategic alliances, partly because he deplores the negative potential of mergers and acquisitions, and partly because of the now generally recognized fact that sophisticated and complex industries such as telecommunications and large projects like the Channel Tunnel require financial resources and expertise beyond the capabilities of one organization. It could also be said that in the more cautious, recession-conscious 1990s, the risk-sharing appeal of joint ventures has increased.

The importance of applying the highest ethical standards to strategic alliances is illustrated by the treatment of Honda in the BMW/Rover takeover. Rover, the last British car manufacturer, enjoyed a productive strategic alliance with Honda from 1980, and in 1990 Honda took a 20 per cent stake in the Rover Group, and Rover became the owners of 20 per cent of Honda UK. The equity stake was seen as symbolic of the 'cement' in their unique relationship. Unlike its Japanese rivals, Honda preferred the strategic alliance to relying totally on direct investment, and gained from it a way into the European market; in return, Rover gained the benefit not only of Honda's engineering expertise, but also of its way of doing things – setting up relationships with suppliers, working across functions, etc. The whole was a *tour de force* of Kay's idea of 'architecture'.

However, after the alliance was forged, Rover became owned by British Aerospace, which in February 1994 sold BMW a controlling stake in the Rover Group, for which it paid £800m. Honda, bitter rivals of the German group, were not consulted before the deal was struck. After being allowed belated consultation with BMW, they decided to withdraw their minority shareholding. Other facets of the strategic alliance – because the architecture of it was so complex and so fundamental – would take longer to dismantle, but it was clear that the basis of trust on which it was built had been breached, and that, in spirit, the relationship was at an end.

On the face of it, Honda then occupied the position of Porter's classic 'loser' in such a situation. Though it was certainly true that their European strategy had taken a severe blow, and that they had 'lost face' by placing their trust in an alliance that had been unethically breached by failing to observe the openness that is essential to joint ventures, they would certainly not be the only, and possibly not the greatest, victims. BMW had lost the Honda engineering expertise, which was calculated into the price they paid for Rover; Rover itself now had further to climb (either on its own or with BMW's help) to attain world-class standing; and Rover's reputation as a fair dealer had been damaged, with incalculable effect on its customers and other stakeholders – even though it was a helpless pawn in the hands of its parent, British Aerospace, the organization that was really guilty of unethical behaviour; and many other current and potential Anglo-Japanese alliances might have been jeopardized. The example illustrates that, although building effective networking into architecture does not safeguard a company against anti-ethical practices, it does mean that ethical transgressions will have far-reaching implications for the many organizations feeding into the network. The more that companies realize the true significance of networking (which has been brought home by the Honda/Rover case), the less likely they are to risk the withdrawal of expertise, goodwill and good reputation that unethical behaviour will bring.

Networking: foreign direct investment (FDI)

Classic foreign direct investment takes place in Third World countries by companies from developed nations, and the traditional (if patronizing) view of it, based on the tenets of neoclassical economic theory, is that it makes a benign contribution to the companies selected. Moran (1985) summarizes the reasons for this: it brings new, scarce resources (capital, technology, management and marketing skills); it increases competition and improves efficiency; its adds jobs to the economy; and improves distribution of income. However, recent research, augmented by dissent from the host countries, suggests that companies engaging in FDI have a much stronger bias towards exploitation than development. To quote Moran:

> In the extreme, foreign companies might capture the commanding heights of the host economy, soak up indigenous sources of capital as they drive local firms out of business, create a small labour elite for themselves while transferring the bulk of the workers into the ranks of the unemployed, and siphon off oligopoly profits for repatriation to corporate headquarters.

That such a chain of events produces ethically undesirable consequences can only be contradicted with some very specious pleading. What may at first be less apparent is the strategic undesirability of such behaviour. This can be explained by developing an awareness of how the global business environment is changing, and also a familiarity with one of the major sources of competitive advantage that Kay identifies in conjunction with that of strategic architecture: the able deployment of strategic assets. (By 'strategic assets', he means any tangible or intangible assets – plant, capital, location, skills, goodwill, brand names, etc. – which make a significant, preferably unique contribution to a company's strategy.)

To tackle the issue of the changing global environment first, it is perhaps only in Africa (and even there it is becoming less blatant) that the wholesale pillaging of the host country in the manner Moran describes is still possible. This is not only due to political pressures, but also to the chain of cause and effect that foreign direct investment produces.

What has happened in Japan offers a good example. The combination of a strong yen, relatively high standard of living, and skilled workforce in the home country caused Japanese companies to set up so-called 'screwdriver' plants, i.e. factories largely for the assembly of products, where few complex components are made and little or no research and development takes place, in other South East Asian countries where the standard of living was lower, and skilled and semi-skilled labour cheap and plentiful. This situation did not remain static, however. The influx of cash raised the standard of living in those countries, and the pressures exerted forced the Japanese companies to give a higher status to the plants, and better training to the workers. The eventual result was not only that new companies grew up in countries such as Taiwan and Malaysia in direct competition with the Japanese, but also that the indigenous Japanese workforce was becoming 'hollowed out', or deskilled, because the coalface activity was taking place elsewhere.

Today Japan is faced with two alternatives – either moving production again to another area of the world where labour is cheap, or of building more meaningful relationships, i.e. developing better networking architecture, in the countries in which it already operates. If the first alternative is taken, the situation will merely repeat itself, and yet other suitable host countries will ultimately have to be found. This clearly does not represent the intelligent deployment of strategic assets that the second alternative offers, and many Japanese companies have realized this, altering their strategies accordingly. True cooperation means playing fair – hence, the importance of ethical values to this strategic perspective.

Third world countries have of late asserted that their viewpoint concerning a range of ethical issues should be taken into account by the industrialized nations, and with some success. At a world conference on 'green' issues, which took place in 1993, India refused to reduce the level of harmful emissions for which her industries were responsible unless the West gave substantial aid, in the form of cash, technology and expertise, to enable her to do so without undermining her economy. Steidlmeier (1993) has written thoughtfully on the moral legitimacy of the western practice of patenting inventions, presenting the third world view that the conditions that enabled developed countries to form their 'intellectual property' probably owed something to the exploitation of the underdeveloped ones; and that, further-more, underdeveloped countries **should** be granted access to new technolo-gies, because the use of these would promote far faster growth than in developed ones (owing to the law of diminishing returns), and give such countries independence from the charity of the international community. On the other hand, it has to be said that the breaking of patents by third-world countries cannot automatically be condoned on the grounds that they are following their own ethical rules, based on a perception of what is 'fair' that disregards international law; and it should also be remembered that the distri-bution of wealth is very unequal in developing countries – in itself a thorny ethical problem that needs to be tackled.

The changing balance of world economic power, and the complex trail of related ethical and cultural concerns it carries in its wake, is illustrated by the controversy over the Malaysian Pergau dam project, which the British govern-ment faced in the Spring of 1994. Malaysia is a rapidly developing country that has many contracts to award to developed-world countries on its path of progress. In recent years contracts awarded to British companies had all but dried up, possibly because the British government had extended little aid to Malaysia. (It is a paradox of the swiftly changing current world scene that newly industrialized countries are simultaneously seeking aid from established industrialized countries, and offering them lucrative contracts.) Following a visit to Malaysia from the then British prime minister, Margaret Thatcher, in 1989, Britain offered to sponsor the projected Pergau dam.

In 1994 a storm erupted in the British House of Commons when it was alleged, first of all, that sponsoring the dam was unethical, because it was specifically intended as a pump-priming exercise to attract contracts for British companies, and, secondly, that this particular choice of project was a prodigal waste of taxpayers' money, not only because it was ill-conceived, but also because it had cost far more than was originally intended. Senior members of the British government vehemently denied both these charges. Whatever the truth of them, and whatever the ethical attitude taken towards the project, any benefit that might have accrued to British industry was probably destroyed by the ensuing acrimony and innuendo, which deeply offended the Malaysian government. It is too simple to assert merely that the British government had shot itself in the foot. What the case perhaps illustrates is that the two countries have different ethical 'norms', and that the British govern-ment, in seeking to approach closer to those of the Malaysians, came under attack from Britons unable to accommodate such a perspective.

All the ethical issues described in the preceding paragraphs are still the source of fierce controversy; they are still to be resolved (and, in common with most debates about ethics and equality will probably never be entirely resolved). They and the ethical issues arising from joint ventures and strategic alliances have been invoked to demonstrate the importance of ethics to 'networking' within the model of strategic architecture.

Conclusion

The range of ethical issues arising from 'external', 'internal' and 'networking' architecture that have been examined in this paper point to the logical identity of the future stakeholder – the 'global stakeholder' who belongs to a sharing world community. If the concept seems a little starry-eyed, it is necessary only to reflect that in the space of less than 100 years the business environment has moved from an ethical stance that did not think it wrong to ignore the interests of all but the shareholder to one which, while still far from perfect, takes account to some degree of each of the stakeholders produced by that environment. We are still novices at coming to terms with the impact of the business environment on the wider environment of the biosphere, and the ethicosocial issues that raises; but a growing number of business leaders now realize the strategic importance of taking this, too, on board. An understanding of the relevance of ethics to 'architecture' – and therefore of the standards that have to be maintained to derive competitive advantage from the resulting complex interplay of relationships – can only accelerate the necessary learning processes.

Epilogue: business ethics and expediency versus altruism

In this chapter we have considered the benefits that taking a strong ethical stance can offer to an organization's strategy, using Kay's concept of architecture as a framework: in other words, we have taken a pragmatic, or expedient, perspective. A purist would say that this is not what true ethics is about; that thinking about how choosing the 'right' behaviour can benefit oneself or the organization, rather than taking the right action because it is right, immediately devalues that act. Therefore should the highest order of ethical behaviour in business be undertaken in a spirit of altruism – and is this indeed possible?

Such reflection brings us into the realm of philosophical and sociological debate on ethics – an area that has deliberately been avoided so far because it requires the introduction of specialized modes of expression and terminologies that 'non-experts' may find uncongenial. Nevertheless, it is important at least to introduce an awareness of the ethical body of knowledge as an 'epilogue', however briefly, since it does help to inform the debate.

'Textbook' ethics nearly always begins with a consideration of **personal moral philosophies**, i.e. the relationship between an individual's concept of right and wrong and the influence it has on the way he enacts his daily life. Problems arise when the individual encounters ethical dilemmas of choice he cannot resolve – an area we have already discussed in relation to the business leader and the conflicts that may occur between his personal moral code and the pressures the organization and particular sets of circumstances impose upon it.

Teleological philosophy says that an act may be considered morally acceptable if it produces some desired result – pleasure, knowledge, etc. It therefore assesses the moral worth of behaviour by looking at its consequences. This is the general perspective that we have taken in looking at ethics and strategy.

Teleological philosophy is often divided into two branches: **egoism** and **utilitarianism**. Egoism defines right or acceptable behaviour in terms of its consequences for the individual. Egoists believe that they should make decisions that maximize their own self-interest, which will be defined differently by each individual. ('Individual' in the business context could read 'organization'.) What this paper has tried to establish is that such a philosophy, which ultimately depends on the law of the jungle, is not only bad for various stakeholders, but is unlikely to result in the development of a healthy strategy.

A more enlightened form of egoism takes the long-range perspective, and allows for the well-being of others, though personal self-interest remains paramount. It could be argued that this was the stage reached by Royal Dutch Shell when it incorporated a medium-term ethical perspective into its strategy in the 1970s.

Utilitarianism is also concerned with consequences, but the utilitarian obliges himself to consider what is the greatest good for the greatest number of people. Utilitarian decision-making relies on a systematic comparison of the costs and benefits to all affected parties; it has sometimes included the rights of animals, though, when applied to business, not yet the wider considerations of the effect of activities on the biosphere. This is a limitation; nevertheless, utilitarianism is approaching much closer in spirit to what we mean by taking an architectural perspective on ethics and strategy, though with the important difference that it is reductionist in approach – painstaking cost-benefit analysis militates against the creation of the synergy that results in the hard-to-replicate output of the architecture.

Deontology is concerned with moral philosophies that focus on the rights of individuals, and on the intentions associated with a particular behaviour (not its consequences). Fundamental to deontological theory is the idea that equal respect must be given to all people. Unlike utilitarians, deontologists argue that there are some things that we should not do, even to maximize utility. Deontologists believe that individuals have certain absolute rights:

freedom of conscience, freedom of consent, freedom of privacy; freedom of speech, due process. Here, indeed, we encounter the moral high ground. In one sense, an acceptance of deontological precepts is what we have been arguing for for the future, in the argument that enlightened businesses will be trying to reconcile their activities to the needs of the 'global stakeholder'. It was, however, pointed out that this ideal was unlikely to be attained absolutely, because there are likely always to be inequalities of power and prestige. There are other inequalities, too, which might not make an outright deontological commitment appropriate: inequalities of talent, of grasping and making use of information – in short, inequalities of the energies that power organizations. In the last analysis organizations are likely to be dependent on leadership – leadership at various levels, but nevertheless leadership that carries both privileges and responsibilities. We have come full circle in the argument, and returned to our first premise that much depends on personal morality, and how the organizational culture fosters or stifles it. Their personal morality is therefore of the greatest relevance to the question whether it is possible for leaders to be altruistic when developing a business strategy, and whether it is even desirable.

Blau and Homans' *Social Exchange Theory* says that all interactive human behaviour is based on the premise that 'there is a price for everything, and everything has its price'. This is not to state dogmatically that human beings behave cynically or with overt self-interest in all their dealings with each other; it can be taken as an observation of the complex web of motive, anticipated outcome, and desire to please (or do harm) that every social act implies. Ultimately, it is a statement of survival; a statement therefore of what it is in human nature that enables humans to survive. Survival must be the first aim of any organization; some survive through perpetrating unethical acts, but by doing so they are isolating themselves and are therefore unlikely to flourish. Increasingly, others are learning to survive through developing a strategy based on architecture, and cemented by the strong ethical values needed to make the architectural relationships work – and they often then go on to flourish. Establishing that 'pure' altruism can be said to exist is beyond our scope, but it is possible to assert that there may be a less disinterested, but perhaps more socially productive 'business altruism'; and that the concept of architecture offers a strong route to the willing commitment to a pursuit of ethical values in business.

References

Barry, A (1992) Days of Wine and Roses, *Purchasing and Supply Management*, October, pp. 22–9.

Bebbington J and Gray, R (1993) Corporate Accountability and the Physical Environment: Social Responsibility and Accounting Beyond Profit, *Journal of Business Ethics*, 12.

Blanchard, K and Peale, N W (1991) *The Power of Ethical Management*, Heinemann, London.

Blau, P. *Exchange and Power in Social Life*

Brooks, L J, Jr (1993) No More Trial and Error, *Chartered Accountant Magazine*, March, pp. 43–5.

Cyert, R M and March, J G (1963) *A Behavioural Theory of the Firm*, Prentice-Hall, New York.

Drucker, P (1979) *The Practice of Management* (revised edition), Macmillan, London.

Drucker, P (1993) *Post-Capitalist Society*, Butterworth-Heinemann, Oxford.

Economist, The (1989) According to Plan (the story of Shell's 'green' strategy), *The Economist*, 22–8 July, pp. 74–5.

Ewin, R E (1993) Corporate Loyalty: Its Objects and Grounds, *Journal of Business Ethics*, 12, pp. 387–96.

Fraedrich, F (1991) *Business Ethics*, Houghton Mifflin, London.

Frederick, W C and Weber, J (1990) The Values of Corporate Managers and their Critics: an Empirical Description and Normative Implications, paper published in *Business Ethics: Research Issues and Empirical Studies*, Jai Press, London, pp. 123–44.

Grant, F (1993) Ethics: Fundamentally Important to Civilisation, *CMA Magazine*, February, p. 4.

Gray, J (1992) Why Banning Advertising is Wrong, *The Campaign Report*, September, pp. 41–2.

Hanly, K (1992) Hostile Takeovers and Methods of Defence: a Stakeholder Analysis, *Journal of Business Ethics*, 11, pp. 895–913.

Heaston, P., *et al.* (1993) The Ethical Environment of the Internal Auditor, *Internal Auditor*, June, pp. 18–23.

Homans, G (1974) *Social Behaviour: Its elementary forms.* Harcourt Brace and Company, London.

Jack A and Dickson, T (1993) Laying Down a Code of Honour: NatWest Publishes its Principles. *Financial Times*, 26 May.

Kay, J (1993) *The Foundations of Corporate Success.* Oxford University Press, Oxford.

Ludwig, D C and Longenecker, C O (1993) The Bathsheba Syndrome: the Ethical Failure of Successful Leaders, *Journal of Business Ethics*, 12, pp. 265–73.

McCuddy, M K *et al.* (1993) Ethical Pressures: Fact or Fiction? *Management Accounting*, April, pp. 57–61.

Madison, R L (1993) The New Ethical Guidelines from an International Perspective, *Management Accounting*, April, pp. 32–7.

Meade, N L and Davidson, D (1993) The Use of 'Shark Repellents' to Prevent Corporate Takeovers: an Ethical Perspective, *Journal of Business Ethics*, 12, pp. 83–92.

Miles G (1993) In Search of Ethical Profits: Insights from Strategic Management, *Journal of Business Ethics*, 12, pp. 219–25.

Moran, T H (1985) *Multinational Corporations: the Political Economy of Foreign Direct Investment*, Lexington Books, Mass.

Osborne, J (1992) The CAASE for Problem Solving, *Accountancy*, September, p. 139.

Pattakos, A N (1989) Growth in Activist Groups: How Can Business Cope?, *Long Range Planning*, Reproduced in Mercer, D (Ed.) (1992) *Managing the External Environment*, Sage, London.

Pizzolato, A B and Zeringue, C A, II (1993) Facing Society's Demands for Environmental Protection: Management in Practice, *Journal of Business Ethics*, 12, pp. 441–7.

Porter, M (1985) *Competitive Strategy*, Macmillan, London.

Porter, M (1990) *The Competitive Advantage of Nations*, Macmillan, London.

Prince, S J and Denison, R A (1992) Launching a New Business Ethic: the Environment as a Standard Operating Procedure, *International Management*, November/December, pp. 15–19.

Rickard, P (1993) Fraud Control, *Australian Accountant*, August, pp. 26–9.

Riley, K (1993) Telling More than the Truth: Implicature, Speech Acts and Ethics in Professional Communication, *Journal of Business Ethics*, 12, pp. 179–96.

Schein, E H (1985) *Organisational Culture and Leadership*, Jossey Bass, New York.

Singer, A W (1993) Can a Company be Too Ethical?, *Across the Board*, April, pp. 17–22.

Smith, N C (1990) *Morality and the Market: Consumer Pressure for Corporate Accountability*, Routledge, London.

Solomon, R C (1991) *Business Ethics*, Blackwell Companion to Ethics, Blackwell, Oxford, pp. 354–64.

Stark, A (1993) What's the Matter with Business Ethics?, *Harvard Business Review*, May–June, pp. 38–48.

Steidlmeier, P (1993) The Moral Legitimacy of Intellectual Property Claims: American Business and Developing Country Perspectives, *Journal of Business Ethics*, 12, pp. 157–64.

Sturdivant, F D (1981) *Business and Society* (revised edition), Irwin, Illinois.

Truell, P and Gurwin, L (1992) *BCCI: The Inside Story of the World's Most Corrupt Financial Empire*, Bloomsbury, London.

Vogel, D (1993) The Globalisation of Business Ethics: Why America Remains Distinctive, *Journal of Business Ethics*, 12, pp. 30–49.

Welch, I (1992) Preys Hitch a Ride with the Hunters, *Financial Director*, November, pp. 57–60.

Yeager, P C (1990) Analyzing Corporate Offences: Progress and Prospects. Reprinted in Frederick, W C and Preston, L E (Eds) *Business Ethics: Research Issues and Empirical Studies*, Jai Press, Connecticut.

Young, A T (1993) On Linking Ethics and Quality at Martin Marietta, *National Productivity Review*, Spring, pp. 133–7.

8

The dark side of excellence: managing strategic failures
Denis Smith

Introduction

The collapse of organizations, many of which had previously been considered to be extremely robust, has focused the attention of strategists on the nature and mechanisms of failure. Along with the work concerning chaos, studies of crisis that challenge the more traditional paradigms are beginning to provide new perspectives on the strategic management process. There are clear parallels between the collapse of natural and technical systems, on the one hand, and organizational failures, on the other; and the former group of events should serve to inform our thinking on the latter. For example, when the *Titanic* hit an iceberg on her maiden voyage in 1912, it illustrated the inherent fragility of complex technical systems. The belief in the ship's supposedly unsinkable nature; the lack of lifeboats in sufficient numbers for passengers; the failure to heed the warnings of ice transmitted by other ships in the vicinity; the confusion surrounding the interpretation of white distress rockets from the stricken ship by another ship lying relatively close by; the time taken to effect the rescue of survivors; and the process of legitimation and scapegoating that occurred after the event, are all indicative of the complex process of crisis management (Smith, 1994). They show how crises become incubated, how the events exceed the planner's worse-case scenario, and how legitimation and scapegoating occur after the event. Despite the popular image to the contrary, crises are not just limited to such catastrophic systems failures. In recent years a series of corporate collapses, financial scandals and major product failures and contaminations have borne testimony to the range of potential crisis events that can befall the modern corporation. Not surprisingly therefore, crisis management has recently begun to attract the attention of business academics, who see a relevance of the process in informing more mainstream management thinking.

The sinking of the *Titanic*, to which we will return in more detail later, illustrates a number of issues that underpin the strategic management process. These include, an inherently flawed belief in both the reasons behind success and the technical rationality that is often held to be an essential part of strategic management. There was an almost unshakeable belief in the robust nature of the *Titanic* and other ships of its type, which compares to the belief, after articulated by managers, in the invulnerability of the modern corporation. The strength of this belief can be gauged from a statement made by the Captain of the *Titanic*, some 6 years before that fateful voyage, when he observed that:

'I cannot imagine any condition which would cause a ship to founder. I cannot conceive of any vital disaster happening to this vessel. Modern shipbuilding has gone beyond that' – Captain Edward Smith of the SS *Titanic* after crossing the Atlantic in the *Adriatic* in 1906. Cited in Lord (1978), p. 55.

A similar belief in the invulnerability of organizations has characterized what we can term the dark side of excellence (see, Carroll, 1993; Heller, 1994). Organizations fail with alarming regularity and yet much of the theory on strategic management makes little reference to the dynamics of this process. Our aim in this paper is briefly to explore the concept of failure as a means of providing a better understanding of the strategy process and to suggest ways in which a knowledge of failure can improve management decision-making.

In terms of theoretical developments, the management literature of the 1980s was typified by the search for excellence and a striving for what appeared to be a 'quick fix' solution to complex problems. While some of this literature offers powerful insights into the management process, in many cases it also runs the risk of luring managers into a false sense of security as a false belief concerning the transferability of excellence becomes engendered. If the 1980s represented the exposition of excellence as a theoretical construct, then the 1990s seem to be characterized by the need to manage chaos and complexity. Given this shift in emphasis, we need to ask how we can develop management competencies to cope with the range of issues that face organizations in the 1990s? In response, the study of crisis management has emerged in recent years as a systematic attempt to examine the ways in which organizational failure occurs and how managers can develop competencies to deal with chaos and complexity (see Pauchant and Douville, 1993). While the process has received increased attention within the management literature, there would still appear to be much more work needed before we can begin to move towards a more effective, and potentially diagnostic, approach to the problem and take us away from the current, largely theoretical base.

In its present stage of development, the crisis literature has understandably tended to focus upon the development of empirically grounded, but perhaps theoretically immature, case material. That such a process has been necessary in the early stage of the subject is beyond debate. However, there is a need to move this process onwards as a means of facilitating further developments in throwing light on the management process. This movement has been aided considerably by a significant number of spectacular corporate failures and crises occurring over the last 15 years, which have provided a wealth of empirical data for analysis. The intention here is to outline some of the recent concepts that have been developed in order to frame the crisis management process and perhaps to move us more towards a practical focus for the problem. In so doing, it will be necessary to detail some of the problems with the more popular management theory in terms of its ability to cope with crisis precipitation and incubation. In addition, the chapter also attempts to offer some speculative suggestions concerning the developments of new framework and diagnostics for use within the crisis management process.

Searching for the holy grail? Excellence in management

The general literature on management theory is highly diverse in terms of its base philosophical approaches. The research activity concerning the more specialized study of strategic management clearly illustrates this point, as there are a number of schools of thought relating to the strategy literature, and healthy debate and disagreement exists within the discipline (see, for example, Mintzberg, 1990a, 1990b, 1991, 1994; Ansoff, 1991). In broad terms we can identify two main generic groups of thought within the literature, although a number of sub-groups exist within them. The main paradigmatic camps can be considered as the rational planning group, in which the assumption that strategy can be developed and planned for in a logical manner is made; and the entrepreneurial and emergent strategy group, in which the search for excellence and learning has predominated (see, for example, Pascale and Athos, 1981; Peters and Waterman, 1982; Hampden-Turner, 1990; Pedler *et al.*, 1991; Senge, 1990; Waterman, 1994). More recent work has recognized that, while much of this entrepeneurial management theory has certain merits, there are inherent problems for managers with simply trying to learn from success (see Pascale, 1990).

The single biggest problem is that 'excellence' and similar constructs only provide a unidimensional perspective on a complex phenomenon. Of particular importance is the notion that excellence is temporarily defined – it is not guaranteed to perpetuate itself *ad infinitum*. Additionally, there is no assurance that the strategy for excellence that works in one organization and culture is transferable to other settings. The more popular management literature has a tendency to extol the virtues of excellence without really offering a meaningful insight into the sustainability of the process. Such a sterile study of excellence also fails to offer a learning experience from failed strategic decisions, which potentially represent a major resource for management development and organizational learning. Consequently, there has been a growth in recent years of a complex literature that explores the dynamics of failure as an antidote to the potentially arid popular culture of excellence that has emerged.

That this has been necessary is evidenced by the growth and decline in management concepts and the fall from grace of many of the excellent companies identified in earlier studies (Pascale, 1990). This is not to say that concepts of excellence are redundant – indeed, one might argue that the search for excellence is essential – but that such a search must be accompanied by some caveats. The first such caveat is that we need to recognize the importance of understanding failure as a learning medium. The second is that excellence does not equate with immortality – organizations have a natural tendency to die (see De Geus, 1988; Senge, 1990). An excellent, and therefore by definition a learning company, would ensure that a transformation or transfer of organizational assets would ensure a rebirth of another organization (see Burgoyne, 1994).

In what proved to be a seminal text Peters and Waterman (1982) outlined their theories behind what makes for an excellent company. This work, which was closely related to that of Pascale and Athos (1981), spawned a whole generation of managers who were preoccupied with the search for, and maintenance of, excellence. The synthesis of this work lies in the 7S framework that was developed while the authors were working for McKinsey in the United States. In assessing the performance of the top companies, they found that the elements portrayed in the 7S framework were common to all excellent organizations. Since then, the McKinsey 7S framework has become an accepted element within the strategic management process. This research has continued to evolve since the early 1980s and a number of subsequent studies have been published. However, over time, a number of the companies previously defined as excellent have experienced severe crisis (Pascale, 1990) and this has begun to raise questions concerning the sustainability of excellence as an organizational construct that can effectively inform practical management thinking.

The risk of corporate decline and failure should come as no surprise when one considers that the average lifetime of an organization is only some 40 years (De Geus, 1988). Despite this, failure has never really adopted a central place in management theory, although a number of writers have highlighted the potential risks of demise that face organizations. However, it should be noted that no amount of 'corporate health care' can guarantee organizational immortality, and that the risk of failure will be forever present. What work has been undertaken has largely focused on the financial processes that come into play in turnaround and corporate collapse (see, for example, Radell, 1990 and Slatter, 1984 for a review of this literature). In more recent years the focus of this attention has shifted towards the more 'human'-centred realizations of failure (Byrne *et al.*, 1991). Indeed, as Weir (1993), observes, human intervention is an essential component of technical and business failures as:

> . . . over 70 per cent of airline accidents involve human agency and the bulk of these involve communication failure. Studies of business failure show a similar pattern. Inadequate management is involved in 85 per cent of cases of corporate failure and 73 per cent are connected with failures of senior management. This compares with 7 per cent, for example, of cases due to exogenous changes in the pattern of demand for a company's products (Weir, 1993, p. 47).

According to Reason (1990), this human intervention in the failure process can result from violations, errors or lapses on the part of individuals. To this can be added the impact of group-think (Janis, 1972) as an underlying construct on the human component of failure. Whether the excellence paradigm effectively accounts for the frailty of human intervention in decisions is a matter for debate. The negative impacts of those decisions taken by management can remain dormant, or incubated (Turner, 1978), within the organization – akin to what Reason (1987) terms resident pathogens. Such pathogens remain dormant until the convergence of circumstances conspire to create a complex matrix of failure that has the human component at its centre. Failure is, therefore, a natural phenomena within organizations and needs to be incorporated into the core paradigm.

While this may seem obvious to natural scientists, there are many who seem to espouse the view that corporations can somehow be exempt from the risks that face biological entities: in this context survival simply becomes a matter of excellent management practice. While the quality of the management process is obviously crucial to survival, the point needs to be made that even the supposedly excellent companies face difficulties due to human frailty, non-controllable, or external factors. In reflecting upon the demise of companies that had previously been espoused as excellent, Pascale (1990) observes that 'Simply identifying attributes of success is like identifying attributes of people in excellent health during the age of the bubonic plague . . . The true path of insight, of course, required a study of both the sick and the healthy' (p. 16).

The biological metaphor is therefore a strong one. Organizations run the risk of acute and chronic illness, or failure, and need to be managed accordingly. In order to understand the way in which organizations work we need to look at both their positive and negative attributes. While the conventional approach to excellence is well-established within the literature on strategy, the study of failure – often expressed as crisis management – is still generally seen as being in its infancy (see Pauchant and Douville, 1993).

Intellectually, the process of crisis management can be seen to be at the interface between the strategic management literature and the more narrowly defined work on risk assessment and technology management. While there is undoubtedly a close relationship between these disciplines, in practice each of them has distinct and virtually separate theoretical origins. Risk assessment, for example, owes its development to early work on reliability for missile systems and in the understanding of natural hazards. In contrast, strategic management draws upon the whole field of business administration and finance, along with certain writings in the field of military strategy. As crisis management is clearly related to both areas, then it will, by definition, draw upon a multi-disciplinary literature that is both rich and varied. However, in general terms the subject lacks the theoretical maturity of its parent disciplines and much current research is aimed at trying to redress that imbalance and in testing recently developed theoretical constructs against empirical data.

The literature relating to crisis management has developed considerably over the last 10 years (Pauchant and Douville, 1993) and a trend in the development of the research can be observed. In its early stages the research in this area was primarily concerned with case analysis and the development of conceptual frameworks, and operated largely through grounded theory. As such, the work has much in common with the early developments in the field of strategic management, which has long been case-driven. Building upon this early material, the body of research went on to construct theoretical frameworks in order to explain the mechanisms by which the crisis process works. The next stage is concerned with verifying these theoretical perspectives in the light of further case material. The final stages of the development of the subject are likely to be taken up with the development of diagnostic techniques and tools for practising managers, the verification of such diagnostics and, possibly, with the development of competing paradigmatic perspectives as the literature begins to mature.

There is a strong relationship between the crisis management literature and that concerning the strategic performance of firms (Argenti, 1976; Pauchant, Mitroff and Pearson, 1992; Smith 1992b). The work in this field can be grouped into five broad areas: turnaround management; organizationally based disasters and catastrophes (technological failures); environmental crises; ethics and corporate crime; and corporate collapse. The literature on each of these topics is extremely broad and the confines of this chapter inevitably prevent a full discussion here. Within this diverse area we can encompass the full range of organizations, from small-to-medium enterprises through to transnational organizations, and the research inevitably cuts across the public/private sector divide. With this broad background in mind, and the research area contextualized within broader academic regimes, this chapter now seeks to outline a framework for the crisis management process in order to suggest a pathway by which learning from disaster and failure may inform management theory.

Crisis management: managing on the edge of darkness?

Owing to the inadequacy of our understanding as to what sustains success, we are unable to help organizations sustain performance with any reliability. This is evident when we take stock of how poorly our assessments and predictions stack up with the results – Pascale (1990).

If success is difficult to define then its alter ego, crisis, suffers equally from the same malaise. Crisis is perhaps among the most commonly misused words in the English language, often trivialized to such an extent that its use borders on the bland and it has an inherently negative image. Despite this, its original meaning (in both Greek and Chinese) referred simply to a point of change. In this context, change is usually traumatic and rapid, and also has the potential for harm. Common academic usage of crisis has refined this meaning to assume the mantle of catastrophic change that is not positive in its orientation.

Within the academic literature the word is also used in a variety of contexts and to describe a variety of meanings (Smith, 1990b). Again, this creates problems of definition, as the term often assumes different characteristics within particular disciplinary contexts. Perhaps the most thorough definition of the term, and the one that will be adopted in this paper, comes from Shrivastava et al. (1988), who argue that crisis refers to 'organizationally-based disasters which cause extensive damage and social disruption, involve multiple stakeholders, and unfold through complex technological, organizational and social processes' (p. 285).

In this context the issues of organizational threat and the inherent complexity of the process are highlighted. Put simply, a crisis is a complex phenomenon that threatens the integrity of the organization that plays host to it. As an event, it inevitably threatens the strategic aims of the organization. The sheer complexity of the process beguiles our attempts to model it succinctly, while the emotional threat associated with the potential consequences makes many managers reluctant to take on board the risk of facing such an event and planning for it. The process is often clouded by denial and complacency among many corporations, and crisis has become associated with managerial failure and the scapegoating that is related to it. While there is an element of managerial inadequacy associated with crises, there is also a certain inevitability that organizations will be exposed to such events (Greiner, 1972) – their ability (or otherwise) to cope with such demands is a different matter entirely.

In a series of articles Smith (1990b, 1992a, 1993a; Smith and Sipika, 1993) has argued that a model (or perhaps more accurately a framework) of the crisis management process can be outlined, and this is shown in Figure 8.1. Here it can be seen that the process of crisis management is essentially circular, starting with a crisis of management, moving into the operational phase, and then feeding back into the organization via a process of legitimation and learning. Each of these phases is perceived as being driven by seven factors, akin to the 7S framework, and these are referred to as the 7Cs of crisis management. Like the 7S framework, the 7Cs can be grouped into a 'cold', technocratic group and a 'warm', more organic group (see Figure 8.2). The validation of this framework has taken place across a number of sectors and in a number of organizations (Smith, 1992a, 1993a; Elliott and Smith, 1993; Sipika and Smith, 1993); while there is still much work to do, in terms of developing a diagnostic element, it is held that it does adequately describe the process and highlights the potential causes of events within a broad framework. In order to illustrate this it is necessary to explore the various dimensions of the model, in an attempt to understand how it operates within the context of actual organizational crises.

In discussing the nature of large corporate failures, Hambrick and D'Aveni (1988) outline a series of critical factors that contribute to the failure process. These factors are fourfold: the extent of domain initiative, i.e. changes in the organization's product and market portfolio; the extent of environmental carrying capacity, i.e. the number of firms that the specific environment can support; the amount of slack within the organization, i.e. the extent of resource surplus over that required for survival; and, finally, the performance of the organization in terms of its profitability, a process that Hambrick and D'Aveni argue is closely related to the amount of slack that is present within the organization. These factors are deemed to operate in four main phases of the failure process – the 'origins of disadvantage'; 'early impairment', 'marginal existence', and 'death struggle' (Hambrick and D'Aveni, 1988). In their empirical research they found that the failure process took place over what could be as much as a 10-year period and that the various phases could be generally grouped into discrete time bands. An adapted form of Hambrick and D'Aveni's model, which ties into earlier work on crisis management from Smith (1990b), is shown in Figure 8.3.

The focus of Hambrick and D'Aveni's research was on a 6-year period prior to the collapse of the company. As a result, Hambrick and D'Aveni acknowl-

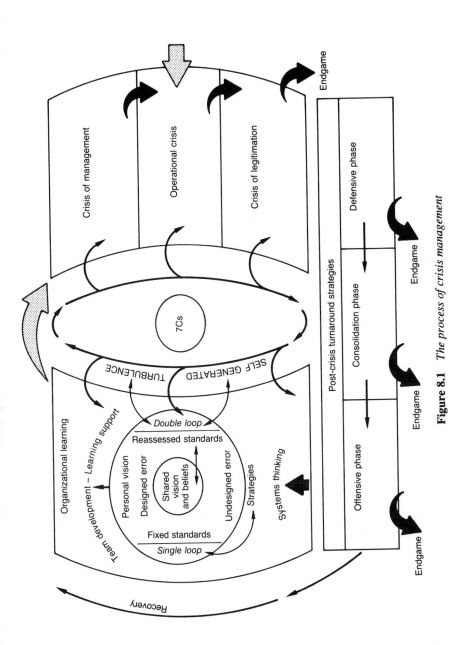

Figure 8.1 *The process of crisis management*

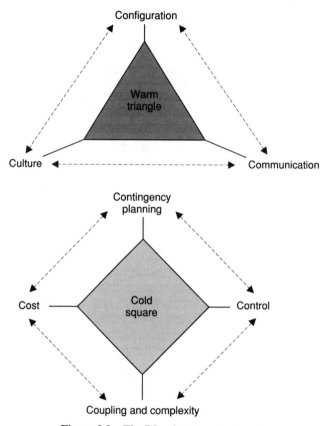

Figure 8.2   *The 7Cs of crisis management*

edge that the early stages of the model need to be developed further. Figure 8.3 adds some detail to this work (evidenced by script in italics) in an attempt to suggest possible factors that may prove to be influential in the failure process. What the empirical work of Hambrick and D'Aveni suggests is that failures seem to be incubated over a long period of time but that they only become apparent (from comparison with the surviving firms) in the last 4–5 years, by which time it would appear to be difficult to affect a turnaround. Of particular importance seems to be the equity-to-debt ratios of the firms, with failed companies having a considerably lower ratio across the time period than survivors. Even by year t-10, failed firms are deemed to be showing reductions in slack and impaired performance. This condition degenerates further until break-even performance is reached around t-6/t-3. It is at this point that changes in environment and strategy assume critical importance in affecting

The crisis process and the downward spiral of failure

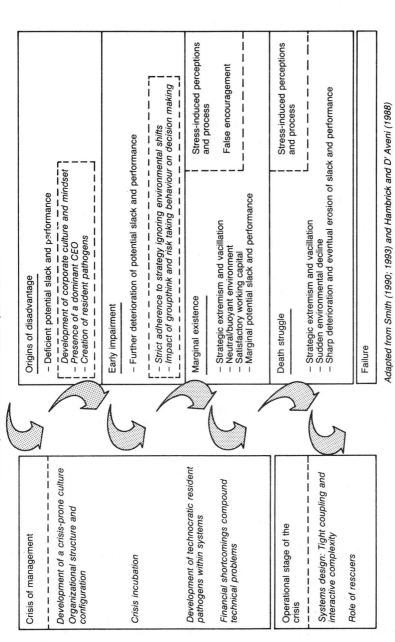

Figure 8.3 *The downward spiral of failure*

Adapted from Smith (1990; 1993) and Hambrick and D'Aveni (1988)

the ultimate demise of the organization. While Hambrick and D'Aveni have focused upon the financial aspects of corporate collapse, other writers have largely attempted to assess the broader influences upon corporate performance and this work now needs to be reviewed.

The crisis of management

> Most of the studies of business failure agree that it is *internal* factors rooted in the management system and its ability to recognise signs of impending problems before they become catastrophic failure that are most worthy of attention – Weir (1993) p. 47.

The period leading up to a crisis event is perhaps the most neglected aspect of the whole crisis management process. It is here that the potential for crises is incubated within organizations and the extent of that crisis-prone nature is often not apparent to managers until the crisis is realized (Turner, 1978; Smith, 1990b). However, this does not mean that proneness to crisis cannot be identified. A number of authors (Kets de Vries and Miller, 1987; Miller, 1992; Pauchant and Mitroff, 1992) have attempted to show how various elements of organizations interact to create a profile of crisis-preparedness – with the crisis-prone organization being easily identified but perhaps difficult to remedy. The reasons for this can be found in the role of culture, power – expressed in terms of hierarchical position and through technical expertise – (Fischer, 1980, 1990; Smith, 1990a) and the role of the CEO (Byrne *et al.*, 1991) in determining the way in which an organization considers the range of its activities with respect to crisis management.

A number of writers have identified a common core of factors in crisis precipitation (Kets de Vries and Miller, 1987; Miller, 1992, Pauchant and Mitroff, 1992). The principal organizational elements identified by Pauchant and Mitroff are strategy, structure, culture and core assumptions/beliefs. These are equivalent to the characteristics of strategy, organization, culture and executive identified by Kets de Vries and Miller. Mitroff and Pauchant argue that these organizational characteristics can be considered to be akin to an organizational onion – a cursory glance at the surface shows the strategy and structure of the organization but, as one peels back the layers, one begins to see the deeper beliefs and assumptions that contribute to the degree of crisis-preparedness. It is manifestly obvious, at least with hindsight, that an organization's strategy may lead it into crisis. However, at the time the decisions are taken within organizations they are often only considered in isolation and, as a consequence, the complex interactions that occur between sets of decisions only become evident later.

Within the context of strategic failures the aetiology of decision-making is of critical importance. How managers take those decisions that degenerate to catastrophic levels plays an important role in both the crisis of management phase and the process of organizational learning. Dixon (1994) suggests a series of reasons for 'disastrous decisions' within organizations. The first group, after Reason (1990), centre around cerebral processes and are composed of illusions/delusions, slips/mistakes and lapses, to which can be added violations (Dixon, 1994; Reason, 1990). Dixon goes on to highlight the negative relationship between stress and the possible disruption of effective decision-making, pointing to the role of information overload in impairing the performance of an individual in conditions of task complexity. Such a relationship would hold equally within the strategic management process as much as in the management of complex technologies. A second reason underpinning catastrophic decisions given by Dixon (1994) is that of group decision-making, or, as Janis (1968) termed the phenomenon, group-think. Finally, Dixon points to the human tendency to display greater irrationality over those decisions that are emotionally important to the decision-maker (Dixon, 1994). The culture of the host organization can serve to compound these inherent human flaws in decision-making. Again, the example of the *Titanic* serves to illustrate the complexity of the process. This 'Titanic syndrome' (Smith, 1993b), where the organization hurtles headlong into catastrophe, almost oblivious of its final end, is well documented in the literature relating to corporate collapse and crisis. It is the development of the crisis-prone culture which ensures that, when the crisis occurs, it exceeds the abilities of the organization to cope with the demands placed upon it. This moves the process into the operational phase of crisis in which containment and control become critical issues for survival (see Figure 8.4).

The operational crisis

The operational phase of any crisis is the one that usually attracts the most attention. It is here that the drama unfolds. To use the example of the *Titanic* again, the operational phase is that period after the ship hit the iceberg – it was here that the implications of the event exceeded the abilities of both the ship and its crew, i.e. management, to control the resultant consequences. This phase is typified by what Perrow (1984) refers to as 'tight coupling' and 'interactive complexity' – or, put another way, the complex interactions inherent within the system cascade the crisis at such a speed that it becomes impossible to control. Others have referred to this process as the outcome of 'resident pathogens' (Reason, 1987) within the system, which have arisen out of the crisis incubation process that takes place within the crisis of management phase.

This operational phase is also typified by the role of rescuers within the

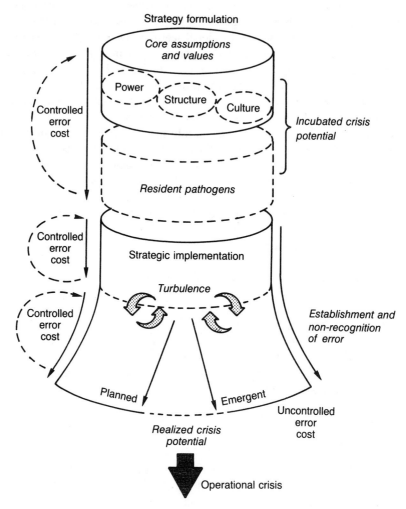

Figure 8.4 *The crisis of management*

crisis – these can be internal or external to the organization. The rescuers may take the form of an internal crisis decision unit, a government agency, or external management specialists (for turnarounds), or they may be the emergency services or some other disaster agency. It is at this level that most of the crisis management literature has been focused. The development of contingency plans, disaster recovery strategies and off-site and on-site emergency plans, along with the growth of local-authority emergency planning have generated a new industrial sector. While there is no doubt that these activities are a necessary component of the crisis-management process, there is concern that many organizations see the development of contingency plans as the limits of their crisis-preparedness. The notion of 'prevention rather than cure' still needs to be encouraged among organizations. Without doubt, the reason for the concentration on this phase of the process is that it is possible to create plans for an organization's response.

Planning for the operational phase can take place in a systematic fashion

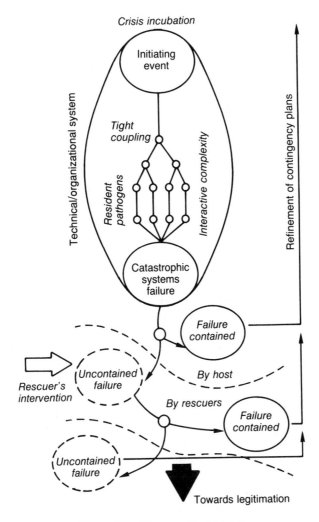

Figure 8.5 *The operational crisis*

and can be effectively monitored and tested. Dealing with the softer (more preventative) side of crisis management is a difficult, time-consuming process, which does not guarantee an easy return on the investment of time and effort. In addition, any move towards cultural change in the preventative process will need to have the approval of senior staff within the organization. The problem here is that many of these senior managers will not see the need for any form of cultural change in themselves – the paradox being that they are likely to be the root cause of the prevailing culture of crisis. Such intransigent organizational members actively contribute to the development of a crisis-prone organization (see Figure 8.5).

Crisis of legitimation

The final phase in the process of crisis management is the legitimation phase (Figure 8.6), which includes the process of turnaround and organizational learning. There is a large amount of literature relating to the process of turnaround within the business administration area. However, there has been less work done in the broader field of crisis turnarounds, i.e. turnarounds occurring after major crises that may not be explicitly caused by financial issues alone. Such events would include product tampering (Tylenol), product contamination (Perrier), pollution events (*Exxon Valdez*) and image impairment (Pepsi and Michael Jackson; Hoover and the free air ticket promotion). This phase of the process also sees the implementation of turnaround strategies intended to ensure organizational survival. A framework for assessing such turnarounds has been proposed elsewhere and tested against a number of cases (Smith and Sipika, 1993; Sipika and Smith, 1993). Figure 8.7 illustrates the various stages through which organizations attempting turnaround pass through; although it should be emphasized that not all organizations go through the stages sequentially and some never manage to achieve an effective turnaround and therefore move into endgame – or total demise.

The first phase of turnaround is concerned primarily with defending the organization against the further ravages of the crisis. Here the main problems are with the effective control of the event and its implications. These are usually seen in terms of information and data-handling and dissemination. There is also a need for organizations to pay attention to the systemic features that contributed to the cause of the crisis in the first place. This needs to be done in order to prevent a recurrence of the event, especially for crises in complex technological systems. Finally, management needs to give due consideration to the problems of divestment as a means of releasing capital needed to fund the recovery process. The financial dynamics of organizational failure have attracted considerable attention within the literature and this pays

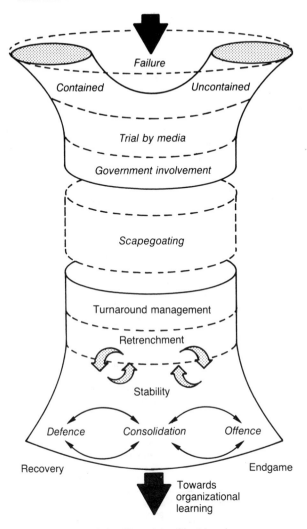

Figure 8.6   *The crisis of legitimation*

testimony to their importance within the process. In essence, this phase is dominated by issues of communications, contingency planning and systems' coupling and complexity.

The next phase of turnaround is the process of consolidation. Here, too, the issue of financial control is important as the organization attempts to arrest its decline and maintain market share. Following on from any divestment strategies that occurred in the preceding phase, management is faced with the need to compensate victims and to engage in financial/investment restructuring. In

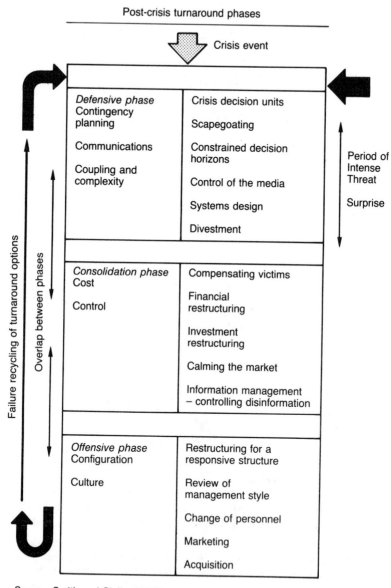

Source: Smith and Sipika (1993)

Figure 8.7 *The process of turnaround*

addition to cost, management needs to pay attention to the various aspects of control. Throughout this period there is a requirement to calm the market, which may be somewhat ill at ease in the wake of the crisis; and also to ensure that any incorrect information, i.e. disinformation, about the corporation is controlled. This both builds upon and extends the need to ensure effective communication within the defensive period.

The final phase within the turnaround process sees the organization moving towards a more offensive strategy in an attempt to rebuild market share and restore corporate performance to pre-crisis levels. What is required here is the ability of the organization both to restructure and change its culture in order to move towards a crisis-prepared state. This may inevitably call for a change in both key personnel and management style. In the final stages, the organization has to develop its marketing capabilities to ensure that market confidence is recovered. Where necessary, the organization may follow a strategy of acquisition if it is to manage to achieve its pre-crisis strengths – inevitably a protracted process, given the capital requirements for such a strategy. It is also important to note that organizational requirements prevailing in the wake of crisis will be fundamentally different from those needed when the crisis is active. This period is also fundamental in ensuring that the learning from the event is incorporated into the management strategies of the organization. It is here that much of the potential for effective crisis management exists. Organizations will have to learn and adapt in order to overcome the *Titanic* syndrome.

Organizational learning for crisis – a *Titanic* syndrome?

An often neglected aspect of the crisis management and turnaround process is the notion of organizational learning from such events. The implications of our apparent inabilities to learn from disastrous events is a matter that has begun to attract attention from both academics and practitioners alike (see Toft and Reynolds, 1994; Toft, 1992; Smith, 1993b). Numerous well-publicized disasters during the 1980s illustrated that it was the rapid interaction between a number of technological and managerial factors that precipitated the failures. These factors, outlined earlier as the 7Cs, seem to be present in most disasters and an examination of such events reveals common threads that provide the opportunity for learning. Like the McKinsey 7S framework, it is held that these elements provide a structure within which managers can seek to 'audit' their organizations. It is not a diagnostic framework *per se* but rather a means of organizing a critical appraisal of the decisions and attributes of an organization.

In common with the 7S framework, it is possible to group these characteristics into both a 'cold' (or technocratic) group and a 'warm' (or humanistic) group, as outlined earlier in Figure 8.2. However, as a society we show a marked reluctance to learn from the mistakes of the past and we seem destined therefore to continue down the path of crisis. But why do we fail to learn from disasters? Perhaps the greatest barrier to learning is the tendency for managers to search for technocratic solutions to the problems of failure rather than seeking to adopt a more holistic approach. Such a reliance on the power of technocracy has attracted considerable criticism within the literature (see Fischer, 1980, 1990; Collingridge and Reeve, 1986; Smith, 1990a) in a form that parallels the critique of the rational planning approach to strategic management (see Mintzberg, 1994).

We need to ask therefore how we break into the cycle of complacency that seems to operate within many organizations? The key to the problem rests in ensuring that organizations *act* upon the knowledge that arises as a consequence of crises. In discussing this process, Toft (1992) argues that there are three main forms of learning with regard to crises. These are organization-specific learning (for those who experience the crisis directly), isomorphic learning (in which general lessons can be drawn from events) and iconic learning (in which individuals and organizations are simply informed about the events via the various media). The essence of effective crisis prevention centres around isomorphic learning, and the challenge of management education rests in overcoming these barriers.

A possible solution to this dilemma of learning barriers lies in changing the way that we recruit and train managers. There is a tendency for all managers to select colleagues who share the same views on the management process. Consequently, it becomes difficult for groups of managers, possibly preoccupied with the search for excellence, to accept any challenges to their core paradigm, as those essential 'organizational irritants' will not be present within the organization in sufficient numbers to question the underlying logic of the managerial decisions taken. In addition, there are intrinsic elements of the human psyche that create the potential for catastrophic decisions. These elements, which were referred to earlier, include the influence of group-think, the potential for errors/mistakes/slips, along with illusions/delusions and violations. The dilemma is that if we focus only on the technocratic group of elements, then we will, by definition, leave the dangerous human elements free and active within the system. The eradication of these 'resident pathogens' (Reason, 1987, 1990) is key to the effective management of organizations and, ultimately, the reduction of crisis potential within them. This will require a shift in the current dominant corporate mindset in order to recognize that both the 'warm triangle' and the 'cold square' elements (as identified in the McKinsey framework) are critical to organizational learning for crisis.

If we explore the proposed 'model' of organizational learning outlined in Figure 8.8, we can see that culture, communication and configuration are key drivers for the process. The need for external verification of both likely decision outcomes and fundamental processes, and the learning that comes from 'self-generated turbulence' within organizations, are all areas that have

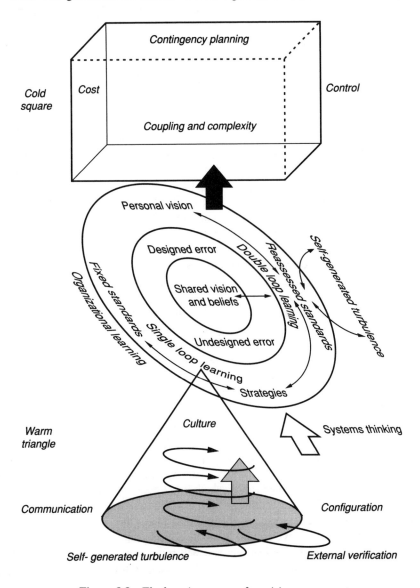

Figure 8.8   *The learning process for crisis management*

been largely neglected until recently. External verification is essential if we are to move away from the predominance of single loop learning within our organizations. This essentially restrictive process of learning fails to explore the fundamental mechanisms by which decisions are taken. It emphasizes the decision outcomes and the decision inputs but does not question the process, or mental model, that drives decision-making.

A move towards double-loop learning would ultimately lead to a questioning of the fundamentals of the mental model itself (see Stacey, 1993) and a recognition that a gold standard against which we can judge our decision-making does not generally exist. By definition, this will require a quantum shift in the core beliefs, assumptions, and shared vision of the organization's senior managers. The generation of turbulence, which is created by constantly questioning the underlying mental model, will ultimately lead to the development of reassessed standards for decision-making that are constantly in flux and open to criticism from those outside the decision body. The aim should be to move away from undesigned error within the system towards providing opportunities for restricted and contained forms of error to become a vehicle for learning. The impact that such a changed corporate mindset would have on the 'cold square' elements would be considerable. In essence, we are advocating turning the learning process on its head and, rather than immediately focusing on the technocratic elements of the supposed solution, beginning to question the basis of technocratic rationality in organizations.

From the viewpoint of the idealized, theoretical ivory tower, such a shift in the learning process may seem to offer much for practising managers. However, barriers to effective learning so obviously exist within organizations and Garvin (1990) suggests three basic steps that need to be taken to ensure learning. The first of these centres around the fostering of an organizational environment that allows learning to take place. The second step entails the removal of the organizational boundaries that will inevitably inhibit the learning process. Finally, Garvin advocates the creation of learning forums or interdisciplinary teams that seek to challenge the core paradigm of the organization. The question that remains is, how can these changes be implemented?

South and Matejka (1990) highlight a phenomena they term 'multiple weak links', which are akin to Reason's resident pathogens within organizations. They advocate six key strategies by which we can inhibit the development of such weak links. The first strategy calls for the creation of organizational watchdogs, which can serve to identify potential weak links and provide mechanisms for corrective action. In essence, these individuals will serve as change agents for effective learning and will provide a challenge to the core beliefs and assumptions that underpin the potential for failure. A second strategy involves the practice of multiple sourcing for both information and personnel. Managers tend to appoint in their own image and feel comfortable with colleagues who share their own beliefs and assumptions. However, as South and Matejka (1990, p. 22) observe, 'Typically a weak manager in the chain tends to foster the development of other weak links, usually at lower levels'. Consequently, the potential for failure as a result of these weak links runs the risk of becoming self-perpetuating unless personnel practices are modified.

A solution to this problem, and the third strategy offered by South and Matejka, is in the practice of management rotation. This should allow for a more interdisciplinary and, ultimately, less technocratic approach to decision-making and will aid in the process of breaking down organizational barriers. A fourth strategy is in terms of team-building – both in the horizontal and vertical dimensions – which, again, breaks down organizational barriers and encourages more interdisciplinary cooperation among managers. Fifthly, the use of performance indicators needs to be extended to cover the more human dimensions of performance, such as managerial attitudes, rather than adopting a narrow focus on profit and efficiency alone. Finally, South and Matejka see education and training as being of fundamental importance in inhibiting the development of weak links. Inevitably this education process will provide a fundamental challenge to the core management paradigm that will be uncomfortable but essential if we are to cope with the demands of failure better than at present.

The points made above can be quickly illustrated by reference to our example of the *Titanic*. The development of the crisis throughout the three phases is shown in Box 1 and, while categoric proof is beyond the scope of this discussion, it is hoped that the points raised will at least stimulate debate over the issues. If we take the 7Cs and apply them to the case of the *Titanic*, then a number of factors emerge as causal agents in the disaster (Figure 8.9).

The *Titanic* sinking was a result of a complex interaction of factors. In the crisis of management phase, the elements of cost, configuration, control and culture were prominent in creating the climate within which the potential for the crisis was set. The inability to communicate effectively the various ice warnings to the captain and adapt both his and the ship's behaviour as a result; the power of captains at sea and the reluctance/inability of sailors to question the orders given; the design of the ship and the materials used therein, were all contributory factors in the precipitation of the event. In the crisis of management phase the size of the ship, its inability to take avoiding action in time, the failure of the lookouts to spot the iceberg earlier and the speed of the vessel, were all major factors in ensuring that the vessel, did strike the iceberg. Parallels with modern corporations are quite obvious – their size, inadequate environmental scanning, poor internal communication, an inability to adapt to changing conditions and the bounded nature of decision-making are all lessons that can be learned from the *Titanic* tragedy.

Once the *Titanic* hit the iceberg, then the contingency planning, control and coupling/complexity inherent within the system combined to ensure that the ship would sink quickly. The use of low grade steel in the construction of the vessel meant that the buckling of the plates on impact and the subsequent flooding of six of the watertight compartments would result in the rapid sinking of the ship. The lack of lifeboats, despite the number exceeding the regulatory requirements of the day, resulted in the considerable loss of life associated with the event.

Table 8.1   The 7Cs applied to the sinking of the Titanic

Culture	– Officers of the watch (*Californian*) failed to wake the captain and the Marconi operator – considered to be normal operating procedure to continue at speed (in the zone of the sinking)
Control	– inability to take corrective action after the iceberg was sighted – inability to prevent the ship foundering as the compartments flooded
Communications	– failure to make use of ice warnings sent by Marconi operators from other ships – failure to wake the Marconi operator on board the *Californian* – failure of *Californian* watch to realize the meaing of the rockets
Configuration	– intense rivalry between the various shipping companies. White Star seeking to gain competitive advantage. – ships' captains were the ultimate power at sea: difficult to question their decisions
Coupling and complexity	– iceberg buckled the *Titanic*'s hull plates below the waterline – intake of water over six compartments resulted in the ship sinking in 1 hour 45 minutes
Cost	– only one Marconi operator on most ships that had a machine – *Titanic* only single-hulled – inferior steel used in the construction of the *Titanic*. This led to brittle steel fracturing due to the cold temperature
Contingency planning	– too few lifeboats for the passengers – six of the *Titanic*'s watertight compartments flooded *Titanic considered to be unsinkable*

While much attention has been focused on the role of the *Californian* in the sinking, it is apparent that its failure to respond to the rockets seen by officers on the watch was only a minor aspect of the disaster. The *Californian* would have been unable to traverse the icefield in the dark and reach the stricken

Titanic in time to offload the remaining passengers before the *Titanic* sank. In a similar vein, once slack has been eroded within an organization it is usually too late to bring in external rescuers – the course of demise is often irrevocably set. Finally, the *Titanic*'s sinking also illustrates the process of legitimation that occurs after an organizational crisis. Witness events such as BCCI, the Guinness/Distillers affair, Polly Peck and the collapse of the Maxwell empire, all of which display the key elements of the legitimation process.

Table 8.1 illustrates the way in which the 7Cs can be used to frame an analysis of failure events. While this has been undertaken for the *Titanic* with the benefit of hindsight, it serves to illustrate the potential that these elements have in crisis generation. The contention here is that if attention is paid to these issues within the strategic management process, then the propensity for failure within organizations may be significantly reduced.

BOX 1   **The *Titanic* syndrome**

Crisis of management

The main cause of the *Titanic* disaster was that the ship sailed at speed (22 knots or 15 mph) into an area that was known to have ice within it. Boats within the vicinity, including the SS *Californian*, used Marconi equipment to warn the *Titanic* of the dangers of ice. The management of the ship seemed to ignore this advice, although the reason why is uncertain. Compounding this initial problem, the *Titanic* carried too few lifeboats to evacuate all the passengers on board the vessel in an emergency. As a result, once the ship hit the iceberg, it was almost inevitable that the loss of life would be high. The cause of the sinking – the speed at which the *Titanic* steamed into the known icefield and the actions thereafter – rested entirely with the management of the *Titanic* and the operators of the ship. In addition, the design of the ship was also a contributing factor to the build-up of the disaster. Far from being unsinkable, the *Titanic* proved itself to be extremely vulnerable to the iceberg's impact. It has been suggested that had avoiding action not been taken – and the ship had ran head-on into the iceberg – then the ship would have sustained damage to the first few compartments and resulted in some loss of life, but probably would not have sunk. A ship of this nature, striking an iceberg would seem to be an accident that was not factored into the design. The ship was single-hulled and constructed of low grade steel. This, combined with the cold temperatures on the night of the sinking, resulted in the phenomenon of brittle steel fracturing. It was this inherent weakness that resulted in the catastrophic failure of the hull upon impact with the iceberg. Similarly, the lack of lifeboats on the ship, despite exceeding Board of Trade requirements of the day, proved to be the critical factor in determining the number of dead. When all these components are put together, the potential for the *Titanic* disaster was incubated from the moment that the ship left port. The chance meeting with the iceberg, the failure of the lookouts to see it in time, the failure to heed the ice warnings, along with the speed of the ship and the angle at which the vessel struck the ice, were all contributing factors in the complex web that constitutes a disaster. Any one of them in isolation would be insufficient to cause such a massive failure. However, combine them, add the design problems and the outcome is catastrophic. So it is with all disasters – it is the accumulation of small factors and their interaction that result in the calamity.

Operational crisis

The amount of coupling and complexity inherent within the disaster is illustrated by the way in which the *Titanic* sank after it struck the iceberg. Following on from a warning by the lookouts, which came too late to take any real avoiding action, the officer on the bridge tried to steer the ship around the iceberg but struck it a glancing blow. The result was that a large non-continuous hole was made along the side of the ship below the waterline. This breached five of the ship's watertight compartments and meant that it would sink in a matter of hours. Had only two compartments flooded, then the ship would not have sunk. Similarly, had the ship ran straight into the iceberg, then it is likely that she would have survived with just a crumpled bow and a much reduced loss of life. From the point of impact, it took the ship almost 4 hours to sink, during which time the crew fired no less than eight distress rockets in the hope of attracting attention from nearby vessels. While there is proof that officers on board the *Californian* saw rockets and that these were, with hindsight, undoubtedly fired from the *Titanic*, there still remains the issue of whether the *Californian* could have made her way through the ice in time to offload all remaining 1,500 passengers on board the *Titanic*; (the majority of whom remained below decks) and been clear of the vessel before she foundered. Given that it took the *Californian* between 1 hour 45 minutes and 2 hours 30 minutes (according to different witnesses onboard the ship) to reach the reported position of the *Titanic* in conditions approaching daylight, and given that from the time of the first rocket being fired (0045) to the time of the ship sinking (0225) was some 1 hour 40 minutes, one has to question the validity of claims that the *Californian* could have saved all on board the *Titanic* or even got there before she sank. Within the context of the literature on crisis and disaster management, the role of Lord and the *Californian* would have been one of rescuer. His function would have been to intervene after the crisis had started, and his role would have been both to provide relief and attempt to mitigate the consequences of the event. However, in order to satisfy this role, Lord would have had to get the *Californian* to the *Titanic* almost at the point of impact in order to ensure an effective evacuation.

The crisis of legitimation

Following the sinking, the resultant 'crisis of legitimation', which remains a constant aspect of all such events, took the form of two public inquiries (one in the USA and one in the UK), an extensive press coverage of the accident and its likely causes and an academic debate (largely over the role of the *Californian* in the sinking and including a reassessment of the *Californian* case by the UK Department of Transport in 1990) that stretches to the present. Both the US inquiry (chaired by Senator Smith) and the UK inquiry (chaired by Lord Mersey) were critical of the role of the *Californian* in the tragedy. That the official UK inquiry, held on behalf of the state, should focus on the actions of a third party, rather than the adequacy of its own legislative requirements, will perhaps not come as a surprise to those observers of recent disasters and their aftermath. In that respect little has changed within the field of disaster management.

Material used within Box 1 is taken from Smith (1994).

The complexity of disaster is there for all to see in the sinking of the *Titanic*. The failure of the regulatory agencies effectively to ensure that passenger safety is provided for and their subsequent involvement in the public inquiry process in the aftermath of disasters, raises the same questions today that were present in 1912 across a range of activities. Were the Maxwell pensioners adequately protected by legislation and the associated regulatory bodies? Was scapegoating a fundamental process in the Distillers takeover? Can the state effectively intervene to prevent a recurrence of such events or are more radical changes necessary within organizations themselves? Salutary lessons are present for all managers and decision-makers in the story of the *Titanic*. What is clear is that all disasters and crises are a complex mosaic of calamity and miscalculation which usually interact with devastating consequences. It is the lessons provided by such interactions that ensure that the case of the *Titanic* has a relevance and poignancy today across the range of managerial functions and business activities.

For those of us concerned with the analysis of events, the disaster illustrates the often controversial roles of corporate power, technical expertise and the media in shaping our understanding of complex events. That lessons are there to be learnt is beyond question. However, managers still appear to believe in the omnipotence of their decision-making and will continue to pay the price of their complacency until events prove the folly of such an endeavour. The issues of effective communication between managers and within organizations is still as much of a problematic today as it was in the Atlantic Ocean in 1912. The accident at Bhopal in 1984 illustrates the difficulties that corporations still have in controlling all aspects of their activities. The technology of communications has moved on apace, but the human frailty that lies behind it remains as flawed as ever. Witness the sinking of the *Herald of Free Enterprise*, the loss of the space shuttle *Challenger* and the accident at Bhopal to see how the lessons of the *Titanic* remained unlearned. Whether organizations have the willingness to learn such lessons is of course a completely different matter entirely.

Conclusions

This paper has briefly outlined a framework for crisis management that moves from the causal factors in crisis generation, through the operational stage and into the processes of legitimation, learning and turnaround. As such, it only represents a statement of work in progress because, although a considerable amount of work has been carried out in this area, there are still gaps in the theoretical framework that has been outlined and these need to be filled before the process as described can be fully validated by empirical data. The next, and perhaps the most important stage in the development of the theory, is to try and construct a diagnostic for the identification of the crisis-prone organization. This would allow managers to move beyond broad-based frameworks and models, and allow them to try and adopt a more strategic approach to the problems that face them. It may be that such a process is akin to a search for the Holy Grail and may even be beyond our abilities. Perhaps the most successful strategy that can be adopted is to raise the awareness of managers to the range of problems that can befall their organizations. Unfortunately, the apparent reluctance of many managers to consider the implications of the worst-case scenario has been a major factor in the development of a crisis-prone culture in many organizations. Breaking into that cycle of complacency is likely to be a critical but difficult task.

There is a need for managers to examine the causes of crisis and to change the way in which their organizations are managed as a consequence. There is much that can be learnt from failure, and if we are to overcome the *Titanic* syndrome within organizations, then that learning needs to be both widespread and effective. The ramifications for business education and practice are considerable, although one needs to question whether business schools have sufficient 'irritants' within their own ranks to mount an effective challenge to the dominant view of the world. If this paper serves to stimulate debate over the various issues associated with crisis and failure, then it will have achieved its aim. As with all academic writing, the message is usually flawed. This chapter is obviously no exception to this rule and much work is needed to develop the arguments articulated here and change business practice in the process. When the good management theory hits the fan, it is then too late.

Acknowledgements

The author is grateful to a number of people who commented on earlier drafts of this paper. These include Dominic Elliott and Josephine McCloskey. As always all errors of omission and interpretation remain mine.

References

Argenti, J (1976) *Corporate collapse: The causes and symptoms*, McGraw-Hill, London.

Ansoff, I (1991) Critique of Henry Mintzberg's 'The Design School: reconsidering the basic premises of strategic management', *Strategic Management Journal*, 12(6), pp. 449–61.

Burgoyne, J (1994) The development of the learning organization, Paper presented at the NW Regional Institute for Personnel Management Conference, Warrington.

Byrne, J A Symonds, W C and Flynn, J (1991) CEO disease: Egotism can breed corporate disaster – and the malady is spreading, *International Business Week*, 198-527 (1 April), pp. 38–44.

Carroll, P (1993) *Big Blues: The unmaking of IBM*, Weidenfeld and Nicolson, New York.

Collingeridge, D and Reeve, C (1986) *Science speaks to power*, Francis Pinter, London.

De Geus, P (1988) Planning as learning, *Harvard Business Review*, March–April, cited in Stacey, R (1992) *Managing chaos: Dynamic business strategies in an unpredictable world*, Kogan Page, London.

Dixon, N F (1994) Disastrous Decisions, *The Psychologist*, July, pp. 303–7.

Elliott, D and Smith, D (1993) Football stadia disasters in the United Kingdom: Learning from tragedy, *Industrial and Environmental Crisis Quarterly*, 7(3), pp. 205–29.

Fischer, F (1980) *Politics, Values, and Public Policy: The Problem of Methodology*, Westview, Boulder, Colorado.

Fischer, F (1990) *The Politics of Technocracy*, Sage, Newbury Park, CA.

Garvin, D A (1990) Building a learning organization, *Harvard Business Review*, pp. 78–91, 1993.

Greiner, L (1972) Evolution and revolution as organizations grow, *Harvard Business Review*. Reprinted in Asch, D and Bowman, C (Eds) (1989) *Readings in Strategic Management*, Macmillan, London.

Hambrick, D C and D'Aveni, R A (1988) Large corporate failures as downward spirals, *Administrative Science Quarterly*, 3, pp. 1–23.

Hampden-Turner, C (1990) *Creating corporate culture: From discord to harmony*, Economist Books/Addison-Wesley, Reading, Mass.

Heller, R (1994) *The Fate of IBM*, Little, Brown and Company, London.

Jarvis, I (1972) *Victims of Group-think*, Houghton Mifflin, Boston, Mass.

Lord, W (1978) *A Night to Remember*, Penguin Books, Harmondsworth.

Kets de Vries, M and Miller, D (1987) *Unstable at the top: Inside the troubled organization*, Mentor, London.

Miller, D (1992) *The Icarus Paradox*, Harper, New York.

Mintzberg, H (1990a) The Design School: reconsidering the basic premises of strategic managment, *The Strategic Management Journal*, 11(3), pp. 171–95.

Mintzberg, H (1990b) Strategy formation: schools of thought, in Frederickson, J (Ed) (1990) *Perspectives on Strategic Management*, Harper and Row, New York, pp. 105–35.

Mintzberg, H (1991) Learning 1, Planning 0: Reply to Igor Ansoff, *Strategic Management Journal*, 12(6), pp. 463–6.

Mintzberg, H (1994) *The rise and fall of strategic planning*, Prentice-Hall International (UK) Ltd, Hemel Hempstead.

Pascale, R (1990) *Managing on the edge: How successful companies use conflict to stay ahead*, Penguin, Harmondsworth.

Pascale, R T and Athos, A G (1981) *The art of Japanese management*, Simon and Schuster, New York.

Pauchant, T and Douville, R (1993) Recent research in crisis management. A study of 24 authors' publications from 1986 to 1991, *Industrial and Environmental Crisis Quarterly*, 7(1), pp. 43–66.

Pauchant, T and Mitroff, I I (1992) *Transforming the crisis prone organization*, Jossey Bass, San Francisco.

Pauchant, T, Mitroff I and Pearson, C (1992) Crisis management and strategic management: Similarities, differences and challenges, in Shrivastava, P, Huff, A and Dutton, J (Eds) *Advances in Strategic Management*, Volume 8, JAI Press, Greenwich, Conn., pp. 235–60.

Pedler, M, Burgoyne, J and Boydell, T (1991) *The learning company: A strategy for sustainable development*, McGraw-Hill, London.

Perrow, C (1984) *Normal Accidents*, Basic Books, New York.

Peters, T and Waterman, R (1982) *In search of excellence*, Warner Books, New York.

Radell, W W (1990) Storming: The losing edge, *Scholars*, 2, pp. 24–31.

Reason, J (1987) Cognitive aids in process environments: prostheses or tools?, *International Journal of Man-Machine Studies*, 27, pp. 463–70.

Reason, J (1990) *Human Error*, Cambridge University Press, Cambridge.

Senge, P M (1990) *The Fifth Discipline: The art and practice of the learning organization*, Doubleday, New York.

Shrivastava, P, Mitroff, I, Miller, D and Miglani, M (1988) Understanding industrial crises, *Journal of Management Studies*, 25(4), pp. 283–303.

Sipika, C and Smith, D (1993) From disaster to crisis: The failed turnaround of Pan American Airlines, *Journal of Contingencies and Crisis Management*, 1(3), pp. 138–51.

Slatter, S (1984) *Corporate Recovery: A Guide to Turnaround Management*, Penguin, London.

Smith, D (1990a) Corporate power, risk assessment and the control of major hazards, *Industrial Crisis Quarterly*, 4(1), pp. 1–26.

Smith, D (1990b) Beyond contingency planning: Towards a model of crisis management, *Industrial Crisis Quarterly*, 4(4), pp. 263–75.

Smith, D (1992a) The Kegworth aircrash: A crisis in three phases?, *Disaster Management*, 4(2), pp. 63–72.

Smith, D (1992b) The strategic implications of crisis management: A commentary on Mitroff *et al.*, in Shrivastava, P, Huff, A and Dutton, J (Eds.) *Advances in Strategic Management*, Volume 8, pp. 261–9.

Smith, D (1993a) The Public Sector in crisis? The case of the UK Prison Service, in Wilson, J and Hinton, P (Eds) *The public services and the 1990s: Issues in public service, finance and management*, Tudor Press, London, pp. 142–70.

Smith D (1993b) The Titanic syndrome: Organisational learning in the wake of crisis, paper presented at the Annual Disaster Limitation and Prevention Conference, University of Bradford, September.

Smith, D (1994) Exploring the myth: The sinking of the Titanic: A review essay, *Industrial and Environmental Crisis Quarterly*, 8(3), pp. 283–96.

Smith, D and Sipika, C (1993) A model of post-crisis turnaround strategies, *Long Range Planning*, 26(1), pp. 28–38.

South, J C and Matejka, K (1990) Unmasking multiple weak links in the chain of command, *Management Decision*, 28(3), pp. 22–6.

Stacey, R (1993) *Strategic Management and organisational dynamics*, Pitman, London.

Toft, B (1992) The failure of hindsight, *Disaster Prevention and Management*, 1(3), pp. 48–60.

Toft, B and Reynolds, S (1994) *Learning from Disasters: A Management Approach*, Butterworth-Heinemann, Oxford.

Turner, B (1978) *Man-made Disasters*, Wyhham, London.

Weir D T H (1993) Communication factors in system failure or why big planes crash and big businesses fail, *Disaster Prevention and Management*, 2(2), pp. 41–50.

Part Four   STRATEGY EVALUATION AND CONTROL

Although they have been included in Part Four, corporate governance and control are also *strategic issues* for organizations. The first two chapters in this part have been written by authors with a background and expertise in fnancial and management accounting respectively. Their views on strategy, while complementing the more holistic stance of Chapter 11, lend an important financial perspective to this handbook.

In the 1990s corporate governance and The Cadbury Report, introduced earlier in Chapter 7 **Ethics and strategy** seem synonymous. The debate highlights the need for strategic thinking, control and accountability, focusing on the role of strategic leadership. Corporate governance also raises important strategic issues concerning objectives. Are organizations able to pursue freely chosen objectives, or are their strategies more means of dealing with constraints imposed by powerful stakeholders? Is profit and the return for shareholders the ultimate end, or should it simply be a means of enabling the organization to pursue other objectives?

David Allen takes the wider view of governance, questioning the extent to which UK accounting standards and conventions assist with the strategic demands on organizations. He argues that a short-term perspective, an emphasis on control, and a concentration on the interests of shareholders (who receive priority over other stakeholders) are limiting strategically. Allen re-examines the financial needs of companies when a longer-term, more strategic perspective is adopted.

The introduction to this handbook discussed the nature of the strategic challenge facing organizations as they strive to survive and prosper in the turbulent and competitive 1990s. The final two chapters in this section both examine the implications of this challenge.

Tom Sheridan's chapter on control develops points made by David Allen.

He looks at the ability of the finance function to:

- deal expediently with the pressures of dynamic change and new opportunities which need to be seized quickly,
- balance the need for control with the need for flexibility in times of growth, and
- deal with changes to corporate strategies as companies switch their priorities from mergers and acquisitions to alliances and joint ventures.

Sheridan explores the centralization/decentralization debate and considers the appropriate contribution for corporate headquarters, looking for ways in which organizations can successfully devolve responsibility and empower personnel without sacrificing control. He also argues that cost management must be linked directly with the search for competitive advantage, flagging the critically important role of accurate and timely information in decision-making.

Both David Allen and Tom Sheridan contrast UK accounting practices with those found elsewhere in the world, especially with our leading European competitor, Germany.

The third chapter by Bill Richardson and John Thompson (**Strategy evaluation: a multi-competency approach**) looks behind the increasing turbulence and defines the range of competencies needed by organizations. Thirty competencies in eight separate categories are identified. Richardson and Thompson then take the arguments forward and consider a series of important management theories in the context of the competencies. They conclude that no single view, taken individually, can deal with the complexity of the challenge. The authors contend that organizations and leaders should use the ideas expressed in the paper to establish their own multi-competency approach.

9

Corporate governance
David Allen

The entity and the equity

The idea of the corporation – an enterprise with its own identity, e.g. legal personality – has been a major feature of the United Kingdom's economic development in the twentieth century. In particular, such enterprises have been able to supply goods and / or provide services on a continuous basis, notwithstanding changes in the people involved as owners and employees. As portrayed in Figure 9.1 they exist in the public sector as well as the private sector, and they may not be seeking distributable profits. Within the distributable-profit-seeking segment of the private sector, their shares may be narrowly controlled or publicly traded, i.e. unquoted and quoted, respectively,

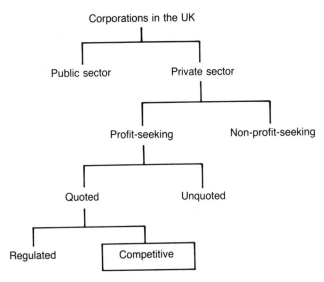

Figure 9.1 *Corporations in the United Kingdom*

and in the latter case the corporations may operate in a 'regulated monopoly' environment or a thoroughly competitive one.

In all these contexts, the way in which the affairs of corporate enterprises are governed is of considerable importance. One way of approaching the question of governance is to think in terms of how the interests of the various stakeholders are balanced. Recent years have provided many examples highlighting the potential conflicts:

- In the public sector, for example, we have seen the separation of purchasing and providing in the National Health Service. In particular, the providers have been established as trusts, with boards of directors responsible for balancing the legitimate interests of taxpayers, employees, patients, etc.

- In the newly privatized utilities, regulators have a responsibility for protecting customers from the monopolistic powers of the suppliers, with particular attention being paid to the conflict between customer and shareholders, e.g. as regards the appropriate rate of return on investment built in to pricing decisions. Public and press comment have also been concerned with the appropriate level of benefits (salary, bonus and share options) accruing to the directors.

- Grave concern has been expressed as to the short termism that characterizes the quoted company sector generally. A modern version of 'hunt the villain' continues to be played, with various interested parties accusing others of being the cause of short termism.

The accountancy profession is embroiled in all of these debates, and has itself been accused of adding to the problem. Without saying which is cause and which is effect at this stage, accounting numbers are invariably associated with short termism. Managers in quoted companies cite the pressures to report high current profits, and those in the public sector the pressures to manage within short-term cash limits, as obstacles preventing them from thinking strategically. Meanwhile, auditors are criticized for aligning themselves with the executive directors, rather than the shareholders to whom they are legally responsible – not the least manifestation of which is the willingness to sanction (or, in some cases, develop) the kind of techniques that have come to be known as 'creative accounting'.

Firms of auditors claiming a mission to bring objectivity to reporting have been happy to sign off balance sheets dominated by subjective judgements, e.g. valuations of properties and brand names. The purpose of such manoeuvres is to circumvent requirements for directors to seek shareholder approval for substantial increases in borrowings or acquisitions. A London Business School report described the practice (of augmenting net assets by brand valuations) as corrosive of the standards process, but it continues.

Concern for corporate governance generally has been sufficient to mount a number of enquiries. A committee looking at the financial aspects thereof, chaired by Sir Adrian Cadbury, produced some ideas that were commended if not exactly welcomed. More recently, and in more depth, the Royal Society for the encouragement of Arts, Manufactures and Commerce (more popularly known as the RSA) has been researching 'Tomorrow's Company', and its interim report majored on the need to adopt an inclusive approach, i.e. take account of the interests of the broad spectrum of stakeholders, rather than thinking exclusively of the interests of one particular group (sometimes shareholders in general, sometimes a sub-set thereof, namely those who intend to sell their shares in the near future).

Though many of the points made will be relevant to all kinds of enterprise, the primary focus of this chapter – in line with the broad aims of this handbook – will be on the competitive, quoted, segment of the private sector of the economy, i.e. that highlighted on Figure 9.1. The context is the United Kingdom, but opportunity will be taken to draw some comparisons with other cultures.

If we look at such a corporation as an entity, its stakeholders can usefully be collected in two groupings. On the one side we have customers, suppliers and employees; on the other hand we have lenders, tax authorities and shareholders. The interplay of the first three creates the wealth of the entity, which is appropriated as between the last three. Significantly, management accounts naturally focus on the entity, but financial accounts have been realigned in recent years to focus on the shareholders. The balance sheet, for example, deducts from the operating assets of the entity the amounts owed to lenders and tax authorities in order to arrive at the 'net worth' of the business to its shareholders. The profit statement, likewise, deducts from the operating profit of the entity the amounts attributable to lenders and tax authorities in order to arrive at the 'profit' attributable to the shareholders. The links with the added value concept are strong, as is brought out in Figure 9.2.

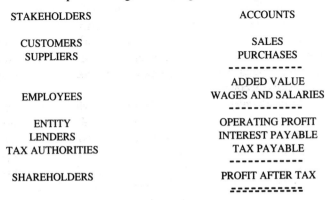

Figure 9.2   *Stakeholders*

There may be other recognizable responsibilities, e.g. to the local and wider community, as regards the avoidance of nuisance and pollution of the environment; but there being no contractual relationship, their influence is of a very different kind, and outside the scope of this chapter.

It is worth stressing, given the current situation, that:

● Directors do not comprise a separate group of stakeholders, since they are responsible for achieving balance between them. Executive directors happen to be part of the employee grouping, but this merely draws attention to the conflicts of interest (and perhaps the need for ethical codes) inherent in the unitary board that prevails in the UK.

● Financial analysts and journalists are not stakeholders. It is surely a cause for concern that finance directors of quoted companies are prepared to provide such people with confidential forecasts, i.e. information they are not prepared to share even with their shareholders.

Meanwhile, any information sought by customers and suppliers will be dealt with on a normal trading basis, and employees will have their own channels for information relevant to them. Lenders will be able to specify their requirements, and the tax authorities' requirements are spelled out in the legislation. Understandably therefore, those bastions of corporate governance, the UK Accounting Standards Board and the International Accounting Standards Committee, see their roles as being primarily concerned with the information needs of shareholders.

This is not so easy as it sounds, however, given the wide differences between shareholders' perceived needs. The average individual shareholder is probably already overwhelmed by the information that must now be provided in accounts, and would ideally like a concise distillation of the numbers, highlighting key issues.

FRS 3's more detailed profit statement and the greater volatility it induces in the profit figure (following the virtual elimination of 'below the line' extraordinary items) was not designed to appeal to such shareholders. This may not matter, given the rapid decline in personal shareholdings and the corresponding growth in institutional holdings (pension funds and the like). This shift has been brought about by the massive tax privileges granted to such institutions. For every 80p of dividend declared by a company, an individual taxpayer has to pay an additional tax of up to 20p (to bring it up to the top rate of 40 per cent), whereas a pension fund can reclaim 20p. Thus, any prospective dividend stream is worth 100 / 60 as much to the fund as to the individual, i.e. 67 per cent more. Little wonder that institutions are net buyers and individuals net sellers.

This has a very significant, but thus far largely ignored, effect on corporate governance. The fact is that the primary responsibility of these funds is to their members, i.e. pensioners and prospective pensioners. Their attitude to a company in which they hold shares therefore tends to be passive – in the sense that, were they to suspect that it was about to go through a difficult time, the best thing they could do for their members would be to sell (quietly) the shares and invest elsewhere.

Indeed, the attitude of many fund managers to investments *per se* is passive. Many believe in a version of the Efficient Market Hypothesis and in 'random walks'. Specifically, they believe that the price of a share at a point in time already encapsulates all relevant information, and that it is therefore impossible to predict share-price movements so as to beat the market by selective buying and selling. This is a large and rapidly growing school of thought, as evidenced by the rapid spread of what are actually called 'passive funds', i.e. ones that set out to track the index. The decisions they make are not influenced by accounting data.

Another school of thought, however, comprises those fund managers who believe that they can identify shares that are under- or over-valued, i.e. will surely rise or fall, respectively, in the near future, and therefore make money by buying and selling at the right time. Some use zodiac horoscopes or other fortune-telling techniques but most:

● Claim to be able to project where a company is going on the basis of information as to where it has come from (a process often referred to as 'reading a balance sheet') and to be able to assess the 'quality' of last year's earnings.

● Believe that it is only a matter of time before:

(a) less capable people come to recognize the company's prospects;
(b) the quality of earnings becomes reflected in the price / earnings ratio;
(c) and hence the price will move so as to provide an opportunity for capital gain.

They all claim to be able to achieve above-average performance, but the majority underperform the index to the extent of the costs of churning their investments. If they are stakeholders, they have no commitment to remaining so, since dividend income (the reward of the loyal shareholder) is dwarfed by the scale of potential capital gains. At the time of writing (Spring 1994) the dividend yield on the London stock markets is around 4 per cent per annum, but it is not unusual for share prices to move up or down by 50 per cent per annum.

The worrying thing is that, by a process of elimination, we have identified this group as the ones for whom accounting standards are being developed. Before probing the consequences of this, we need to clarify the links with strategy.

The financial aspects of strategy

At the strategic level managers are concerned with questions as to *what* to do, such as the markets to serve and the products (goods or services) to offer. As the rate of change in the environment has speeded up, these questions arise ever more frequently, and need to be addressed ever more quickly.

Gone is the era when it could be assumed that tomorrow would be very much like yesterday. Gone therefore is the era when tactics (concerned with questions as to *how* to do what is to be done) was the predominant level of control, and hence the halcyon days for people skilled in analysing a certain past. The current environment is characterized by volatility, when the safest starting point is that tomorrow is going to be different from yesterday. In such an environment the need is for skills in synthesizing judgements about an uncertain future. As financial services advertisements are bound to say, past performance is not an indication of future potential.

The rate of change, having its roots in scientific discoveries, technological developments, etc., has been reinforced by globalization. The removal of exchange controls, the liberalization of money markets and the moves towards free trade have enlarged the arena in which the competitive struggle for existence is played out. As they strive to regenerate themselves, enterprises seek world-class capability in all that they do – along the lines of Figure 9.3.

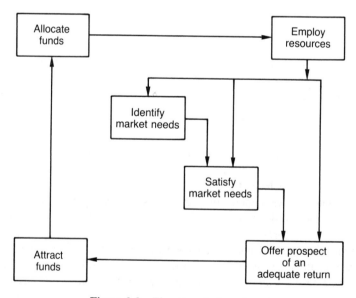

Figure 9.3   *The struggle for existence*

The bottom right-hand box – the need to offer the prospect of an adequate return – is especially important in the context of the subject matter of this book. Enterprises that can do so will be able to attract the capital required to fund their growth aspirations; those that cannot must inevitably shrink. Note the forward looking connotation: survival is not about *having made*, but about *offering the prospect of*, an adequate return. In general terms, i.e. so as to be applicable across the various kinds of corporation, including not-for-profit organizations and the public sector, an adequate return implies that the value of outputs exceeds the value of all inputs, including capital.

What constitutes an adequate return on capital varies over time, and according to time frame, summed up in prevailing interest rates, and portrayed in the familiar yield curve. To the individual enterprise, this is seen as 'the cost of capital' and either incorporates, or is accompanied by, an allowance for the uncertainty of the outcome of the investment. The higher the rate of interest, the higher the return required to justify a given investment, and the lower the rate of growth. See Figure 9.4.

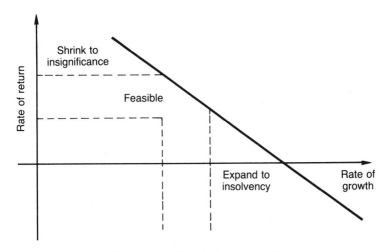

Figure 9.4   *The ultimate trade-off*

Given its overwhelming strategic importance, it is surprising that few boards of directors are prepared to go public on their perception of the cost of capital. Off the record, most UK quoted companies think that a return in the 'the mid-teens', i.e. around 15 per cent per annum, is necessary to warrant the employment of funds. When you consider that the public sector uses 6 per cent or 8 per cent per annum, depending on the proximity of private-sector activity, the shift of resources in recent years (and the consequent public-sector deficit) is not surprising. Moreover, when you consider that German and Japanese companies also use single figures, the UK's relative economic decline is also clearly explained.

Indeed, globalization has drawn attention to the fact that there are basically two species of corporate governance: English-speaking and non-English-speaking:

- The English-speaking model, in evidence, for example, in the UK and USA sees the publicly quoted company as the appropriate form for the wealth-seeking corporation, and equity investors as comprising the principal stakeholder grouping. The main medium of communication from the company to this grouping is the document containing the annual accounts, based on standards set in the private sector (the accountancy profession being large and broadly based). A company's share price is seen as an objective measure of its performance but, in practice, shows a high degree of correlation with reported profits or, more precisely, with those 'confidential' short-term forecasts thereof provided to analysts.
- Germany and Japan provide obvious examples of the non-English-speaking model. There bank finance is the main source of funding. Quoted companies exist but only a small proportion of their shares are traded, the majority being owned by loyal investors, including the banks. Communication with banks is by way of confidential briefings of a forward-looking nature. Accounting standards are set by government (the accountancy profession being small and restricted to auditing). Significantly, management accountancy (the branch of the profession that is oriented to the needs of management) does not exist and there is no demand for it.

It is perhaps because of the sharing of foward-looking judgements with their principal financial stakeholders – the banks – that managers in the German and Japanese model tend to use a lower cost of capital (specifically, a lower augmentation for uncertainty) than their English-speaking counterparts. This enables them to rate long-term investments, e.g. market building strategies, more highly, and hence to grow at a faster rate. British bankers are uncomfortable with cash-flow forecasts, preferring the 'security' of charges on tangible assets shown on last year's balance sheet. Meanwhile, the diffuse and (as we have noted) largely passive body of shareholders is provided with virtually no forward-looking information whatsoever.

Nature abhors a vacuum and, in this case, the gap left where company law assumes that there are active shareholders has been filled by none other than the directors themselves. Arguing that their security depends on the share price, and that the share price is strongly influenced by reported profits, they have begun to measure performance, and reward themselves, on the basis of accounting numbers. This brings us back to a point made in the first section of this chapter, namely the disturbing connection between two features characterizing the English-speaking model: its short termism and the importance attached to backward-looking accounting numbers.

What are accounts used for?

The uses to which the accounting model are put (or to which it is advocated that it be put) can be classified as follows:

1   *As an input to taxation computations.* Although there are some obvious differences – capital allowances v depreciation, for example – the starting point for taxation computations is the profit after interest shown in the (historical cost) accounts. For privately owned businesses this is probably the most important use, and leads naturally to the application of the most prudent accounting policies: where there is a choice, the treatment that results in the lowest possible profit is to be preferred.

2   *As a means of determining distributable profits.* This has its roots in company law and, in particular, the protection of creditors (from overdistribution). Again, the more prudent the figures, the better this purpose is served.

3   *As a means of reporting on stewardship,* i.e. what has been done with the money entrusted to the directors. Here disclosure is seen as the key, since the aim is to protect the shareholders' interests vis-a-vis those of the directors. The shareholders seek reassurance, in the form of the auditors' report, that the disclosure complies with current requirements, e.g. as laid down in standards.

4   *As a means of denominating directors' powers and freedom to act without prior shareholder approval.* Articles of association, borrowing, covenants and stock exchange listing agreements specify the limits, invariably expressed as a proportion of the net assets of the business as shown in published accounts. This has been a major contributory factor in the spread of 'creative accounting', as directors seek to maximize their freedom of manoeuvre. Revaluations of tangible assets and inclusion of intangibles are examples of these pressures at work.

5   *As a basis for monitoring progress.* Profit as a percentage of sales, of assets, of budgeted profit or of last year's profit, have all been popular focal points, especially in quoted companies. Their importance has been magnified by their use in determining the pay of managers and directors, including those who sign off the accounts. Again, this has acted as a spur to creative accounting, as directors seek to maximize their own wealth by

reporting the highest possible profit, notwithstanding the fact that it means that the company pays taxes earlier than it need do.

6   *As a basis for assessing the wealth created by the business, and hence its value at a point in time.* Where directors have chosen to spend shareholders' money on obtaining a consultants' valuation of their brands and to include such value as an asset on the balance sheet, for example, they often argue that they have made the net worth of the business closer to its 'true value', though, for some reason, they never state what they think that true value is.

7   *A source of information on which outsiders can base decisions, e.g. to buy or sell shares in the company.* This is the most contentious use to which it is advocated that accounts be put, especially in an age of discontinuity, but, as we saw in the first Section (p. 198), provides the foundation on which both the UK Accounting Standards Board and the International Accounting Standards Committeee have built their programmes.

The use to which accounts are put shows significant correlation with the identity of the promulgator of standards. In Germany and Japan accounting standards are set by government – and tend to be used for purposes 1 and 2, i.e. the determination of tax and distributability. The more the accountancy profession gets involved in the standard setting process, the further down the list of uses the process falls, and the more likely it is that creative accounting techniques will emerge.

More generally, it seems most unlikely that one set of accounts can possibly serve all seven purposes. To probe this more deeply, it is useful to contrast the contents of the accounting model with the information needs of the manager, particularly at the strategic level.

The first point to make is that the accounting model is designed to report on what has happened, telling investors what has been done with their money. Endorsement by impartial and passive outsiders (the auditors) is an important corollary, as is the standardization of the treatment of like transactions so as to ensure comparability. Contrast these features, however, with those of management, where the emphasis is on making things happen. Managers are proactive insiders, and they need information that is customized to the strategies on which the enterprise is embarked.

Reporting is, by definition, a backward-looking process. Verifiability is a key feature, which explains the preoccupation with realized profits and tangible assets. It comes as a surprise to many non-accountants to learn that accounting statements are not designed to assess the wealth created by the enterprise, but e.g. as laid down in SSAP 2 in the UK, how much of it has been realized in the form of tangible assets.

What the accountant calls an asset, however, the strategist often sees as a liability: property in the wrong place but unmarketable, plant that is obsolete but not fully depreciated, work-in-progress in a just-in-time factory, etc. Conversely, what the strategist sees as assets are those investments that bring competitive advantage. In a rapidly changing environment these are likely to be the ones that enhance awareness, anticipation and adaptation, like research, development, marketing, training and information. Significantly, these are the very ones the accounting rules say have to be charged against current profits. Courses of action aimed at maximizing current profits (or achieving budgeted profits, or keeping within cash limits) will almost certainly damage the long-term financial health of the enterprise. To counter this, managers need to pay due attention to judgements, unrealized gains and intangibles.

Accounting numbers are also totally inward-looking, seeking objectivity – the viewpoint of the outsider. This explains the focus on costs, which can be objectively verified, and on capital maintenance: profit for a period is defined as what you could afford to distribute and still be as well off as you were at the beginning of the period. Meanwhile, managers are insiders looking out and the judgements they make are therefore inevitably subjective. They need to put values on expected outcomes – and value, like beauty, is in the eye of the beholder. The question of how much could be distributed is not a meaningful one; the real question is how much will need to be distributed to justify the investment of the capital required to fund the growth of the enterprise.

In short, accounting is a static model, based on an apportionment of income and expenditure between relatively short, discrete, periods of time. The basis for this apportionment is the concept of capital versus revenue, i.e. what can be carried forward, as opposed to what must be charged immediately, leading to a quantification of assets and profits. Meanwhile, strategic management is a dynamic activity, concerned with the long-term continuum. As practitioners will know, the focus is on anticipated cash flows, discounted (at the cost of capital) to allow for the passage of time.

The purpose of these contrasts is not to denigrate the accounting model, nor to support suggestions put forward for its revision (for revaluations of tangible assets and the inclusion of intangibles destroy objective verifiability). Rather, it is to position financial management as something distinctive. The two go together: accounting is a legal necessity but the level of investment in financial management is itself judgmental.

Readers might like to think of the relative importance attached to the two sides in their organizations. Accounting logic appeals to people with strong left sides to their brains and therefore good at analysing what exists or has happened. Financial management, conversely, appeals to people with strong right sides to their brains, and therefore good at synthesizing what does not yet exist. Many finance people say that they spend the first 3 weeks of every month on passive reporting, and are only available for making things happen in the fourth. Needless to say, their colleagues and general managers do not think this makes sense, and this has led, in many instances, to the separation of the two functions: managers seeking the objectively verifiable truth about a certain past go through the door marked 'accounting' while those seeking help in synthesizing judgements about an uncertain future go through the door marked 'financial management'.

In the context of corporate governance, however, we need to recognize that the English-speaking model is almost exclusively left-sided. As mentioned earlier, the main vehicle for communication between directors and their principal stakeholders is the backward-looking, inward-looking, static, accounting model, with its emphasis on realized profits and tangible assets. This might have been tolerable when the future was thought of as a projection from the past, but in a volatile environment it is so misleading as to be unacceptable.

Two aspects of financial management

It was noted in the second section (p. 190–91) that the prospect of an adequate return on investment is pivotal in the working of the economy. Enterprises offering such a prospect are able to attract the capital need to fund their growth aspirations; those not able to do so must inevitably shrink. Financial management, at the strategic level, requires not only that one heeds that discipline but harnesses it as a criterion for the allocation of resources within the enterprise.

In more stable times this criterion was expressed in the form of an accounting rate of return, i.e. profit as a percentage of assets employed. Some organizations still use this, as evidenced by the still-popular pyramid of ratios. It has also been adopted in the public sector: note, for example, the requirement for the UK's National Health Service Trusts to make a 6 per cent annum return, and for the railway infrastructure to make 8 per cent per annum. In this age of discontinuity, however, this can be seriously misleading. Growth almost always brings a 'front-end' increase in assets and/or reduction in profits before the benefits show through in results.

The easiest way to improve return on assets therefore (as is quickly spotted by people with profit-related pay) is to skimp on those investments that produce intangible assets. Other things being equal, a shrinking business will always show a higher return on assets than a growing one. Where return on assets is used to measure managers' performance and, what is even worse, determine a significant component of their income, the resulting bias against growth is plain to see.

Managers who seek to manage strategically, and for the long term, need a way of expressing the criterion so as to recognize the long-term continuum, i.e. the long term as a series of short terms, and the value of time (otherwise known as the cost of capital). In the private sector this is facilitated by the recognition of two distinct but interrelated aspects of financial management:

- The *treasury* aspect, which, at the strategic level, is concerned with the relationship between the enterprise and its financial stakeholders (shareholders, lenders and tax gatherers) and, in particular, with:

  (a) *identifying* sources of funds – from borrowings through various hybrids, to equity – which may be denominated in any of the world's leading currencies;
  (b) *assessing* the likely expectations of rewards in the minds of the various providers of such funds: interest, dividents and the apparently inevitable taxes;
  (c) *employing* the chosen source and in the proportions deemed appropriate in the light of the forecast cash flows of the enterprise; the aim is to have the capital structure that is best for the principal financial stakeholders, and in English-speaking culture this is normally taken to mean the shareholders.

- The *financial control* aspect, which, at the strategic level, is concerned with the relationship between the enterprise and its constituent business units (usually defined in terms of products, markets and/or locations) and, in particular, with:

  (a) *identifying*, i.e. proactively seeking, opportunities to invest in, or withdraw funds from, particular business units;
  (b) *assessing* the likely returns from (i.e. benefits of) each opportunity;
  (c) *deploying* funds in support of those opportunities deemed to be financially viable, i.e. ones offering the prospect of an adequate return (a return in excess of the cost of capital) and denying them to those not able to do so.

The links between the two aspects are brought out in Figure 9.5.

The financial controllers provide the projections of cash flows that trigger the treasurer's realignment of capital structures, and the treasurer quantifies the all-important cost of capital. What the treasurer sees as the rate of return necessary to warrant the employment of funds, the controller sees as the criterion for their employment. Both are playing their part in maximizing the value of the enterprise to its principal stakeholders – for all practical purposes, in a private-sector organization, the net present value of its projected cash flows. Individual business units seek to maximize their value to the entity, and

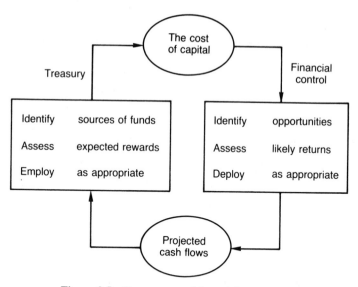

Figure 9.5   *Two aspects of financial management*

the treasurer seeks to maximize the proportion thereof that is attributable to the equity.

This 'value attributable to the equity' is sometimes referred to as shareholder value, but care needs to be taken because this expression is used by others, including the pioneers of shareholder value analysis, to mean last night's capitalization (the number of shares in issue multiplied by the price that brought supply and demand for small lots of shares into equilibrium towards the end of yesterday's trading on the stock market). As well as being restricted to quoted companies, this is totally backward-looking. How can you influence what has already passed? Worse, all the evidence is that share prices conform to the semi-strong form of the efficient market hypothesis, i.e. they reflect published information.

There is an artificial mountain of academic literature built on the hypothesis that in a perfect world (in particular, one in which the future was precisely and accurately predictable) the price of a company's shares would provide a valid indication of its capacity to generate cash for its shareholders. As has been shown by various spectacular collapses in recent years, however, it is possible to report increasing profits for quite a while, while starving a business of investment in its infrastructure. Only when the resulting difficulties become public knowledge, e.g. when the company becomes insolvent, does the share price move, showing it to be a lagging (rather than leading) indicator of financial health.

Nevertheless, the theory provides a veneer of respectability for share option schemes. Directors may well see the maximization of the short-term share price as an objective consistent with maximizing their personal wealth, but remember that for every seller there is a buyer. The price at which a share changes hands is part of a zero-sum game:

- buyers of shares want the price to be as low as possible;
- loyal shareholders are indifferent, their focus being on future dividends, i.e. projected cash flows, net of any pre-emptions for interest and tax;
- only sellers want it to be as high as possible, and this is the group with whose interests directors are prompted to conform by share options, with predictable consequences.

For the sake of completeness, it should be noted that although most public sector enterprises (including agencies, departments, etc.) are said to have a responsibility to achieve value for money, it is very rare for one to make any attempt to quantify the value of their outputs. As far as cash flows are concerned therefore, value is either or assumed to equate with cost. National Health Service providers, for example, are bound by Department of Health regulations to charge purchasers prices that equate with total costs plus that 6 per cent per annum return on assets. The criterion of maximizing (net present value) is still tenable but, as things stand, needs to be divorced from cash flows.

A front windscreen view

In the private sector, however, cash flow does reflect value to paying customers. It also reflects the two aspects of financial management introduced in the previous section:

- The treasurer sees cash flow in terms of a 'balance of payments' with the financial stakeholders. If distributions (interest dividends and tax) exceed financing (new capital, be it equity or borrowings) the enterprise is clearly a net generator of cash. If financing exceeds distributions, conversely, it is a net absorber of cash.
- The controller sees it as subdivided into two components: profits and expansion. If the enterprise is a net generator of cash, profits will exceed expansion; if it is a net absorber of cash, profits will fall short of expansion.

It is one of the accountancy profession's best kept secrets that cash flow is known, unequivocally, within hours of the end of the period in question. What takes weeks or months is the accounting task of segregating capital from revenue, etc., so as to arrive at the closing assets and hence expansion and profit figures. The various attempts to recognize the impact of changing price levels made this clear to a wider audience. Setting aside that element of the expansion calculated by reference to historical costs, which merely reflected the fall in the value of money (current purchasing power), or changes in specific prices (current cost accounting) had a corresponding effect on profits but the unequivocal cash flow was obviously not affected. Interestingly, accounting statements invariably follow the sequence profits/assets/cash flow – the exact opposite to their chronological relationship – because accounting specialists see reality reflected in a rear view mirror: the last thing they passed is in the foreground of the mirror.

To counteract this, we need to consider 'the three Ps' inherent in any control system: performance, potential and progress, differentiated and linked as follows:

- *Performance* is something measurable, which means that it has already happened – in this case, the cash flow that has occcurred in a particular period of time. On its own of course this is not very meaningful: considerable cash could have been generated, for example, by a rapid shrinking of the business. In recent years there has been much talk of 'the balanced scorecard': a weighted average of various (but, by definition, equally backward-looking) measurements, e.g. market share, repeat business, labour turnover.

- *Potential* on the other hand, is not measurable, since it relates to something that has not yet happened; but it is nevertheless quantifiable. Called upon to establish the price your business could justify paying for a gold mine, for example, you would put together the judgements of geologists (how much gold there?) engineers (how difficult to extract?) marketeers (value of output) etc. You would not, would you, apply a multiple to the value of gold already extracted? You would not evaluate a company, would you, by applying a multiple to profits already realized?

- *Progress*, then, can be defined as performance plus or minus the change in potential. The first part is measurable but the second is not: it is quantifiable, but is best described as an assessment. Under this terminology, profit is an expression of progress, amounting to cash flow plus expansion. The cash flow is measurable, but expansion depends on the accounting convention applied. Define expansion in terms of historical cost, purchasing power or current cost, for example, and you will derive three different profit figures from the same cash flow.

What is not widely appreciated, however, is that there is an inherent contradiction in all the conventions mentioned: they all purport to assess expansion by reference to the objectively verifiable costs of unconsumed tangible assets, and hence are totally backward-looking. You need to recognize that, by the time you can measure something, it is too late to do anything about it. At the strategic level of management therefore you cannot wait for objectively verifiable facts: monitoring needs to be continuous and forward-looking. Moreover, it will be found that the most important features of strategy, though quantifiable by way of an assessment, are the most difficult (sometimes impossible) to *measure*.

Potential is, by definition, a forward-looking concept – in this context, future cash flows, the net present value of which just happens to correspond with the criterion recommended as a basis for resource allocation. Many managers are familiar with this concept as a basis for making strategic decisions, but most fall into the trap of using the quite different accounting model for monitoring progress.

Hence the devastation caused by using accounting numbers 'beyond their design spec.', i.e. as though they were valid measures of performance (and hence sound bases for determining rewards) or indicators of progress. What is required, if we are to encourage the strategic thinking required to compete in this increasingly borderless world, is an approach to progress monitoring that is forward-looking, and keyed in to what is to be maximized, i.e. net present value in the private sector of projected cash flows, for example.

Let us build up a simple example to bring out these differences. Imagine a company, whose balance sheet at the end of year 1 could be summarized as follows:

	£'000
Operating assets	10,000
(Borrowings)	(2,000)
(Taxes payable)	(582)
(Dividends payable)	(558)
Net worth	6,860

Imagine further that, a day or two after the end of year 2, the treasurer of a company is able to identify the cash flow of the entity as a net generation of £1.250 million, comprising:

	£000
Distributions	
Interest paid	310
Tax paid	582
Dividends paid	558
	1,450
Financing	
Increased (borrowings)	(200)
Net cash generation	1,250

This enables a benchmark to be established against which to compare the assets at the end of year 1. Given that £1.250 million of the opening assets have been converted into cash, the closing assets figure needs to be more than £8.750 million for the company to show an operating profit. If, for example (a few weeks later) the financial controllers quantify the assets as £11.000 million, the company will show an operating profit of £2.250 million, appropriated as follows:

	£000
Operating profit	2,250
Interest (payable)	(310)
Profit before tax	1,940
Tax payable (say 33% of accounting profit)	640
Profit after tax	1,300
Dividends payable (say 10% up on year 1)	614
Retentions	686

Note the chronological sequence: cash flow, expansion, profits:

	£'000
Opening assets	10,000
Cash (generation)	(1,250)
Benchmark	8,750
Closing assets	11,000
Profit	2,250

Collecting the figures in this rational, if unorthodox, way makes it easier to see why accounting numbers are inappropriate to the monitoring of strategy. They ignore the value of the business, and the value of time. A strategic approach to progress monitoring would correct both these deficiencies. Say, for simplicity, that the real cost of capital is assessed at 10 per cent per annum constant, and inflation at 5 per cent per annum constant (implying a nominal cost of capital of 15.5 per cent per annum) and that the cash flows are projected to increase at a rate equivalent to five points ahead of the inflation rate e.g. year 2's cash flow is expected to be £1.375 million.

On this basis, the value of the entity would be put at £1.250 million / 5 per cent, i.e. £25.0 million at the end of year 1 and (assuming the expectations were reconfirmed) £27.5 million at the end of year 2; figures would be articulated as follows:

	£'000
Net present value at end of year 1	25,000
Cost of capital, 15.5% thereof	3,875
Cash (generation)	(1,375)
Net present value at end of year 2	27,500

These figures could be reconciled with the accounting numbers as in Figure 9.6.

	Accounts £'000	Unrealized gains £'000	Cost of capital £'000	NPV £'000
Opening position	11,000	14,000	–	25,000
Cost of capital	–	–	3,875	3,875
Cash (generation)	(1,375)	–	–	(1,375)
Benchmark	9,625	14,000	3,875	27,500
Closing position	12,100	15,400	–	27,500
Profit / net strengthening	2,475	1,400	(3,875)	–

Figure 9.6   *Reconciliations*

Such a reconciliation – adopting, it will be noted, the financial-control viewpoint – can serve to direct attention to important strategic issues. Take, for example, that closing 'unrealized' figure of £15.4 million. From the accountant's point of view this could be seen as a quantification of intangible assets such as the investments in research and development (resulting in innovation), marketing (resulting in a reputation in the market place that facilitates that innovation), training (resulting in the quality that underpins the reputation) and information (resulting in faster responses). The strategist, meanwhile, would see it as a quantification of the sources of competitive advantage, or the barriers to entry, which investments in tangible assets are unlikely to provide.

But one of the most enlightening, and alarming, uses of this model is from the viewpoint of the treasurer. If the value of the entity is a function of its projected cash flows, then, since these can be attributed to the various stakeholders, so can the entity's value, as shown in Figure 9.7.

	Lenders £'000	Taxation £'000	Equity £'000	Entity £'000
Opening position	2,200	11,636	11,164	25,000
Cost of capital	341	1,804	1,730	3,875
Cash (generation)	(121)	(640)	(614)	(1,375)
Closing position	2,420	12,800	12,280	27,500

Figure 9.7   *Revelations*

Thus, this company, whose financial profile is not untypical of a successful manufacturing business, making a 22 per cent return on assets, opting for 20 per cent gearing and growing at around 5 per cent per annum in real terms, is worth more to the Inland Revenue than it is to its shareholders, whereas, on the balance sheet, the tax liability amounted to less than 10 per cent of the equity. The faster the rate of growth, the greater the proportion of the value attributable to the tax authorities, thanks to a tax system based on the (historical cost) accounting model.

We have reached the ridiculous situation where investment opportunities may have positive value as far as the entity is concerned, even at the UK's high cost of capital, but are being spurned because they would reduce the net present value of cash generated for shareholders. The result is a further discouragement to growth and investment for the future, but the preoccupation with backward-looking accounting numbers, as distinct from forward-looking financial management, successfully obscures a serious problem for corporate governance defined broadly. The economy, and especially employment levels, shrink and more money has to be siphoned off the wealth-creating sector to shore up uneconomic activities.

In some cases businesses are only able to maintain their level of activity by asking for their money back in the form of rights issues. Apathy among shareholders, the costs of any alternative action and the power of the arithmetic of rights issues combine to leave the shareholders with little option but to subscribe. Merchant bankers earn fees by providing underwriting facilities, which guarantee the directors the funds they seek even if the shareholders do not subscribe, and insulate directors from any questions as to what will be done with the money.

The way forward

Pulling the various strands of thought together:

- In sharp contrast to the cultures showing the greatest propensity to grow, the English-speaking cultures see the quoted company as the preferred form of economic activity, equity capital as the principal form of funding, and last night's share price as an important measure of performance.
- The UK tax system, by favouring institutions such as pension funds, has resulted in the passivity of the holders of the major proportion of equity shares.
- Directors have filled the resulting vacuum and, among other things, have developed performance measurement and reward systems based on accounting numbers. The accounting standard setters condone this, even claiming that accounts should provide outsiders with information on which to make economic decisions like buying shares (but the law protects auditors from claims for damages by anyone silly enough to believe it).
- Because the accounting model ignores the increasingly important intangible assets, short termism is encouraged: setting out to maximize short-run profits will almost certainly damage the long-term health of a business.
- Conflicts of interest therefore arise between what is good for directors' personal wealth and the long term health of the enterprise.
- It is not clear that the auditing wing of the accountancy profession is, as has traditionally been assumed in company law, oriented towards protecting the shareholders from the actions of the directors.
- Much greater risk is associated with the UK's preferred form of capital, i.e. equity, as distinct from the bank lending, which is seen as the primary source on the continent and the Far East. Hence the discount rate, which is used to trade off between current and future cash flows, is much higher in the UK than elsewhere.
- Hence the rate of growth is lower, with a particular bias against those tangible investments – research, development, marketing, training and information – which enable a business to be more aware of its environment, to anticipate changes therein, and to adapt accordingly (the three As of strategic management).
- The public sector, however, is insulated from many of these pressures, its investment opportunities being evaluated at a much lower discount rate, and its cash flows ignoring such embarrassing factors as inflation, taxation and the volatility of interest rates. Hence this sector grows at the expense of the private sector.

- Public-sector growth is partially financed by a corporation tax system that discourages private-sector growth. Growth by retention means ploughing back profits that have already been taxed to generate further profits that will also be taxed. Successful companies in the UK are worth more (in terms of cash flows) to the Inland Revenue than they are to their shareholders.

In short, if the question is 'Does the UK's collection of corporate governance influences – accounting standards, banking and stock exchange practices, taxation system, and the current approach to performance measurement and reward – help or hinder the country as it competes with others?', the answer is emphatically the latter. It is not obvious, however, which is cause and which is effect. Does the UK have the governance appropriate to its short termism or is it short termist because of its governance?

There are some arguments in favour of the former interpretation, such as the fact that the prevailing management ethos rates problem-solving very highly. Many managers clearly get considerable satisfaction from solving problems – problems that could, with forethought, have been avoided – and do not enjoy the thinking process that would enable them to identify opportunities. But if this is the case, the consequences are sombre: the economy's comparative decline will continue, and may even accelerate, since the various factors are mutually reinforcing. Evolution tells us that some species shrink to extinction while others develop.

The optimist would support the second interpretation and argue that the failings identified can be dealt with. The accountancy profession, currently seen as part of the problem, could actually be part of the solution. The first step is to recognize that there is far more to accountancy than accounting. Though a large proportion of the membership of the profession actually enjoy being passive outsiders, reporting objectively on what has happened, there is a significant minority who are keen to be members of the teams that make things happen. People in this group see their roles in terms of financial management rather than accounting. As a general rule, they are concerned with maximizing the value of their businesses, given all the constraints, rather than getting involved in any action to remove those constraints.

In particular, there is a need to acknowledge that backward-looking accounting numbers do not provide a valid indication of either financial health at a point in time, or of progress over time. Neither do they provide a valid input to the making and monitoring of decisions. Care needs to be taken, however, to avoid the obsolete, but still taught, theory of corporate finance, which was promulgated in America a decade or two ago (and, presumably, partly responsible for some of the corporate disasters there) and gives prominence to short-run share prices. Financial management is at least as important to unquoted businesses and not-for-profit organizations, including the public sector, as it is to quoted companies. There is a need to learn lessons from other economies, especially other members of the European Union.

Elevating the importance of value, and positioning the cost of capital as the rate at which society trades off between time frames, are the ways this can be done. Maximizing (net present) value is applicable across the whole spectrum (and compatible with European thinking) and the profit-seeking sector can bolt on the secondary objective of maximizing the proportion of entity value attributable to the equity. UK bankers will need to get to grips with forecast cash flows if they are not to lose ground to overseas competitors.

The conventional wisdom that the private sector should be taxed according to success and growth must be challenged. By highlighting cash flows rather than accounting profit, it is easy to show the adverse effect that the current regime is having on economic vitality of the country. This would provide a platform from which to address the distortions brought about by the imputation system of taxation and, in particular, the tax breaks given to shareholders whose objectives mean they must inevitably be passive.

Active shareholders would be motivated to stem the tide of directorial self-interest. When a rights issue is announced, for example, they might avoid getting bogged down in the false arithmetic of the price, and seek clarification of what the directors intend to do with their money. In return, they might acknowledge the inappropriateness of net assets as a basis for denominating directors' freedom to increase the company's borrowings or to acquire other companies, and, by having a more rational denominator, thereby eliminate the need for such devices as 'brands on the balance sheet' to circumvent their articles of association.

It would surely then be only a matter of time before directors began to share forward-looking judgements with their principal stakeholders. Were they to publish the cost of capital they use for evaluating strategies, and their assessment of the rate of dividend growth this would engender, this could be distilled into a valuation of the business to its shareholders. Financial analysts and journalists might also be prompted to be forward-looking and to identify any remaining anomalies.

What is stopping us?

10

Control in organizations
Tom Sheridan

Introduction

The classical description of the function of control is that it deals with the tasks associated with restricting, coordinating and regulating action in line with a plan to achieve predetermined goals. The need for restriction is to keep the actions broadly within the limits of the plans, and the regulation is to maintain progress in relation to the planned time-frame. Control, in this context, is exercised by establishing some kind of standard against which actual performance can be compared. Clearly, the ultimate purpose of control is to help the organization achieve its mission and goals through carrying out the strategic plan. The shorter-term objectives, however, are to achieve the level of performance set out in the various standards through well coordinated actions, while minimizing any deleterious effects resulting from deviations from the plan.

This was the rather restrictive view that was popular with organizations perhaps only a couple of generations ago, epitomized by Geneen's ITT, with its strong control culture, where the Controller was dubbed the 'abominable no-man'. The emphasis was on numbers, on certainties, and on a stable environment, where the belief in the sheer arithmetic of the DCF calculations was an article of faith with financial managers. It is a very different world today in the mid-1990s. Today's uncertainties are putting great pressures on financial managers. Control is still essential but it exists in an entirely new environment. Financial managers and controllers need entirely different skills from their forebears of just a couple of generations ago.

It is impossible to discuss control in the 1990s by merely looking at organizational structures and operating methodologies on their own, divorced from the business climate. We have to examine the framework within which the control function is operating. This chapter therefore starts by discussing the general business framework and the factors that are impacting on financial managers. It then goes on to look at financial management in general and its control/controllership component in some detail, with a discussion of the key methodologies currently used by organizations. It concludes by surveying some national differences in approach, emphasizing the human relations aspect that is now so important in the management of the control function.

This chapter discusses financial management, (and its sub-set, controllership) a term that is used quite deliberately. It is important to emphasize that financial management is much more than accounting, and that financial managers are increasingly coming from all disciplines. Treasury management, for instance, has become an important element of financial management, and there a banking background is just as important as an accounting one. Most important of all, there are any number of MBA and business courses teaching financial management. The modern financial manager and controller has to be skilled at planning, at managing people, and in handling risk, just as much as in the minutiae of financial reporting. Already a significant and increasing number of financial directors in Britain's top companies are not chartered accountants.

The business climate in the mid-1990s

Votality, instability, the improbable, even the incredible, are all words used by management theorists to describe today's business climate. Global competition, ever-newer technology, shorter product and market cycles, combined with the increasing weight of regulation as companies trade across frontiers and meet new requirements, are all putting new pressures on managements. Risk has increased as the current recession has cruelly exposed business weaknesses, while, paradoxically new opportunities are opening up in the Second and Third Worlds. The finance function has a key responsibility to ensure that companies successfully meet these challenges. What it has to do is to marshal the information needed to drive the business while maintaining flexibility to react to both the threats and opportunities. It might be said that this was always the function of finance. What is new, however, is the pressure on the finance function from the sheer speed of change. The very rapidity of change is impacting on information systems and the bureaucratic structures of corporate business. At the same time cost pressures are reducing the number of staff in the finance function to deal with such issues. The pressure on the finance function is from both sides.

Moreover, financial managers are torn in different directions. They are regarded as business partners by their colleagues in the management team, who see the job of finance as not just to deliver the numbers but to deliver the appropriate numbers and to demistify them into understandable language for other managers. At the same time as being asked to play a proactive role in making things happen, they are also required to report according to both the external and internal rules. The pressures of corporate governance demand a policeman role from them. How can financial managers satisfy all these requirements? Already the ICAEW is having to deal with the ethical problems of financial managers pulled in different directions. There are internal problems, too. How can control be combined with decision support, and how should they balance strategical considerations with short-term reporting? It is a commonplace of informed comment that financial managers have moved into the mainstream of business management. But how does this match up to their role as corporate watchdogs, re-emphasized yet again by a whole series of financial losses in the late 1980s and early 1990s, from Volkswagen, Allied Lyons and Shell's Japanese Associate to name just a few? Vigilant control is needed as much as ever. One wonders how finance directors and controllers can sleep easily at night.

How businesses have reacted to the new pressures

In this new situation companies are facing three basic issues:

- How to combine big company synergy with the flexibility, entrepreneur-ship and motivation of small units.
- How to satisfy a whole range of increasingly vociferous stakeholders with often incompatible demands: the authorities (and the various different authorities), the community, the 'greens', the employees.
- How to ensure that information systems keep up with the relentless and endless changes, and how to ensure that they are timely and appropriate while not being over-burdensome and costly.

The corporate response has been more or less a standard one, characterized by six essential elements:

- Endless and apparently never-ending reorganizations. In the 1993 CIMA multinational survey of Europe's twenty-five top multinationals, virtually every company contacted had either recently been reorganized, was undergoing reorganization or was about to be reorganized. ICI has split itself into two; Hoechst is considering spinning off its fibres business; ABB has reorganized itself from the classical matrix of functions, businesses and regions into fourteen separate businesses; Ciba-Geigy has its 'Vision 2000'; and so on.

There is a direct impact on the finance function, both in regrouping the information systems to take account of the ever-changing organizational patterns, and also in paying for the changes. ABB's 1993 profits were hit by a non-recurring restructuring charge of $596m, which reduced profits to $68m (as against $505m in 1992).

- A retreat to core business accompanied by contracting out non-core activities, which can even include accounting and financial operations. The structural change can be quite fundamental, as with BAe selling its Rover Division to BMW.
- Moving to new forms of association: linking up with suppliers and customers, joint ventures, mergers, partnerships, alliances, as well as cross-border linkages on the lines of Reed-Elsevier. All these sound very fine in international seminars. In practice there are considerable headaches for controllers:

   (a) the problem of coping with joint ventures in which, even though they are 50/50, the other partner has operating control and is able to impose his business systems and operating requirements, e.g. Ford's control of Autolatina, a joint venture with VW, now being unwound;
   (b) the need for extra audit capability on the lines of oil companies' auditing joint ventures where they are not the operators;
   (c) the issue of deciding on the method of the financial calculations;
   (d) the profit allocation (how calculated, when paid, in what currencies, etc).

The risk of failure is high. Volvo posted a loss of SEK 2.64bn (£222m) in 1993, which financial analysts regarded as reflecting the first tranche of the cost of unwinding the alliance with Renault.

- Reorganizing all the operating systems, often coupled with a reduction in the size and functions of the central bureaucracy and head office. This process is often linked to the 're-engineering' of all the systems in the company.
- Changing the whole nature of the business: privatization is the best example of this.
- In all organizations there is a growing recognition that information is a critical factor in business success, and that business managements need information on non-financial items such as service, safety, quality, timeliness, etc. It is significant that the first item reported on in London Underground Ltd's monthly management report is the achievement of service levels.

The concept of corporate federalism

The organizational form companies have increasingly been moving to in order to reconcile these contradictions is a federalist structure, which combines local flexibility with world-wide synergy. Think global, act local, is the popular catch-phrase.

Per Barnevik, CEO of the Swiss-Swedish multinational Asea Brown Boveri, described his company's organization as multidomestic, both national and multinational, being both big and small at the same time. The need in business as in politics is to balance out the tribal region with the nation state. Small may not always be beautiful, but it is the most comfortable. People want to identify with a hunting pack, not a massive bureaucracy.

Federalism is more than just divisionalization, however. It is not that power is devolved from the centre but it is assumed to belong to the lowest point of the organization. The centre governs with the consent of the governed as in a federalist nation such as the United States. Power has to be distributed, with the services and facilities needed by all located at different units, not just at the centre.

The theory is all very fine but the US federal example shows the need for rules. It has to be accepted that the price of local autonomy is some measure of central control, discipline and coordination. There is a very delicate balance between central synergy (as for example, in company-wide R & D) and the local autonomous 'skunk works' so beloved by Tom Peters. There has to be some power at the centre to allocate resources. Rules are necessary and the finance function is the key to this, because when we are talking of allocating resources, we are basically referring to funding. In a federalist company, with a minimal central organization, it is the finance function that is very much the cement that holds the company together as the only central organ left. This is because, despite all the organizational gurus and the encouragement of empowerment, an organization is still legally bound to maintain accounts and produce financial statements, taxes have to be accounted for, statements passed to the relevant authorites and consolidations prepared. There is no escaping from the need to have corporate rules and principles for doing things in common and reporting in the same way. These are more difficult to realize in a federalist 'democracy' than in an old-fashioned autocracy.

The first absolute essential is the definition of the checks and balances and of the boundaries of power, determining who has the authority to do what, where, and within what limits. This is the framework within which finance works, and the finance function looks to management to provide this definition. Every major company has its manuals and definitions: ICI/Zeneca have their finance manuals, which specify the costing principles in some detail; ABB has its 18-page 'bible', while Grand Metropolitan works through a group of itinerant business ambassadors.

These rules deal largely with financial responsibilities, definitions, transactions and reporting requirements. Best corporate practice is to agree:

- The roles, powers and responsibilities of the head office and the different business unit or divisional head offices. These have to be clearly defined. It is all very well for CEOs to talk of being both big and small, at international conferences. These are fine words, but their exact meaning has to be carefully defined.
- The common language. In many cases this is business English and non-Anglophone companies take great care to ensure that their people (just like their PCs) are compatible with each other. Globalization means uniformity in reporting but it has to be accepted that this is particularly difficult in international companies with international staffs of different nationalities and financial cultures. Readers are asked to consider the problems of a Danish bank, for instance, whose business language has to be English. When the bank's inspectors go from Denmark to review the operations of, say, the Kuala Lumpur branch, the conversations will be held in English, of course, *between two groups of persons neither of whose first language is English*. The scope for errors and misunderstandings is enormous unless careful precautions are taken.
- Common units of measurement and a common understanding of terms. One of the issues faced by CMB, the Anglo-French merger in the canning industry, was the lack of understanding and rapport between the British and the French financial staff. The merger was eventually unwound in the early 1990s.
- Reporting timetables and common reporting formats. Here we are talking of discipline that has to be imposed by the centre, and accepted by the rest of the organization.
- A definition of what is regarded as good and bad performance and how this is to be measured. This is essential for any company-wide reward structure whether financially based or not.

The impact of the finance function

The finance function is at the receiving end of all these influences and changes. A conference of European Financial Managers held in Paris in Summer 1992 summed up these new influences on finance as follows:

1980s	*1990s*
Growth	Rationalization
Debt	Liquidity
Income	Risk

Profits	Cash flow
Asset volumes	Asset quality
M & A	Strategic alliances
Diversification	Core businesses and competences

There is intense pressure on finance. It is all very well for the combination of business change and macho managements to force organizational change on a company, but such changes have to be recorded, documented and reported on without losing continuity with either the past or with current plans for the future. Every reorganization has to be accompanied by a restructuring of the systems and the reporting. Systems have therefore to be extremely sophisticated. They have almost to be three-dimensional as companies seek to organize their information to identify the trouble spots in detail while giving their managements the total picture at the same time. Nor is it just a question of reporting on events within the organization. New forms of organization, whether networking with suppliers and customers, or joint ventures and alliances with third parties, have also to be regulated financially, controlled, monitored and reported on.

These new factors have affected three areas of financial management:

- *Business planning and control.* A combination of market pressures, the need for flexibility and speed, new organizational structures and groupings, combined with the 'federalist' movement have stressed the importance of proper business planning and control. It has been said that in the long term all planning is financial planning and financial managements have, of necessity, become increasingly involved with corporate strategy. In the short term the focus is on management direction through the budgetary system *handled properly*. We shall discuss this later on in this chapter.
- *Cost pressures.* Businesses have to cope with cost pressures from all sides and from opponents with significant cost advantages (from anywhere in the globe it seems, but particularly from the Second and Third Worlds), coupled with the speed of changes in the market and in customer requirements.

The current recession has forced multinationals to cut their costs, but at a macro level, not just a trim. What this means is that cost-cutting is no longer just a financial measure. It has become strategic. The question all companies have had to face is, how does one cut out the fat without severing an artery? The trouble is that the easy things have already been done, often a long time ago. Morale, particularly at middle management level, is bound to be affected by continual waves of cost-cutting. The experience of Robert Horton, who was forced to resign as Chief Executive of BP after initiating dramatic change, is a salutary lesson in this respect.

- *Information,* Information is power, but it has to be the right information for the circumstances, which are continually changing. We have concentrated so far on internal information to run the organization, but there is the external aspect as well. The authorities are continually pressing for more transparency in reporting, spurred on in the UK by a whole series of scandals and business failures, and on the Continent by pressure from the EC and by the need to conform to the requirements of the US authorities, sitting on top of the world's largest capital market.

There can be no better summing up of the new focus of financial managements than that given by Professor David Allen (1994):

Managerial megatrends affecting the finance function:

FROM	TO
Stability	Volatility
National	Global
Tactical	Strategic
Functionalism	Generalism
Centralized	Devolved
Confrontation	Teamwork
Tangibles	Intangibles
Quantity	Quality
Products	Customers
Direct	Indirect
Analysis	Synthesis
Reactive	Proactive
Accounting	Financial management
Static	Dynamic

In controllers' conferences three issues come up again and again in the discussions:

- How to reconcile central strategic planning with passing responsibility down the line.
- How to balance central financial control and the reporting requirements relating to corporate responsibilities with the need for business unit operational flexibility in their financial management and entrepreneurship in their operations (including financial operations).
- How to balance the need for demonstrable profit now with the requirement for investment for profit later, in other words the familiar short-term pressures so much agonized over in the Anglophone world.

The strategic importance of the finance function

It has been said that the two most important relationships that any CEO has are with his chairman and his finance director. One has only to look at the business press to realize the keen interest that is taken in the appointment of finance directors in any company. Too rapid a turnover in FDs is taken as a bad sign: not the least of the unfavourable press comments at the end of 1993 on the problems of Fisons was due to the apparently premature departure of its finance director.

Apart from the chief executive, the FD is the one other director that has to be consulted on every strategic decision made by the company, and it is therefore almost a matter of course that the FDs have to be members of their company's top strategic decision-making cadre. This enhancement of status has been recognized by a change in title, whether CFO in US companies or managing director finance in companies such as Enterprise Oil or the Italian oil multinational, AGIP.

There are several reasons for this enhancement in status:

● We have already noted the trend towards a reduction in the size of the corporate headquarters. However lean and mean a company is, it must nonetheless produce its financial results and figures to satisfy its shareholders and the financial authorities. Even such notoriously decentralized organizations as Hanson and BTR need to have financial staff at the centre to carry out these tasks. Indeed in some holding companies, such as the French Danone, with turnovers in billions of pounds, the majority of the central staff are in the financial department. This is even more pronounced at the lower end of the scale. Thomas Jourdan plc is typical of many smaller companies. With some £20m turnover, its group headquarters consists only of the chief executive, the finance director and their secretaries.

● Information is the lifeblood of the business in any company. Corporate managements look to their financial staff to provide the necessary controls. One has only to cite a few cases of the lack of control in recent times to appreciate what can happen: Ferranti, Queens Moat Houses, Metallgesellschaft (which resulted in the departure of the FD as well as the Chairman). The corporate governance 'movement' in the UK is pressing hard to ensure that the FD is more controlled than ever by his company's Remuneration and Audit Committees. GEC-Alsthom recognized the information pressure on its management and took great care to set up monthly management accounting as a priority as soon as possible after the merger of the two companies.

- The trend to contracting out the routine financial operations (such as payroll or consolidations) is another factor. Whether one is talking of oil companies in Scotland or local authorities in England, the contracting out of the routine financial work has left the central financial function as a small, high-powered unit, dealing with financial policy and the financial aspects of corporate strategy.
- Controls are at one end of the spectrum of management, strategic planning is at the other, and in a decentralized, federal company – especially a large one – top management can concern itself with no more than long-term planning. We have already referred to the fact that in the long term all planning can be seen as financial planning. This is yet another reason for the importance of the finance director in a strategic role.
- The pressure on finance directors and their top teams comes from both sides, from within an organization and from outside. The pressure of outside stakeholders and potential stakeholders is increasing. The German company Daimler-Benz is busy selling itself to outside (largely US) institutional investors and the 'road shows' in the United States have to be headed as matter of course by that company's FD. On top of everything else the FD has to be his company's ambassador!

Finance directors and their top teams have to concern themselves with three key aspects of strategy:

- *Strategy implementation*: to ensure that the agreed stategy is proceeding according to plan. Financial managements have to keep the whole company under review. They have to ensure that the necessary control points are in existence, the milestones and responsibilities mapped out, and that everyone is aware of what they have to do. The deployment of funds, often through the capital expenditure programme, is a key element in this, and the capital expenditure programme is one of the most important ways in which a headquarters keeps control in a group. In the best international companies funding is the essential link between strategic plans and their realization. Leading edge companies such as ABB insist that their finance departments should take a proactive role in this respect.
- *Strategic change*. Financial managers have to ensure that their systems remain flexible to reflect the continual changes. The approach has to be constructive, the attitude being not the negative 'How much can we afford?', but the positive 'How much do we need for all the things we have to do?'

- *Strategic flexibility*. It is not just that change comes suddenly, but also that the windows of opportunity are open for only a brief period of time: for instance, a Middle East suddenly with a chance of peace, opportunities in South Africa, or the chance of making a major acquisition such as Nestlé had with Rowntree Mackintosh and with Perrier. Finance has to be ready to respond fast to such opportunities.

The top management interface

It goes without saying that a quality finance function can only operate effectively in the framework of a well-organized company and that its finance team can not exist in a managerial vacuum. There has to be a supportive corporate structure with the total backing of the chief executive. Five key factors are essential:

- There has to be a clear definition of the role of the centre and of the business units, who is empowered to do what, what the responsibilities are, where the frontiers are and what is and is not negotiable.
- There has also to be a clear-cut organization structure with defined ways of doing business between the units, covering such items as intertrading and payment terms. This may sound childishly basic, but one still comes across groups where units can and do withhold payment from other sister units to such an extent that the result is often legal action, *between units in the same group*!
- It is only when the above disciplines have been established that it will be possible to set out the responsibilities of the central financial management as against business unit managements and business unit financial managements.
- There have to be clear cut and strictly enforced procedures for setting objectives, plans and budgets
- Reporting disciplines have to be backed up by top management and insisted upon. This means taking sanctions in cases of indiscipline.

It is virtually a contract. As a *quid pro quo* for its backing, top managements look to their financial functions to provide them with the necessary strategic support in the form of connections with the banks and the financial world, and to ensure that relationships with the authorities are on a proper, that is trouble-free, basis. It goes without saying that top managements expect their finance functions to handle the full range of accounting and financial transactions smoothly and without fuss, and to ensure that there are no unpleasant surprises.

Leading edge companies judge the performance of their central finance teams on their ability to satisfy six key requirements:

- The ability to identify the organization's essential information needs (which may well change with time), agree them with management and provide the information in a way that makes business sense as well as satisfy the legal requirements. This will cover not only the financial data but also the non-financial numbers such as manpower, market share, units of production, and, increasingly, environmental data.
- The correlation of information from the subsidiaries/business units so as to provide a helicopter overview of the business. What is important is that this is a forward view to enable the company to plan ahead. In this respect there have to be reference points such as robust budgets and plans.
- What is produced must be information, to be acted on, and not just a collection of data. Without action, information is useless.
- There must be common practices, common understanding and company-wide principles both for the internal and the external information, to ensure that it is all produced on the same basis. This sounds a business cliché: it is amazing in how many international companies such uniformity does not exist or exists only imperfectly. Dare one say it, this also applies to domestic companies, operating in a single country where all the staff speak the same mother tongue
- Finance has to be able to manage the company-wide financial rules so that there is a common agreed basis for reporting and for organizational interrelationships. These rules have to be reasonable and simple so as to be readily understood and accepted throughout the company. They have to be agreed: they cannot be imposed.
- The figures must be robust and reliable. It is sadly true that in too many companies', time is spent at management meetings in discussing whether the figures are valid, not what they mean.

It will be apparent that finance directors are in an extremely exposed position. They are key members of the management team, with a particularly important input to corporate strategy, on the one hand, impartial arbiters between the different business units, on the other, and with, at the same time, important professional reporting responsibilities regarding third parties. All these pressures are yet another reason for the enhancement of their status, but they do not make the job any easier.

The role of the central finance function

We can now define what the central finance function in a company has to do. There are eight key elements:

- Strategic planning, covering the development and monitoring of business plans (details and milestones), the establishment of the optimum capital structure, and ensuring that the necessary funds are available to carry out the strategy.

- Managing the key financial relationships with outsiders: shareholders (particularly the major institutional investors), the authorities, the taxation authorities, the financial world, auditors, analysts, banks.
- Establishing and carrying out financial policy.
- Operational financial planning: capital expenditure programmes, cash and balance sheet planning.
- Treasury management, debt structure, gearing, the management of risk.
- Economic viability: performance measures and the budgetary system.
- Intra-group policies, reporting and performance related bonus schemes
- Control, including quality control, information systems, standards and procedures.

Finance is the language of business. It is the job of the central finance team to define that language, however decentralized the organization and however much autonomy has been given to the business units.

The finance team

At this point it is appropriate to look at the work of the finance function. Inevitably, as is only to be expected, the organizational permutations are endless. In some continental companies there is no FD at all, and the senior members of the finance team are the controller and treasurer, reporting directly to the company's president; in other companies the FD has a wider role and is in charge of administration, planning, and even purchasing; in some German companies in particular planning and control are seen as a separate function. However, despite all these qualifications it is possible to make some tentative generalizations as to the division of work in the majority of multinationals. This is set out in Figure 10.1.

The finance director, or whatever the title may be, is a member of the top management team. He (or she) is concerned with the strategic direction of the business, with managing the finance 'team', as it is increasingly coming to be called, and with outside relationships, such as with banks and investing institutions, and their confidence in him will be an important factor in determining their confidence in the company. He will concentrate on the big picture, detail being the affair of the next level of management, which is why an important part of the FD's job is to ensure that the right people fill the senior posts in financial management.

In general, control is delegated downwards to the business units, Treasury, on the other hand, (usually also consisting of taxation and insurance) is nearly always centralized. It is a common saying that profit belongs to the business units, but that cash belongs to the centre. And of course it goes without saying that control of cash is power. This is a critically important area for many companies. ABB's treasury, with over 700 staff divided between Zurich and Stockholm, is treated as a separate business unit, and is responsible for as much as one-third of ABB's profit. In many companies, such as BP, Italy's ENI or Sweden's Stora, the Treasury function is a bank, with a full banking licence. We do not go further into the work of the treasurer here, as it is outside the scope of this chapter.

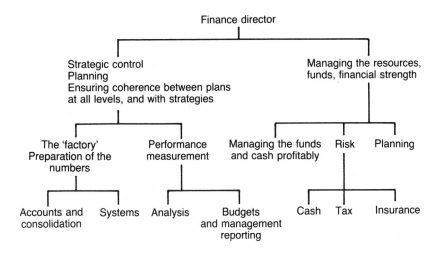

Figure 10.1   *Work of the finance team*

The controller

The rise in the status of the FD has been accompanied by a corresponding increase in the importance of the controller who will also often be part of the core strategy-making group in many international companies, and who increasingly has a crucial part to play in carrying out strategic decisions and implementing performance improvements. Indeed, in many companies the role is very much like that of the FD of a couple of generations ago. The controllers are the internal financial managers *par excellence*, even though the current pressures for business unit autonomy have left them with only a small number of direct reports. They have to operate at a 'socratic' level through business unit controllers whose formal reporting is to their own chief executives. The emphasis has to be on their managerial skills.

The role of the controller is to manage five key areas:

- Basic bookkeeping and accounting.
- Financial consolidations, reporting to the authorities and to shareholders, etc.
- Budgets and planning.
- Internal reporting, costing, analyses.
- The 'rules', definitions, procedures, timetables.

> These more routine tasks are often referred to as the 'factory'.

The work of the staff engaged in routine accounting and consolidation has been shown separately. Software developments have resulted in a downgrading of the importance of this type of work. It is no longer a question of highly skilled accountants poring over long sheets of paper to consolidate a group's results. All this can be handled by computer systems, either in-house or bought-in. We have shown this routine 'factory' task as part of the head office, but in theory the work can be located anywhere, provided the computer links exist. Corporate practice differs as to the reporting relationships of this department. In some companies it is a stand-alone unit, but in most, for convenience, it has been brought under the management of the controller.

An interesting more recent development has been an increasing emphasis on the proactive nature of the controller's role, as shown in Figure 10.2, which sets out the organizational philosophy of a leading Swiss-based chemical multinational.

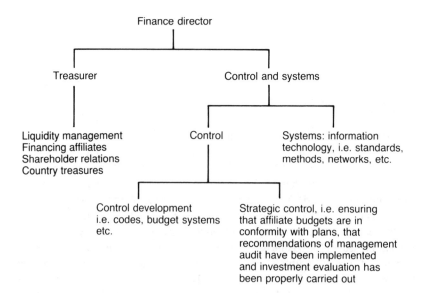

Figure 10.2 *A type of organizational philosophy*

Asea Brown Boveri (ABB) is an enthusiastic proponent of the proactive role of the control function. The company insists that its controllers should not be just mere providers of the figures, but should play their part in taking action on them. ABB divides its control departments into two: accounting control, which deals with the production of the financial figures, and business control. Even the former is not just an accounting numbers factory. Its staff have to get behind the reasons for differences and have to go so far as to act as troubleshooters in digging out information. Business control is an even more proactive function. At head office its role is strategic, looking to profitability and risk management; in the business units its task is to work actively with management to assist in reaching profitability targets, using the information produced by accounting control to formulate and initiate action programmes.

Divisional business unit controllers

The corporate controllers certainly do not have the staff these days to be able to check and evaluate the figures reported to corporate headquarters. In the CIMA survey one British controller said that he only looked at figures with six noughts attached to them! For the rest he had to rely on the heirarchy of subordinate controllers, which is why we said, earlier on, that there was an almost socratic relationship with them. The control is exercised through ensuring that the right people are appointed to the posts and that their thinking is on the right lines.

This relationship is a very delicate matter. The finance directors and corporate controllers exert their influence through their contacts with business unit chief executives, through finance conferences and through 'looking after' the subordinate controllers. In one major French company the group controller sees his job as very much influencing through networking. Even the largest multinationals recognize the power of these personal relationships and cement the personal ties by transferring their finance staff around the world, and in and out of head office, so that these personal links are strengthened and fostered.

The subordinate controllers (as we shall call the divisional or business unit controllers for convenience) therefore have a dual reporting line in reality, whatever it says in their job descriptions. They report to their line manager, the local chief executive, and they are key members of his management team. However, they also have a 'dotted-line' responsibility to the central finance team (FD and controller) from a quality viewpoint, and for the proper financial management of their areas. This is a professional link and in most well-run companies causes no conflict with line management. It usually works smoothly, provided the basis is well-established and understood by all concerned. It is only when there is a conflict of interest between the subsidiary and head office (as apparently, between VW and its Spanish subsidiary SEAT at end 1993) that the subordinate controllers find themselves pulled apart by conflicting loyalties. There are no easy answers, and one can only recognize that this is an ethical situation in which financial managers, both FDs and subordinates, are increasingly finding themselves in.

The focus on control

In one sense the control function in any major company, especially one that has an international business, faces the same problems. There is the central issue of the centrifugal pull of the subsidiaries against the centripetal pull of the head office; there is the management of an increasingly complicated network of country, market, product and functional financial relationships, allied to the need to monitor subordinate controllers and ensure quality reporting. A matrix management system is the rule in most large companies, but this too can be difficult to manage. Many companies report that when they move to a matrix management system, particularly for the first time, there were bewilderingly conflicting demands on the finance function that could cause crises if not foreseen and handled properly.

We need to emphasize also that one can not talk of control in the abstract. The impact of orangizational styles and cultures, as well as financial cultures, is very important. Four factors appear to be determinant:

- *The industry*. In the food industry the different units can be run as a federation of often smallish companies manufacturing different and stand-alone brands, which is the approach of the French multinational Danone. This is also true of holding companies, such as Hanson plc, which can be managed on largely a financial control basis. Other companies, such as airlines, oil or chemical companies, require a much greater degree of integration.
- *History* is also, not surprisingly, a major factor, and often is the explanation for a powerful head office in one company, and an ineffective one on another. A company that has grown organically, such as Shell, has an entirely different control culture from one that has made major takeovers such as BP. AEI, the British electrical conglomerate taken over by GEC in the late 1960s, was almost a case study of corporate disunity and of the inability of the centre to control. Its components were warring subsidiaries, which rendered the centre almost totally ineffective. It needed only a takeover bid for it to fall apart.

- The GEC take over of AEI emphasizes the importance of *business leader-ship*. There can be no doubt that the control cultures of their companies have been powerfully affected by dominant business leaders such as 'Tiny' Rowland (Lonhro), Lord Sheppard (Grand Met) or Lord Weinstock (GEC), for instance.
- *Shareholding:* the existence of a dominant family or single shareholder is often a key driver of the corporate control culture. The business world abounds with examples, particularly on the continent, where one notes the influence of the 'families': the Wallenbergs in Sweden, Mellos in Portugal, Agnellis in Italy, and so on.

The controller under pressure

It has to be said that the word 'control' does not sit easily in a business world dominated by the currently fashionable theories of federalism, decentralization, empowerment and teamwork. But even the most star-studded football team has to have rules to coordinate the efforts of the team to best effect and to ensure that its members play together. Teamwork does not do away with the need for discipline and control. Rather, it increases it, but discipline and controls have to be imposed in an entirely different way. A company just like a team, has to be clear as to how it defines victory, what constitutes good and bad performance, and how these should be recognized, rewarded or dealt with. In addition, companies have to live in a disciplined world of rules and regulations to which they have to adhere. The controller has to operate in this environment.

The task is not an easy one because the rules have to be accepted, and cannot be rigidly enforced. Managers have to buy in to them. But it is not just a question of disciplines and rules. There are also strategic pressures the control function has, somehow, to balance. In every international business there is an inevitable tension between economic imperatives, on the one hand, and host government demands, on the other. The former drive companies towards global business integration, coordinating their activities to achieve synergy through large-scale efficient operations, focusing on cost reduction and the achievement of the optimum investment intensity to link up to the increasingly insistent demands of multinational customers and competitors. At the other end of the scale there is political pressure from host governments as well as local market demands for local responsiveness, local content, local customers and local requirements.

Controllers complain that their CEOs are asking the impossible of them. But then, the CEOs themselves are under intolerable pressures too. They need information to help them manage their businesses in these turbulent times. No business can afford to be smug when even IBM and VW can hit trouble. In particular CEOs are asking their controllers to define and to report against:

- *New company organizations.* Reorganizations have become a normal feature of corporate life today as has already been pointed out. Here one is talking not only of internal reorganizations but also of the formation of new organizational structures, such as joint ventures, cross-border alliances, mergers, demergers, link-ups with other companies, state entities and even governments. The controller has to make sense of the new structures and to report against them fast, and in a meaningful way.

- *Market changes.* Global, regional and local markets: new structures, new markets, new regulations and now deregulation, new products and new customers. All this requires information, quality systems, careful costing and meticulous analysis.

- *New standards of information transparency.* These are increasingly being insisted on not only by shareholders and investors but also by the authorities, both national and international.

A major problem for controllers is that today information has to serve so many different, and perhaps conflicting, purposes: local statutory versus consolidated results, internal reporting conventions versus external reporting according to international standards, holding company versus local accounts. It is a major task to reconcile the legal with the operating figures, something that the merged CMB was never finally able to accomplish satisfactorily. Ciba-Geigy, on the other hand, is an example of a company that has invested heavily in resolving this issue. It presents its figures in different ways: the holding company accounts are, obviously, reported according to Swiss accounting rules, while at the same time each national entity has to produce its figures according to its own national reporting standards. The internal management reporting is produced according to the internal (Ciba-Geigy) rules, while consolidated group accounts are also produced for the benefit of analysts and the international financial world, according to international accounting conventions. What is important is that Ciba-Geigy has developed its software systems so that these different reporting formats reconcile with each other. It is interesting to note that the pressures of changes in information technology in Ciba-Geigy have also brought about a restructuring of the company's systems.

The tools of the trade

1   Budgets

The methodologies are still the classical ones:

- The budget remains the centre piece of control, linking long- and short-term planning, inputting into cash and capital expenditure planning, and plotting progress against the plans, usually monthly, in what is often called the board reporting 'package'.

- The use of the appropriate performance indices – an increasing number of them non-financial – is an important basis of the reporting structure.
- Costing has always been an important feature of corporate management. It is of critical importance today when cost management has become such an important issue as companies strive to gain and maintain competitive advantage. Cost management, indeed, is now a a strategic issue.

However, while the methodologies are unchanged, they are being used in an entirely different way today by leading edge companies.

Budgetary control, including capital expenditure and cash budgeting, is at the heart of companies' management systems; indeed, when viewed as a short-term profit plan, the budget links strategy with capital expenditure programmes. A properly managed budget system answers three questions. 'Do I have the correct plans in place and do they address the correct issues?' (direction-checking); 'How is each part of the business contributing to the performance of the whole?' (score card); 'What has affected the results in each part of the business recently, what is likely to affect them in the near future and what will be the impact?' (attention-directing).

The importance of the budget (done properly and taken seriously) is that it is a forward-looking document that can serve so many purposes:

- Variances between budget and actual are the means by which top management can monitor the business(es) and prioritize the areas for action. Managements therefore need to spend a considerable amount of time in defining the budget assumptions and parameters. In this way, too, budgets are a means of coordinating the different units of an organization (helped by activity-based techniques).
- The use of variance analysis combined with flexed budgets and an activity-based approach can enable management to identify trends and get a fix on the year-end results: when combined with regular reappraisals and reforcecasts, this can go some way towards guarding against unpleasant surprises.
- Performance to budget is the standard tool whereby top managements measure both business unit performance and managerial performance, the latter often being linked – in British companies at least – to bonus payments. It is not uncommon in British companies for bonus schemes to add some 25–60 per cent to managers' base pay, based on a mix of profit achievement, cash flow, working capital and physical indicators. Many public companies now set out the basis of the top management reward systems in their annual reports for all to see.

● At the very minimum, and most negative, budgets also serve to fix managers' spending targets in discretionary areas such as PR or training.

A federalist system would be chaos without a budget. The budget system enables head-office managements to balance delegation with control, while, at the same time, giving the subsidiary levels of management the freedom to act within the defined guidelines. In that sense, used properly, the budget system can be a great motivator. The cash budget, in particular, is often used to define how far a subsidiary business may act on its own without head-office approval, and – dare one say it – it is used as a means of bringing over-independent and troublesome subsidiaries back into line. The budgetary control system is an essential interface between head office and the business units, within which the finance function plays a leading role.

The finance function manages the budget, sets the rules and the timetable, and pulls it together, but the budget belongs to the managers, not to the finance function. It is important to stress this point, because the whole system will become worthless if abused or politicized. It must be an honest budget: head office must accept the subsidiaries' viewpoints (admittedly after tough discussions) and the subsidiaries must present 'true' figures and not try to keep something in reserve, hidden from the centre. In all too many companies and public authorities the budget system has become hopelessly corrupted by corporate politics, so that the annual budget round resembles nothing so much as trench warfare between head office and the businesses. The result is that the budget has become a bone of contention, it is worthless as a plan and it becomes an active demotivator. On top of everything the central finance team is forced to prepare its own, private budget for the organization as a planning guide because it cannot trust the budgets it has been given.

Leading edge organizations work hard to prevent this happening. Almost universally in Anglophone and continental companies managers refer to the budget as a contract between head office and the businesses. It is taken extremely seriously and, inevitably as a result of this, the outcome is, in the words of one British chief executive, 'three months of hell for all concerned'.

If the budget is regarded as a contract, the implication is that the subsidiary has to adhere to it, and work to correct deviations and meet budget except in the most exceptional circumstances. Even so, most companies contacted in the CIMA survey admitted that, whatever the excuses – and however valid the excuses – a manager who consistently failed to meet budget would not last long in his post in the organization. Their agreed budget is the price for autonomy, and the subsidiary must meet it. But the head office has to pay a price too. Once a budget is agreed, head office has to accept that the operation must be managed by the subsidiary business with the minimum of interference – over-interference would of course give the subsidiary an alibi for failure. It is common practice for international companies to show a subsidiary's budget in two parts: the first part consists of all the items under local management control, for which it is responsible; the second part comprises the total budget, including items imposed or allocated from the centre as properly forming part of the subsidiary's business, but because they are central items, cannot be attributed to local responsibility.

A subsidiary that meets budget – better if it consistently meets budget – has an enviable freedom to manoeuvre and to operate on its own: this is the message from well-managed conglomerates such as BTR, Hanson, Danone, the Belgian Petrofina and the German Preussag. BTR goes so far as to give its subsidiaries considerable freedom in the treasury area as well.

It is common practice for performance to budget to be reported to the top management monthly in what used to be called the 'reporting pack', though nowadays it is more often produced through the computer system. The price for business unit autonomy is that reporting has to be strict, both in format and in timing. On average, multinational companies' head offices receive their reports on the tenth working day after the close of the month, with the fastest being produced within 3-4 days. Flash reports before the monthly results are also very common.

2   Capital expenditure budgets

We have already emphasized the importance of the capital expenditure budget in linking the strategic plan with the short-term budget programme. It generally serves two purposes:

- It is an important means by which the centre keeps control of the businesses. The definition of authorization levels is one of the first priorities in any takeover, and the amount of a manager's spending limit is a key indicator of his status and importance.
- The capital expenditure programme, by defining the priorities, and what should be done, by when and by whom, ensures that the strategic plans are translated into action.

Companies in the heavy industry sector appear to be very much driven by their capex programmes. Capital expenditure proposals are usually evaluated at the business unit or divisional level, and most companies use the main financial evaluation methods, with the most popular being discounted cash flow, payback and internal rate of return. It has to be admitted, however, that financial criteria may well not be the main ones taken into consideration by managements in making their capital expenditure decisions. Strategic fit appears to be extremely important, even if the financial returns are low. Many finance directors echoed their German colleague who complained bitterly how he was overruled on so-called strategic grounds. 'A lot of things can be changed when you use the word strategy. Strategy costs a lot of money.'

3   Performance indices

Today there is a new approach to the identification and preparation of performance indices, which once again focuses on the control function, even though an increasing number of the figures are not financial ones. The starting point is the identification of the business drivers (the critical success factors), which will differ according to the level of the organization being looked at. Once these have been identified and agreed (for the current period), the next stage will be to define the key performance indices (KPIs). This process can be surprisingly difficult, because the KPIs usually have to meet several objectives: obviously they must be appropriate for the business in question, but they must also be comparable both internally and externally to enable the organization to benchmark its results. At the same time they must meet a whole variety of outside requirements, including shareholders and stakeholders. The influence of the latter cannot be ignored; one oil company gives pride of place to safety statistics at its regular monthly management meetings. Car rental companies such as Avis and Hertz place great emphasis on customer service, quality and the occurrence of repeat business.

Figures are useless without action. Increasingly it is not a question of the control organization producing the information for someone else to do something. The controllers themselves have to initiate the action. The trick here is in knowing where to take action for the best effect, in other words to identify the levers for achieving success. These in turn can be monitored by the KPIs.

Table 10.1 gives an example taken from a manufacturing organization, to show how the drivers, KPIs and levers would typically interact. It is to be noted how many non-financial indices there are, and how these become increasingly important as one descends the organizational hierarchy.

4   Cost management

The CIMA survey revealed that concern with their companies' total cost base was the biggest worry controllers have. European companies feel themselves besieged by organizations able to deliver the same product/ service but at cheaper cost. With the changes in Central and Eastern Europe the potential competition is now quite literally on the doorstep of western companies. Cost management has become a strategic issue and the principles of an activity-based approach are well understood and are being extended to areas such as

Table 10.1 Performance indices

Level/ accountability	Critical success factors	KPIs	Controllable factors (levers)
Corporate level Shareholder value	Lowering cost of capital Portfolio management Investor relations	Share value EPS	Capital structure/ gearing Dividend policy PR/ information Diversification
Group Return on equity	Capital investment Funding Integration	Debt/equity ratio Tax rate Cash Net profit	Borrowings/ funding structure Capital allocation Group costs Supply pipeline control
Division Return on investment	Customer satisfaction Delivery performance Product development	Market share Revenue Margin % Asset productivity Customer satisfaction monitors	Cost control Product mix Working capital Overhead costs Customer service Asset management
Department Unit costs	Cost control Product quality	Cost Volume Quality measures Service measures	Direct costs Product mix Maintenance management Statistical process control
Plant area Resource utilization	Plant utilization Yield Efficiency	Availability/ utilization Throughput rate Labour productivity	Operations management Material usage Labour utilization Stock control
Work group Task completion	Planning Scheduling Labour productivity Workforce skills	Schedule achievement Job quality Labour utilization	Work organization Workforce recruitment Training

budgeting and customer costing, even if not too many companies have yet gone to the full extent of installing ABC.

Cost pressures have impacted on three areas in particular:

- Overheads.
- Head-office costs (including the costs of the hierarchy of head offices in a group of companies).
- IT costs.

What this means is that companies are having to rethink their total operations and cost base. This is not just a matter of tinkering, of taking off 5 per cent or 10 per cent. Radical changes are necessary. Sainsbury and Tesco are making whole layers of managers redundant. BP is only one of many companies to have reduced the size of its head office and to have contracted out significant parts of its routine administrative functions. It sounds easy, but managing down is extremely difficult in practice. Cutting out the fat is one thing, doing it without severing an artery or risking a total collapse in morale is quite another. Lean and mean may result in anaemic and sickly. Corporate history is too full of examples of companies that have reduced their headcount and closed offices, only to find too little an impact on their cost structure.

It is a cliché that companies are engaged in re-engineering their business processes, both systems and organization. Costing is an essential input to this and controllers play an important role in it with their knowledge of the horizontal cost interrelationships and cost dependencies throughout the organization. At the macro level the cost calculations cover not only the controller's own company but also its suppliers and customers as well. This is a lesson that Marks & Spencer learnt long ago before it became a fashionable management theory.

5   Some things never change

Too many businesses fail through not heeding the tried and tested rules of control. In this respect some things never change, and finance directors and their colleagues need to watch the classical key business unit indicators:

- Cash flow,
- Inventory turnover,
- Debtor days,
- Interest/ profit,
- Gross margin,
- Added value,
- Disproportionate growth in overheads.

Financially aware chief executives focus on two areas for an indication of problems:

- Consistently missed cash flow forecasts and/or a declining or negative cash flow even if the reported figures show the business unit still to be profitable.
- Profit and return on assets targets regularly missed.

The point made repeatedly to us in the CIMA survey was that the biggest 'crime' a subsidiary unit could commit is not a variance on budget, but trying to hide it. Accounting surprises (whether good or bad) during the year therefore are infallible indications of a lack of control in that unit.

National financial cultures

Continental multinationals face the same issues as Anglophone ones, such as cost pressures, globalization and the IT revolution, and it is therefore inevitable that their methodologies are largely the same: budgeting, for instance, is the universal centrepiece of financial management. That said, however, it has to be emphasized that there are substantial differences between the Anglophone approach to financial management, and the continental approach. Of course one cannot speak of continental attitudes as if they were all alike: it would need a book to do justice to all the different European nationalities and their approaches. One can only skim the surface, and readers will perhaps forgive a certain concentration on Germany, by far the biggest economy on the continent. German attitudes are interesting because they are so diametrically different from Anglophone ones.

It is important to stress that there is a fundamental difference between the Anglophone – British – view of the place of management accounting and the continental approach. In Britain management accounting is part of the accounting continuum, and members of CIMA regard themselves as accountants. On the continent companies have departments undertaking the operations that would be called management accountancy in Britain, but they do not see these operations as being called management accountancy, let alone being a part of accounting. Controllership is the word that is most commonly used to describe these tasks. Accounting, in the continental culture, relates to auditing and financial reporting; controllership is part of management. Indeed in Germany an accountant (i.e. auditor) would lose his practising licence if he left auditing to practise financial management, or management accounting in British terms. An important outcome of this is that while management accounting in Britain is the province of accountants, on the continent the work is carried out by a whole range of persons, from those trained in accounting techniques, to engineers, economists and business graduates. In Germany, in fact, costing is considered to have more in common with engineering than with accountancy.

These differences are reflected in the differences in financial culture between Britain, where the short-term pressures on companies are to demonstrate short-term results, and Germany, where there is much more an industrial view of the company, and the approach is a long-term one.

In a typical German company the financial culture would be to concentrate on the company rather than the shareholders, in that:

- Dividends are regarded as an expense.
- Growth and financial strength are more important than *reported* profit or EPS.
- Cash flow and gearing are key indices.
- Residual after tax income is what counts rather than profits before tax, because that is what finally finishes up in the company's 'pocket'.
- The emphasis is on building for the future and therefore on investing in technical strength in such matters as R & D, training, high tech, efficiency improvements, etc.
- Takeovers are very difficult and contested ones are virtually impossible. National pride is aroused where a foreign owned company is concerned. Readers may reflect on the chances of BAe, or any other foreign company, ever being allowed to take over BMW.
- Asset stripping is on a par with deindustrialization and is regarded as virtually obscene.

The tradition in Britain and the Anglophone world is that of the 'true and fair' view of the accounts according to standards set by powerful accounting bodies. This stewardship aspect focuses on the transparency of reporting on the same basis for all interested parties, from shareholders to the financial media. The German approach is very different. The public accounts are legal and correct according to the rules (which is not the same as true and fair). It is not so easy to compare these with the reported profits of UK public companies as, in general, they understate the profit. It is the management accounts that are true and fair. The objective here is not to maximize the profits at all costs so as to impress the shareholders and influence the share price, but to show the realistic picture to the company's business partners. The Germans dismiss the theory that speculative trading could direct capital in an economically desirable direction as a road leading straight to Polly Peck. Germany company accounts are not there to define some unattainable 'truth' but to achieve the more modest aim of fulfilling legal and fiscal obligations. The emphasis is on long term or 'core' shareholders, including the big banks most of all, and there is not seen to be anything wrong if these are given more up-to-date information than are other investors.

As a consequence of this, the Germans, like other continentals, are not so naive as to believe that the published accounts give the relevant details relating to a company. Only the real accounts, the management accounts, do this. British investors, on the other hand, appear to have a touching faith in published accounts, even though these are regulated by no governmental agencies, and they are genuinely surprised and concerned when self-regulation is found not to work and the accounts are proved defective and – at the extreme – fraudulent.

There are several implications when we compare the British with the Germanic tradition:

- Management thinking in Britain has become very dominated by public reporting, hence the whole 'accounting engineering' movement. The reported group figures, with their emphasis on stewardship drive the business unit ones. The impact of the Cadbury Committee's recommendation on corporate governance has given a further impetus to this trend in that management bonuses have to be publicly linked to the reported results.
- The outcome in Britain is that the publicly reported figures, with their backward-looking view, take precedence over the internal management ones; hence the high prestige of the chartered accountants.
- In Germany the internal and external figures have to reconcile of course, but it is the internal ones that really count. The objective in German companies is to balance technical goals (R & D, quality, technical superiority) with financial goals much more obviously than in British companies. This explains the German insistence on high technical qualifications, particularly in engineering.
- The German view is that controllership is not part of accounting, though linked to it, and therefore it can be much more forward-looking in German companies. Many of the figures quoted are not financial figures at all. In France there is a similar practice, and an important reporting concept is of a control panel of key indices, called the *tableau de bord*, to guide company managements.

Convergence

Attitudes, however, are changing. The continental multinationals contacted in the CIMA survey all insisted that their problems were global, and therefore their attitudes had to be global not purely continental European. The universality of cost pressures has become a great leveller, pushing even engineering-dominated companies such as Daimler-Benz and Volkswagen into taking a very financial approach to business, and to concentrate much more on the short term than ever before.

Anglophone financial concepts have become much more dominant than even a generation ago. The impact of business English (or rather, business American English!) in finance has become a powerful driver. It is the second language of Scandinavia and the Netherlands, and in business it is the language of banking and of treasury. The relentless advance of the English language goes hand in hand with that of the Anglophone reporting concepts, pushed hard by the major auditing firms. Even companies in Central and

Eastern Europe are beginning to realize the importance of having their accounts audited by one of the – inevitably Anglophone – major auditors. It is commonplace for international businesses to produce their reports in English in addition to their national language, and this also applies to many continental domestic companies such as the German department store groups Karstadt and Kaufhoff, even though they may be wholly domestic in their operations. Financial control and reporting manuals are produced in English, and senior members of control departments are expected to speak English as a matter of course. ABB reports its figures in $US.

The American influence has been a great driver. Global companies have enormous financing needs that can no longer be satisfied by the local German or Swiss markets, for instance. They have to go to New York as Daimler-Benz has recently had to do. Its experience is being anxiously watched by other German and Swiss companies needing to go to the US market for finance. They are dreading the tyranny (as they see it) of US reporting detail and the requirement for ever more figures. The price for American funding is the introduction of Anglophone accounting concepts such as quarterly reporting, greater transparency, and higher dividends based on short-term performance. One finds continental companies talking of shareholder value, a concept they have all but ignored until recently. They can ignore it no longer, faced as they are by vociferous US investors who have bought into continental companies and are reputed to have holdings of up to 20-25 per cent of such flagship companies as Deutsche Bank and Siemens. Many Swiss companies such as Nestlé have had no alternative but to swim with the tide and liberalize their shareholding rules.

Convergence works both ways however, and one notes the changes in British practice too. The grip of accountants on financial management is relaxing, though very slowly, and already there have been comments in the press on the number of non-accountants such as MBAs in posts as finance directors. It is recognized that best practice in controllership is to focus on the future, a trend that is emphasized by the new CIMA examination syllabus. Above all it has become very common practice for British companies to report non-financial data in their management information summaries. There is still a long way to go before convergence will become harmonization, if that indeed is desirable, but a start has been made.

People

It is all very well to talk of organization structures and methodologies when discussing control and controllership, but one must recognize the key importance of the human factor. Our discussions with companies inevitably started with culture and people. Three interesting aspects stand out:

- By far the largest number of companies we saw were run by a closely knit group who have worked with each other for a long time. This makes for a very powerful synergy. Thus the position of the finance director often results from his personal relationships with the chief executive and the top management team, as opposed to his nominal position on the organization chart. In many companies it is not uncommon for incoming CEOs to bring in their own finance directors, and for the FDs, in turn, to bring in the key members of their finance team.

- There is often a 'family' feeling about many continental companies, even the largest ones, in particular because of their policy of looking after and nurturing their employees. There is less need for detailed manuals because of the long-standing personal relationships: the controller of a Dutch chemical company explained it in this way: he knows their man in Brazil and trusts him because they have worked together for many years. The FD in Brazil would know exactly when to contact head office and about what, without being prompted by any manuals.

- Such a network of personal relationships between the senior people in finance makes for a very effective cooperation between a head office and the business units' finance staff, and it is often this informal network that enables a matrix organization to work properly.

Control comes down basically to people. It works if the management works properly. Perhaps the biggest change that the fast few years has seen is that financial managers have had to learn to be not just competent technicians, but good managers too. To add to the pressures, top managements are looking for the cost beneficial operation of all their service departments, including the control department. Many have reinforced this by the introduction of service agreements. As a service department, the finance/control department is under pressure from its 'customers' to give good value for money. It can only do this if it is managed well and effectively. Financial management is as much about management as it is about finance.

Looking back, finance directors can reflect that times have changed to an enormous degree and that financial management and control systems and philosophies have certainly moved a long way from the command and control, monitor and check management styles of only a couple of generations ago.

References

Allen, D (1994) *Strategic Financial Decisions*, Kogan Page, London.

Coates, J B *et al.* (1993) *Corporate Performance Evaluation in Multinationals*, CIMA, London.

Sheridan, T J (1993) *Management Accounting in Continental Multinational Enterprises*, CIMA, London.

11

Strategic evaluation: a multi-competency approach
Bill Richardson and John Thompson

Introduction: towards a new view of strategic evaluation

How do we evaluate the strategic effectiveness of an organization? What measurement criteria should we be using?

One popular and important approach is an evaluation of individual strategies, both existing and proposed. Johnson and Scholes (1993) adopt the criteria: suitability; feasibility; acceptability. Thompson (1993) uses similar categories: appropriateness, feasibility, desirability. This approach implies that there are discrete decision points where evaluations can be made. Clearly there are such points and moments, but, as Chapter 4 by Bailey and Johnson earlier in this handbook shows, major strategic change decisions do not provide us with a full explanation of how strategies are created and changed in practice.

Most writers on strategy also make the important distinction between measuring efficiencies ('doing things right') and effectiveness ('doing the right things' and meetings the needs and expectations of stakeholders). Efficiency measures focus on resource management and tend to be quantitative in nature. Effectiveness measures relate to perceived outcomes, not only from a financial viewpoint, but also from the point of view of stakeholders; in the latter case, they are inevitably more subjective.

Kaplan and Norton (1992) suggest that organizations should focus their efforts on a limited number of specific, critical performance measures that reflect stakeholders' key success factors. In this way managers can readily concentrate on those issues essential for corporate and competitive success.

Kaplan and Norton use the term 'balanced scorecard' to describe a framework of four groups of measures, amd argue that organizations should select critical measures for each one of these areas. The four groups, and examples of possible measures, are:

- *Financial* Return on capital employed. Cash flow.
- *Customers* Perceived value for money. Competitive prices.
- *Internal processes* Enquiry response time. Enquiry order conversion rate.
- *Growth and improvement* Number of new products/services. Extent of employee empowerment.

It can be seen that these measures encapsulate both efficiency and effectiveness.

Figure 11.1, from Thompson (1993), illustrates that effective strategic management implies an ability on the part of the organization to create a productive congruence between the nature and demands of the Environment, the organization's Values (the dominant beliefs the organization holds about its role and position in its markets and the way organization personnel should behave), and its Resource base (the resources it has at its disposal, the ways in which it uses these resources, including the skills it employs in adapting to and creating its environments). E-V-R congruence implies that if we are to measure strategic effectiveness successfully, we must also take some account of culture and values.

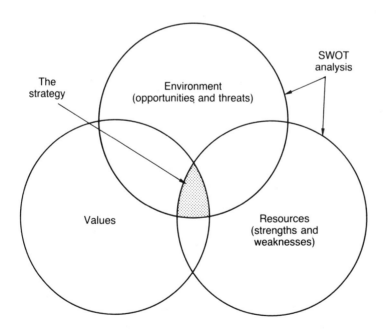

Figure 11.1   *E–V–R congruence*

This chapter takes and develops the above contentions. Before we expand our argument, however, it is useful to consider the following commentary from a manager working in the dynamic 1990s:

In general, competition is increasing and the environment for our business (itself part of a conglomerate) is becoming more unstable.

Globalization and leglislation which is helping to remove market entry barriers have combined with new technology to change the rules of competition in the industry. In recent years, too, demand for our service has levelled off as consumer attitudes have changed.

In this context our basic competitive strategy is not only to differentiate by adding value but to do so with a reducing (or at least a stable) price. Our twin focus on providing high value services whilst continuously driving down costs helps our customers (like us, manufacturers) to gain advantage in their arena. It is simple: if they win then we also win.

Strategy is very much about doing whatever is necessary to maintain our acknowledged position of market leader. Our depth of marketing expertise gives us a distinctive competence. A powerful marketing data base enables us to assist customers in the promotion of their particular programmes and to build very close relationships with them.

The group as a whole is emphasizing *continuous* productivity improvements for all its businesses. Reductions have been achieved through rationalizations and increasingly sophisticated use of technology.

My assessment of our structure is that it is still a bureaucracy but it is in the process of transforming itself and becoming more adhocratic. This is involving a proliferation of project groups for integrating tasks which cross departmental boundaries. As a result of the automation of many of the basic administration and some operational tasks (a continuing process), those tasks which remain are more complex and require mutual adjustment between people working on them. However, there are still significant elements of the organization which carry out routine, formal work. Consequently, the structure does not categorize neatly into either bureaucracy or adhocracy.

Thinking again about our strategies, the picture is complex. We are 'prospectors' in so far as we keep seeking out new market opportunities from a flexible organization structure, but at the same time we also act as 'defenders'. We look to enhance our technological efficiency and focus on an important niche in the market.

The corporate centre controls us through a system of ratios, both financial and non-financial (the latter including, for example, the ratio of managers to front line workers). Simple measures like this create very powerful means of ensuring that overall organizational goals – such as the empowerment of front line staff and the de-layering of management – are taken very seriously by the individual business units. The target figures for each unit are agreed by negotiation. Within our unit, the most obvious control mechanism at work is the budgetary process.

Within this controlled framework, and the push for productivity, the corporation is attempting to create business units where speed, flexibility and innovation are key values. These values are at the heart of our corporate culture and pervade our strategy making processes. The culture which is being created is a very questioning one and this is crucial for ensuring that the strategies which emerge are the ones which adequately reflect the changes in the environment – such that strategic drift does not develop.

The chief executive has said that he aims for an 'open' organization, where everyone has access to the same information and everyone pulls in the same direction. Quality circles, team briefings, weekly telephone conferences and 'best practice' teams are our attempt to share out information on best practice in the group. They are also key ingredients in the attempt to cut across and break down boundaries.

Although the aim is to involve the whole organization, the parent company has established constraints which define the context in which these processes take place. 'Umbrella' strategies are planned by the parent company in consultation with our unit strategists. Within these ground rules the processes are geared towards letting strategy emerge both from changes in the environment and, more particularly, from within the organization. It assumes that people have many good ideas which, given the right mechanisms for drawing them out, will optimize the performance of the company.

The overall direction of strategy is clear but the participative approach leads to it developing incrementally.

On balance, I believe we are well positioned to maintain our market leadership position as long as we remain vigilant and look to be amongst the leaders if there are any major and discontinuous changes in the industry.

These comments reinforce the argument that many strategies *emerge* as organizations learn and adjust in a dynamic, turbulent, competitive and possibly chaotic environment, and that a range of competencies, only one of which relates to choosing successful new product-market strategies, is required for successful, on-going strategic development.

The process of strategic change is sometimes gradual and experimental, but on other occasions more dramatic changes to products and services create discontinuous change attempts in order to establish new rules of competition ahead of rivals. Such dramatic changes require insight, imply risk and again demand a multi-competency approach. Objective appraisal of the implications and outcomes may not be possible at the beginning. Critical for managing strategic change therefore is an organization that is capable of learning, adapting and changing – fast.

This chapter takes the view that an organization is a system of strategic development, and that from this perspective strategic evaluation needs to become a process of identifying, measuring and improving critical organizational competencies. It is clearly more complex than the process associated with a one-point-in-time decision concerning product-market changes. Given this more holistic viewpoint, a primary task for the strategic leader is continuously to measure and seek to improve the organization as a multi-competency system.

The nature and demands of modern business environments

Environmental determinism is a label given to a school of management theorists who see the forces in the environment around organizations as the drivers of organizational change and the adoption of new strategies. The basic assumption of this school is summed up in the words of Lawrence: 'Tell me what your environment is and I shall tell you what your organization ought to be' in *Agyris*, 1972, p. 88).

The nature of modern business environments is characterized by the following traits and trends, which call for associated organizational competencies.

Bigger than they used to be

It is clear that businesses now compete in a global setting. Multinational organizations operate worldwide and the links in this global environment mean that even small, local organizations are connected to or influenced by aspects of the worldwide network. This type of environment inevitably increases the need for enhanced organizational competencies in environmental understanding and for awareness of the changes taking place. This awareness will (*a*) underpin suitable anticipatory responses by the organization, (*b*) help facilitate the motivation and control of the people in the organization who are often geographically distant from head office, and (*c*) support the creation and management of strategic collaborations with, for example, suppliers, customers and governmental bodies who understand foreign markets, provide 'passports' to entry therein or provide vital shared resources or supplementary skills.

In the face of these pressures, organizations need to be skilful in (i) *empowering staff* at all levels to work with motivation and discretion for the organization and (ii) *creating productive strategic alliances and learning communities* that lead to important new products, projects, processes and services.

More diverse than they used to be

Enlarged and interlinked global networks introduce more variables on to the strategic development agenda of modern organizations. This emphasizes even more the need for skills in developing 'helicopter vision' and management systems that motivate personnel to look after their parts of the complex network and to communicate both upwards and laterally the important strategic information coming to their notice at the periphery.

Complex, interactive networks are also the birthplaces of 'wild-swing' crises, and so our naturally diverse, complex and interactive environments of the 1990s require organizational competencies in the functions of *crisis avoidance, contingency planning* and *crisis management.*

In addition organizations need to be highly competent in (i) *strategic analysis*, which provides insight into strategic situations and choice about the ways in which resources, culture and/or environment need to change to ensure successful progression, (ii) *empowered, fast and effective communications,* and ideally, because organizations can damage lives as well as enhance them, (iii) *management based on a considered approach to business ethics.*

Changing more quickly than in the past

Although specific periods in our history have witnessed greater upheaval and traumatic change (as, for example, with the onset of the Second World War), the underlying dynamism of change in the business world is accelerating. When things change fast, communication systems need to improve and more discretion has to be given to (preferably) committed-to-the-organization personnel, who are required to spot, monitor and develop *their own* solutions to the challenges arising, from within their own networks of contacts and colleagues. Such solutions, ideally, should contribute to the achievement of a viable, overriding vision of where the organization is heading – another aspect of modern organization that demands competence in its leaders. In quickly changing and hostile environmental situations a further requirement is that leaders should be open to challenges from parts of the organization which have noticed that the vision is no longer an appropriate – or the most appropriate – way forward, or where it is constraining useful innovatory developments.

Thus, the modern organization needs to be highly competent at (i) *empowering personnel* (again), (ii) *listening* to the concerns of (and perhaps challenges from) its various stakeholders, (iii) *envisioning successful futures*, (iv) *pragmatically developing the vision*, and (v) *changing course* if necessary.

More powerful and threatening than they used to be

In a complex, interactive world there is a natural tendency for parts of the system to experience crises. A change in one part of such a system ricochets through the system, often in a seemingly random and unpredictable way, to impact adversely in another part. For example, a sudden political change in a foreign country may create new export restrictions that significantly affect the small supplier of a bigger supplier to a customer in that foreign country.

Quite apart from this chaos-related hostile characteristic of modern environments, the relationship between UK organizations and parties external to them has tended to change over the past 40 years or so. In general, environmental players seem to have more bargaining strength and so modern organizations need to be increasingly adept at monitoring changing power positions and ensuring the organization has an on-going capability to attract critical resources from suppliers, shareholders, financiers, personnel and customers.

The modern organization needs constantly to improve its competencies in (i) *staying close to the aspirations of powerful stakeholders* and changing organizational activity to meet their new demands as they arise, (ii) *monitoring changing power situations*, so that the organization can respond in a timely manner, (iii) *devising political strategies*, and (iv) *being responsive and adaptive*.

More competitive than they used to be

In this dynamic, turbulent environment the UK has ceased to be the engine room of the world and its dominant supplier of goods and services. Free market governmental policies and the aspirations of new competitors have created a situation where more competitors now provide more choice for customers and constantly seek to gain competitive advantage through innovating new processes, products and services and/or through reducing costs of production. Thus, organizations need to improve their competitive, innovative, productive, quality and customer responsiveness competencies. Where service is a crucial aspect of customer satisfaction, it is essential for staff to also have high levels of service skills. Competitive environments worldwide give rise to opportunities to move into new marketplaces and the necessity of moving out of old ones. Thus, another key competency of the modern organization is one that helps it to understand the need for such changes and enables it to discover, create and develop into new areas of market opportunity and to leave markets that are no longer attractive.

To summarize, intensifying competition implies the need for competencies in (i) *understanding competitive situations* and devising strategies for competitive advantage, (ii) *working closely with customers*, (iii) reducing cost bases and/or adding value and (iv) *target setting and performance ratio improvement*. High levels of competition lead to significant changes in marketplaces, reinforcing the need for additional ability in (v) *making effective choices about when to leave marketplaces and about which new ones to move into*, and (vi) *being innovative* in order to get ahead of the competitive race, or at least to stay in it.

Resources are more limited and more life-threateningly polluted than they used to be

The green movement reminds us that the earth's natural resources are being exploited and damaged to dangerous levels. Organizations have an ethical duty to mankind to improve their resource management in order to reverse their damage to the ecosystem and safeguard the earth for its future inhabitants. This environmental characteristic combines with the competitive one referred to above, to reinforce the need for a competence in continually improving productivity while remaining friendly to the needs of the ecosystem. It also calls into question the organization's socially responsible competence and tests the managerial ethic itself – the very ethic upon which the modern organization is built. This movement requires organizational personnel, and especially organization leaders, to consider their own deep-seated beliefs and personal ethical systems, to seek out wider views about what organizations should be and do, and accede to some extent, at least, to the demands of these pressure groups – *if only because 'it now pays to be good'*.

Thus the modern organization needs to be (i) '*greener*', more environmentally responsive and more productive in its resource usage, (ii) *less selfish and inward-looking* and paradoxically, given most of what we have said earlier about the need for enhanced competitive competency – (iii) *less competitive but, rather, more collaborative and caring*.

These environmental trends, which demand a multi-competency approach, are illustrated in Table 11.1. Readers might wish to use this as a simple evaluator of the nature of the environment in which their organizations operate and for stimulating thought about the extent to which their environments are changing.

It should be apparent that this chapter is based on the assumption that environments in general are moving towards a situation where they are more difficult to manage.

Table 11.1   Nature of the environment

Small and local	1 2 3 4 5 6 7 8 9 10	Big and global
Simple and singular	1 2 3 4 5 6 7 8 9 10	Diverse and interconnected
Slow and Sleepy	1 2 3 4 5 6 7 8 9 10	Quick and volatile
Weak and amenable	1 2 3 4 5 6 7 8 9 10	Strong and demanding
Protected and friendly	1 2 3 4 5 6 7 8 9 10	Competitive and Hostile
Safe and/or uninformed	1 2 3 4 5 6 7 8 9 10	Damaging and/or green-conscious

Generic environments, generic competencies, and key tasks for strategic leaders and information system designers

The authors have concluded that the above environmental developments can be amalgamated into a generic environment that affects almost all our organizations, be they big or small; private or public; industrial, professional, commercial or retail; profit-driven or not for profit.

In Table 11.2 we have listed thirty critical strategic competencies in eight discrete sections. Figure 11.2 illustrates these competency groups and highlights how strategic leadership will ideally bind them into a cohesive whole. The strategic leader is the primary architect and custodian of the organizational system, and a key question for all leaders is 'How does my organization score in terms of its competencies for meeting these strategic challenges?' Managers might also like to use Table 11.2 as a checklist against which to evaluate the strategic effectiveness of their own organization, both generally and in specific competency areas.

The hypothetically super-equipped organization, wholly prepared for today's business situation, would score 'ten-out-of-ten' when evaluated in each of the competency areas. The question that needs to be asked and

Figure 11.2 *Strategic effectiveness*

answered (thirty times) is 'How effectively does my organization perform in this competency area?' Of course the sensible strategist would seek confirmation from other sources and measurement systems of the reliability of any personal or subjectively derived scores.

Thus, key tasks for every leader include those of measuring the level of performance achieved presently in each competency area and of implementing action to improve the existing levels of performance. Given the increasingly dynamic and turbulent nature of the generic environment we have described, performance monitoring needs to be a regular activity. The task of competency measurement raises many implications for information system designers, not least because, traditionally, many of these experts have been preoccupied with the creation of financial performance indicators and their related information systems.

Although it might make sense for evaluation and attention to be paid first to those competencies that are most clearly perceived to underpin the organization's financial and competitive success, it must be emphasized that each competency is important. Resource factors that give rise to competitive advantage, for example, need to be supplemented by a cultural and ethical base that accepts both the need for challenge and change and the right of others to have their say and their place. Without this, the present-success drivers are likely to become outdated and lose potency without anyone in the organization noticing or taking remedial action at an appropriate time. Simply, each of the competencies needs to be evaluated and then action taken as necessary.

Table 11.2   Strategic effectiveness evaluation

Thirty critical strategic problems and related
organizational competency need areas

Strategic awareness and control
1   Ability to think strategically.
2   Ability to maintain an awareness of environmental changes and their implications.
3   Ability to design and operationalize a 'fitting' organization – one whose structures and systems match its environment(s) and stay matched in a changing environment.
4   Ability to avoid the trap of self-enacted reality (whereby the organization drifts into problems because it has an unrealistic view of its position) and to reach more objectively, environmentally aware, informed decisions.

Stakeholder satisfaction
5   Ability to understand and manage the organization as a stakeholder (political) interaction, and goal-setting/attaining system.
6   Ability to diagnose organizational strategic standing, core competencies and strategic abilities – its strength in its marketplace (s), its resource strengths and weaknesses, and the opportunities and threats in its present and future environments.

Competitive strategy
7   Ability to understand competitive situations and to choose where and how to compete.
8   Ability to get closer to the customer – to understand, attract and satisfy him/her better than competitors by adding value more effectively.
9   Ability to choose winning product/market developments.

Strategy implementation
10   Ability to organize for operationalizing and implementing strategy.
11   Ability to create, share and implement a winning vision.
12   Ability to 'commit' and empower organizational personnel and motivate them towards continuous organizational improvement.
13   Ability to foster internally generated synergy through cooperation and sharing.
14   Ability to collaborate in strategic alliances for competitive advantage.

Quality and customer care

15 Ability to provide excellent quality as perceived by the customer.

16 Ability to achieve states of greater organizational productivity, continuously.

17 Ability to 'invoke' a creative, innovative and self-organizing organization climate and state.

Functional competencies

18 Ability to utilize research and development to help create a future for the business.

19 Ability to develop new products and services and bring them to market both effectively and in the appropriate timescale.

20 Ability to reach and satisfy customers with effective distribution of products and services nationally and/or internationally.

21 Ability to harness the potential of information technology for fast, efficient and effective processing and sharing of information.

22 Ability to maintain financial control of the business and access capital for future investment programmes.

Failure and crisis avoidance

23 Ability to avoid business-failure situations.

24 Ability to plan for when things go wrong.

25 Ability to avoid socio-technical (life-threatening) disasters.

26 Ability to manage business-failure turnaround situations.

27 Ability to manage socio-technical disaster situations.

Ethics and social responsibility

28 Ability to manage 'green issues'.

29 Ability to manage socially responsibly.

30 Ability to become more ethically aware and to manage with an ethical underpinning.

A dilemma: can strategy theory support this multi-competency approach to strategic leadership?

There are well-documented theories of management strategy, incorporating a number of branches (see, for example, Mintzberg, 1973 and Richardson, 1994), which highlight the need for particular competencies and also provide benchmarking material against which leaders might measure their own organizational performances. Some of the theorists prescribe or describe, explicitly or implicitly, the organizational characteristics commensurate with high performance in particular competency areas. The features of a 'quality organization' (Deming, 1986), a 'competitive organization' (inferred in Porter's work, 1990, 1985), and an 'excellent organization' (Peters and Waterman Jr, 1982), for example, have all been documented. These branches of theory also contain helpful information on how present performance levels in the critical competency areas might be improved.

The next section of this chapter explores how these different branches of management literature might be helpful for evaluating and improving strategic competencies. What follows is a brief resumé of the branches of strategic management and the nature of the strategic competencies upon which each focuses.

Strategic management and competencies

The classical administrator

The 'classical administrator' is the most traditional of our twentieth-century models of the leader. Henri Fayol (1949) is recognized as a founding father of the 'classical school' of management. Working and writing in the early years of the twentieth century, Fayol derived a set of common activities and principles of management.

For example, he divided general management activities into five elements: planning, organizing, commanding, coordinating and controlling. *Planning* looks at the future, deciding what needs to be achieved and developing a plan of action. *Organizing* provides the material and human resources and creates the organizational structure to carry out the activities of the organization. *Commanding* maintains appropriate activity among personnel and achieves the optimum return from all employees in the interests of the whole organization. *Coordinating* is aimed at unifying and harmonizing the activities and effort of the organization to facilitate its successful operation. *Control* activity verifies that everything is occurring in accordance with plans, instructions, established principles and expressed commands.

The classical administrator therefore is clearly most concerned to achieve progress through carefully planning how order inside his/her organization might be established and maintained.

Fayol's work has been mirrored by other theorists and practitioners. Frederick Taylor (1948), who introduced a 'scientific management' approach to the planning, organizing, commanding, motivating and monitoring of production department work, might be viewed as a production-centred classical administrator. Peter Drucker (1968), considered by many to be the father of modern-day management theory, might also be categorized as a 'strategic administrator'. His starting point was the externally oriented product-market strategies of the organization but, thereafter, in traditional classical-administrator mode, he prescribed the use of an internally oriented 'management by objectives' system, which systematically plans individual employee performance improvements, and motivates, monitors and controls these performances.

Thus, the classical administrator theory base provides help for those who wish to measure and improve internal competencies in organizations that typically feature 'top-down' planning and control, formal target-setting and measurement, programmes for functional improvements through 'scientific' engineering, productivity ratio improvement and a formal organization structure.

The design school planner (DSP)

Kenneth Andrews of Harward Business School has been given credit as a primary architect of the 'design' school of strategic management, along with Alfred Chandler (1962) and Igor Ansoff (1965). They emphasize the leader's role as that of the primary planner of the medium-to-the-long-term development of the organization. This DSP leader designs strategic developments by formulating strategy in a controlled and conscious process of thought. He/she is the leader who attempts to create success by asking and answering the questions: 'Where are we now?', 'Where do we want to be?, and, 'How we are going to get there?' in a process of systematic business planning. The design school planner therefore is an expert at anticipating, with the help of analytical techniques, what future business environments are going to be like, and at devising appropriate product-market strategies that fit productively (economically speaking) with the environmental opportunities and threats facing the organization and its resource strengths and weaknesses. Having planned strategy, the DSP leader then uses the techniques of his classical-administrator forerunners to plan its implementation by subordinates who are expected to work to a blueprint of key tasks and budget-controlled activities.

The design school of strategy helps us to measure and improve organizational competencies for developing 'helicopter vision', choosing appropriate product-market developments, anticipating future scenarios, and generating and writing formal business plans and associated contingency plans – plans for things that might go wrong.

The role-playing manager

Henry Mintzberg challenged the models of the classical and design theorists, arguing they make unrealistic representations of how leadership and organization development actually occurs. He carried out empirical work into the 'real' nature of managers' jobs (Mintzberg, 1973).

Mintzberg therefore was an early advocate of the need to *prescribe through description* to observe the reality of strategy in action and to report this reality and its implications for leadership – rather than to *prescribe by design*. He suggested that not only were the latter approaches unrepresentative of what actually happens in organizations, but also they might not necessarily be the best way of managing strategic change.

Mintzberg thus took a founding-father position for a growing body of theory which portrays the manager's job as being much bigger than that of the 'reflective-calculating-planner-controller'. Mintzberg's findings, for example, produced ten leadership roles – the 'figurehead', 'leader', 'liaison', 'monitor', 'disseminator', 'spokesman', 'entrepreneurial', 'disturbance-handler', 'resource-allocator' and 'negotiator' roles.

Further, these roles are carried out in a continuous and less rational way than is implied by the earlier schools of thought. This view of the strategic development process has been extended by Quinn (1980).

This school of thought emphasizes the leader's attention to learning-by-doing decision processes, a system of strategic development where strategies *emerge* in the context of political and social interactions rather than from deliberate and systematic planning systems. It provides help for those of us who wish to improve our organization's capabilities in political activities such as negotiating and building supportive social networks for the incremental development of strategic ideas and projects.

The political contingency responder (PCR)

A more externally oriented and strategic view of leadership is provided by theorists such as Freeman (1984), Mintzberg (1983), and Pfeffer and Salancik (1978), who emphasize total organizational development rather than more narrow and discrete administrative or operational issues. From this PCR perspective the strategic leader's main tasks are to monitor his/her internal and external environments, to recognize the critical strategic issues (those issues with the potential to affect the security and development of the organization) that are emerging, and to change the organization to meet the challenges as they arise.

For Pfeffer and Salancik (1978), for example, the key skill of the political contingency responder is one of discerning and acting on an *appropriate reality* – one that acknowledges the need to satisfy the aspirations of those parties (as they emerge) who have control over the supply of a critical organizational resource. Too often, they argue, organizations fail to react to changes that create new power balances. Rather they continue to accept, unthinkingly, the continuing importance of traditionally important stakeholders.

This, then, is a power-based perspective of leadership, and the political-contingency leader needs to be an adept power structure analyst. In this view of strategic management the crucial issues for organizations owe their criticality to the existence of stakeholders (customers, governments, suppliers, for example) or other variables (such as environmental variables in the ecosystem) which have the power to threaten organizational survival and which might be disposed to use this power against the organization if appropriate organizational responses are not made. Having performed his/her stakeholder-power analysis the political-contingency leader then requires expertise as a political bargaining strategy designer and manager. He/she aims to become an 'orchestrator' of stakeholder activity (Drucker, 1988).

The PCR theory base therefore provides insights for building additional competencies in stakeholder (power) analysis; awareness of changing environmental circumstances, including political, economic, social, technological and *ecological* changes; the design of political bargaining strategies; and, fundamentally, in challenging any blind acceptance that the organization occupies an enduringly safe place in its environment.

The competitive positioner

The competitive positioner subscribes to the environmental determinism school but focuses almost exclusively on the task of achieving competitive advantage (market power that produces above average profits) in a marketplace where *the* critical contingency is competition. The primary proponent of this view of strategic leadership has been Harvard professor Michael Porter whose books 'Competitive Strategy' (1980), 'Competitive Advantage' (1985) and 'The Competitive Advantage of Nations' (1990) have been extremely influential in shaping the thoughts and activities of management theorists and practitioners. Much attention has been paid over the past decade or so to the question of how an organization can create a better than average wealth-producing position in competitive marketplaces. This attention has, of itself, fuelled and intensified competition.

The competitive positioner's main tasks are to decide where his/her organization is to compete, and then to align his/her organization against other marketplace forces in a way that gains advantage over them. Competitive advantage is assumed to lead to above-average industry profitability.

Competitive forces at work in marketplaces include customers, suppliers, and, very importantly, substitute products and services, as well as traditionally acknowledged present and potential competitors. Our future competitors may not be those we recognize today; the newcomers may well enter by changing the rules of competition in the industry. Successful alignment against these forces depends upon the competitive positioner's ability to create a successful competitive strategy – organizational activity that erects barriers to entry into its marketplaces, attracts price premiums for its goods and services or reduces costs of operation below those of its competitors.

It follows that the theory base here is particularly appropriate for helping to improve competitive competencies, abilities that underpin effective industry analysis, the choice of winning competitive strategies (where and how to compete) and the implementation of functional strategies that successfully operationalize the competitive grand plan. This school's emphasis on least cost and/or differentiated market positions also assists in issues concerning customer (and other important stakeholder) satisfactions, and the achievement of higher levels of quality and productivity.

The visionary transformer

During the 1980s, fuelled by the works of writers such as Peters and Waterman Jr (1982) and Deal and Kennedy (1982), the visionary transformer rose to prominence as a leader for the present age. The theorists who promote this view of leadership describe and prescribe a process of 'vision management', which requires leaders to decide:

- Where the organization should be – in terms of strategic market positioning. The visionary leader takes his/her organization into market positions of greater growth and profitability than has been the tradition for his/her organization or the norm for the industry in which it has operated.
- How the organization should be – in terms of market image, the especially attractive features of its customer interaction strategy; its role in society and how it will be a particularly attractive place in which to work and with which to interact with. The visionary leader 'redefines the mundane', e.g. to make his/her organization's customer interaction strategy competitively attractive even in commodity markets
- What should be the central thrust (and text if it is to be written down) of the organization's mission. The mission conveys to all personnel the central intent behind the 'wheres' and the 'hows' of the organization and the core goals and values to which all personnel should commit themselves.
- How to reorganize the entire organization so that each component part of it – and the organization in its entirety – acts in harmony to live the mission. This requires, in particular, the ability of the leader to empower the personnel of the organization and to imbue them with the commitment and the emotional and physical resource backing required to enable them to work with discretion towards the realization of the organization's goals.

Success in achieving 'vision living' therefore depends on the ability of the 'transformational' leader to (i) envision a successful future (ii) design and manage an appropriate organization and (iii) utilize a range of 'vision *implementation* leadership qualities' (which include high levels of motivation, dogged determination, an enormous capacity for hard work, exceptional communicative skills and the ability to perform as a role model for others to emulate).

This, then, is the theory base that provides particular help for practitioners who wish to measure and improve their own visionary leadership skills in the above areas. It also contains help for those who wish to develop an understanding that will lead to practical improvements in their networking skills; a visionary is adept at making useful contacts and gaining the support of people for his or her projects.

In some ways the visionary transformer illustrates similarities with the design planner, and a competitive strategist with the skills of the competitive positioner. He/she differs from these earlier leader-types, however, in a number of crucial ways:

1   Much of his/her strategic thinking is done covertly rather than in the context of a formal planning process, which makes visionary planning skills difficult to explain or transfer.

2   He/she brings passion and emotional values to the process of strategic development – in contrast to the colder, more calculating, cognitively rational, economically biased, design and competitive planner leaders.

3   He/she is a supreme (and interested and caring) shaper of the organization culture, in contrast to his/her economically rational, and dispassionate, predecessors, who plan and position and then, in a very formal way, pass on delegated activity.

4   The visionary transformer is as much concerned with the implementation of strategic developments as he/she is with their creation.

5   He/she depends much more on personal charisma, empathic understanding and the development of a people- (as well as task-) centred approach to leadership in order to motivate (empower) subordinates to commit themselves to the achievement of his/her preferred organizational goals. This again contrasts with the more mechanistic, directive, impersonal, planned approach to the implementation of strategy charac-teristic of the design planner and the competitive positioner.

6   The visionary transformer adopts a more pragmatic approach to strategy development than does the design planner or the competitive positioner. Although his/her central vision for organizational success remains intact, the route to its achievement is through flexible, incremental and emergent activity, through listening, acting and learning rather than through blueprint plans or 'fixed' organizational approaches.

The literature on the visionary transformer leader also provides lessons about the dangers of self-enacted reality and offers insight into how to avoid this problem. It contains many case illustrations of successful leaders who have become arrogant, over-confident and/or complacent, and whose organizations lose their strong market positions as a consequence. In this way, too, the visionary literature raises ethical isssues and warns of the dangers of very selfish and introverted approaches to life.

The self-organizing facilitator

As the environments around organizations are perceived to become increasingly turbulent and full of surprises (Ansoff, 1984; Peters, 1991), theorists are also emphasizing the need for 'self-organizing, learning' types of organizations (see, for example, Stacey, 1993). Such organizations need to be designed and led by self-organizing facilitators.

Here, the major skill of the organization leader is as an organization designer. This leader is required to create an organization in which its parts (and, first and foremost, its *people*) continually 'self-organize' around emerging strategic issues to develop the organization in a fluid way. In this type of organization, too, the accepted recipes about what it should do and how it should do it are constantly challenged and, if necessary, 'unlearned' (Pedler *et al.*, 1990).

This leader is highly competent at facilitating and taking a role in 'learning communities' – networks of personnel who work together in the absence of traditional command-leadership positions and processes for creating successful innovation. Thus, the literature relating to the learning organization facilitator is particularly appropriate for those who seek to improve their capabilities for innovation, interpreting weak environmental signals, and collaborating – competencies that are particularly appropriate for environments that are difficult to control and changing quickly. It also provides help for those leaders who seek to empower rank-and-file personnel to work for the organization despite the absence of traditional positional power or reward and control systems. This body of theory, too, is useful for leaders who seek to improve their understanding of the more covert ways in which subcultures emerge and develop to influence organizational activity for better *or worse*.

The turnaround strategist

The turnaround strategist is a leader who comes to the fore when it is decided to reorient and 'turnaround' the performance of an organization in decline.

Often the visionary transformer is portrayed as a turnaround strategist –

when he/she is called to practise his/her transforming skills following the removal of a non-visionary leader who has been blamed for the decline. An altogether more autocratic, ruthless and swift-to-act leader is called in to *save*, under crisis conditions, an organization in imminent danger of collapse.

This type of leader rises to prominence when others have failed. He received special attention in the 1980s from theorists such as Slatter (1984) and Grinyer *et al.* (1989). The particular prevalence of business failure turnaround situations in the first half of the 1990s, however, allows him/her a continuing and important role.

The theory base helps in the development of personal skills for implementing new control systems quickly and for the championing of strategic changes to 'sharpbend' (Grinyer *et al.*, 1988) organizational performance.

The crisis avoider

The late 1980s heralded the era of 'a world turned upside-down' (Peters, 1988) and paved the way for the crisis avoider leader. Smith (1990) notes an increasingly crisis-ridden and disaster-prone organizational and societal scenario, and calls for leadership activity aimed at reducing the extent to which organizations and society are crisis-prone.

Central to the model of the crisis avoider leader is the possession by him/her of a belief system that is neither too exclusively introverted and selfish nor too extroverted and generous. The crisis avoider utilizes 'double-sided' belief systems, which are reflected in an array of 'hard' and 'soft' organizational systems and behaviours. This leader acknowledges the *likelihood* of crises and so introduces organizational systems that reflect an understanding that crises and disasters are part and parcel of modern business life. The crisis avoider leader creates an organization which continuously tests how crisis-prone it is, and selects systems and staff for the effective management of any crises that do impact on the organization.

This type of leader, too, is concerned about his/her organization's impact on the ecosystem, he/she working from the positions of both crisis responder and crisis causer. He/she also brings ethical considerations to the fore of strategic decision-making with a greater cogency than is the case with any previous leaders and is beginning to challenge our traditional economic approach to strategic decision-making.

This type of leader therefore is served by a theory base that implies the need for 'double-loop learning', with the challenging and overturning of our dominant belief and ethical system. More than any other branch of theory this one expounds the need to develop competency in listening – to the concerns and aspirations of others.

The strategic leaders discussed above are listed chronologically in Table 11.3, which, incidentally, indicates an on-going relevance for *each* of the leadership styles and the associated skills. The chronological display does not infer a discrete, step-like progression in which as one style and associated repertoire of skills becomes pertinent, previous ones are discarded.

These leader types, and the theory bases focusing on them, provide help for developing an understanding about why particular competencies are desirable, how specific organizational competency levels might be assessed and how improved competency might be developed.

Table 11.3   Strategic leadership types in chronological sequence

	(*Years approximate*)
THE CLASSICAL ADMINISTRATOR	1910 →
THE DESIGN SCHOOL PLANNER	1965 →
THE ROLE-PLAYING MANAGER	1975 →
THE POLITICAL CONTINGENCY RESPONDER	1980 →
THE COMPETITIVE POSITIONER	1982 →
THE VISIONARY TRANSFORMER	1985 →
THE SELF-ORGANIZING FACILITATOR	1990 →
THE TURNAROUND STRATEGIST	1992 → new emphasis
THE CRISIS AVOIDER	1992 →

The sequence is based upon when each type individually gained general acceptance as a theoretical force.

We have concluded that if organizations are to meet all the strategic challenges of the 1990s, the *ideal* leadership contribution is a complex mix of styles. Leaders could usefully reflect on the appropriateness of their current styles in the light of how good their organization is at meeting the demands placed on it by the environment.

Conclusion

Establishing and maintaining the necessary competencies to achieve and sustain strategic success is, we believe, the central challenge for strategic leaders today. We recognize that individual strategic leaders will have preferred styles of management and that their own expertise in particular areas of competency is likely to be reflected in the organization's skill base. The natural tendency in organizations is for particular competencies to be emphasized at the expense of others. As we have indicated, however, the generic environment of the second half of the 1990s is one that will increasingly demand all-round, high-level competency. An associated leadership challenge therefore is that of widening and deepening existing approaches to strategic development to make sure that *the organization* as a whole is well-equipped with all the styles, structures and competencies needed.

Most organizations will be able to find opportunities for strengthening individual competencies and all-round strategic capability. For some the task might be one of incremental adjustment and continuous improvement. For others, however, possibly those that presently score low across most or all of the competencies (and that are therefore presently in, or close to, business failure or crisis), the challenge will be greater and, if faced, will mean changing strategies, structure, management styles – and competency levels – simultaneously, significantly and urgently.

The message emanating from modern business environments is clear. Modern organizational success is to be earned through effective performances across the range of required modern competencies. The theory of management strategy, in its breadth and depth, provides a rich source of help for those leaders who take up the challenge of evaluating and improving their organization's comprehensive strategic competency.

The following comments from Heller (1994) summarize the challenge:

> The roles of chairman, the chief executive, the board, the executive management – all these have to change before any other changes are possible . . .
>
> Everybody knows about the manager of the future. Every guru has been painting much the same portrait for years. Whether the path to the vision leads through quality, or business process-engineering, or modern manufacturing or the search for competitive advantage, or leadership . . . the final picture remains the same: an undeniable formula for 21st century success.
>
> Manager 2000 will practise co-operation and collaboration with everybody, inside and outside the firm, from colleagues and subordinates to customers and suppliers. He/she will be a tolerant teamworker, tolerant of different and new ideas, forgiving of errors made in the cause of progress, putting the objectives of the team above the ambitions of the person. The environment will encourage this by devolution of power and delegation of duties – right down to the empowered, self-managing worker near the top of the inverted pyramid.
>
> The inversion of the traditional hierarchy places top management at the base and the customer at the summit. For the management process will be geared to the non-stop search for competitive advantage . . . it's the ideal but hardly anybody is doing it yet.

References

Andrews, K R (1980) *The Concept of Corporate Strategy*, revised edition, Irwin.

Ansoff, H I (1965) *Corporate Strategy*, McGraw-Hill.

Ansoff, H I (1984) *Implanting Strategic Management*, Prentice-Hall.

Chandler, A D Jr (1962) Strategy and Structure chapters in the *History of the American Industrial Enterprise*, MIT Press.

Deal T and Kennedy A (1982) *Corporate Cultures: The Rites and Rituals of Corporate Life*, Penguin.

Deming, W E (1986) *Out of Crisis*, MIT Centre for Advanced Engineering Study, Cambridge MA.

Drucker, P F (1988) *The Practice of Management*, Pan Piper.

Drucker, P F (1988) The Coming of the New Organisation, *Harvard Business Review*, January–February, pp. 45-53.

Fayol, H (1949) *General and Industrial Management*, Pitman.

Freeman, R E (1984) *Strategic Management: A Stakeholder Approach*, Pitman.

Heller R (1994) The Manager's Dilemma, *Management Today*, January, pp. 42-3.

Johnson G and Scholes K (1993) *Exploring Corporate Strategy*, 3rd edition, Prentice-Hall.

Kaplan R S and Norton D P (1992) The Balanced Scorecard – Measures that Drive Performance, *Harvard Business Review*, January–February, pp. 71-9.

Lawrence P R quoted in Argyris, C (1972) *The Applicability of Organisational Sociology*, Cambridge University Press.

Mintzberg H (1973) *The Nature of Managerial Work*, Harper and Row.

Mintzberg H (1983) *Power In and Around Organisations*, Prentice-Hall.

Pedler M, Burgoyne J and Boydell T (1990) *The Learning Company: A Strategy for Sustainable Development*, McGraw-Hill.

Peters T J (1988) *Thriving on Chaos*, Macmillan.

Peters T J (1991) *Liberation Management*, Macmillan.

Peters T J and Waterman R H, Jr (1982) *In Search of Excellence*, Harper and Row.

Pfeffer J and Salancik G R (1978) *The External Control of Organizations: A Resource Dependence Perspective*, Harper and Row.

Porter M E (1980) *Competitive Strategy*, The Free Press.

Porter M E (1985) *Competitive Advantage*, The Free Press.

Porter, M E (1990) *The Competitive Advantage of Nations*, Macmillan.

Quinn, J B (1980) *Strategies for Change: Logical Incrementalism*, Irwin.

Richardson W (1994) A Comprehensive Approach to Strategic Management: Leading Across the Strategic Management Domain, *Management Decision*, Vol. 32, No. 8, pp. 27–41.

Slatter S (1984) *Corporate Recovery*, Penguin.

Smith D (1990) Beyond Contingency Planning: Towards a Model of Crisis Management, *Industrial Crisis Quarterly*, 4 (4), Elsevier Science Publishers, pp. 263-75.

Stacey, R D (1993) *Strategic Management and Organisational Dynamics*, Pitman.

Taylor F W (1947) *Scientific Management*, Harper and Row.

Thompson J L (1993) *Strategic Management: Awareness and Change*, Chapman and Hall.

Part Five   STRATEGIC CHANGE

Chapter 12 Structural issues and challenges

The final chapter returns to the theme of discontinuous change. While an understanding of past events is an essential aspect of strategic learning, the past itself may be a poor guide to the future. Competitive environments change rapidly and unpredictably; future competition may come from organizations that in the past have not been competitors. Newcomers enter a market and seek to add value in some different and imaginative way. External events can similarly change the rules of competition in an industry; privatization is one such event.

Simon Littlejohn's contribution is an assessment of how privatization has led to simultaneous strategic, structural and cultural change at Yorkshire Water, one of the ten privatized water companies. In the introduction we termed this strategic regeneration. We commented that at times it is necessary, but that it is never easy to implement. It implies major change and consequently it can be uncomfortable and risky.

The UK water industry was privatized in 1989, since when the individual companies have been regulated. Price increases have been restricted by a formula linked to inflation; at the same time the companies have needed to invest substantially in their capital base and in the infrastructure. Quite typically, Yorkshire Water comprises two businesses: the core activity of water provision and dispersal (sewerage); and other peripheral, sometimes diversified, activities where core skills and competencies can be deployed profitably. The corporate strategy has been changed in an attempt to build up a portfolio of non-regulated businesses. More recently there has been a deliberate attempt to spin non-core businesses off into a series of alliances – what is called an onion strategy. Companies which pursue this strategy need to develop competency in managing and controlling a network of independent but inter-related businesses.

In the 5 years since privatization Yorkshire Water's charges for core activities have been held to a rate of increase lower than the other nine main UK providers. In the last 10 years the number of employees has been reduced from some 6,500 to under 4,000, and the number continues to fall. Strategies of rationalization leading to productivity and efficiency gains have implied further changes to structures and management styles.

Yorkshire Water has had to venture into the unknown in its attempt to meet the differing needs of the regulator and its customers, many of whom are also shareholders! It has not been an easy struggle; and the company's results, relative to similar businesses, bear this out (Table V.1).

Table V.1   Financial results – YW compared with other water companies

	Yorkshire Water %	10 company average %	Rank (YW in the 10)
Compound annual earnings/share growth	11.56	9.1	2
Compound annual dividend/share growth	10.31	10.6	8
Share price relative to the sector	−1.3		7

Sources: Financial Times and Yorkshire Water

In this open and honest assessment Simon Littlejohn charts Yorkshire Water's progress and learning. One of the key issues to emerge is that there are no absolutes and that a company needs to become a *learning organization*.

Structural issues and challenges
Simon Littlejohn

'Tidy plans do not work . . . A business strategy is most successfully conceived when it is not quantified . . . The greatest mistake
lies in believing that the subject needs elaborate description and
procedure; strategic planning is a way of thinking.'

'Perhaps the most apposite definition of strategy for me is
drawn from the world of chess: Strategy is knowing what to do
when there is nothing to do; tactics is knowing what to do when
there is something to do.'

These quotes from Sir Trevor Holdsworth (1991) are a sobering lead-in to
a chapter on structural issues and challenges. In the same article, he went on
to observe 'that most businesses started with a vision: an idea. Good administration and organization may prevent a good idea being ruined but I have never
thought of them as being creative'.

Yorkshire Water – background

We are talking about an organization that, in the space of 5 years, has found
itself in a wholly different set of circumstances. It has had to embrace those
circumstances and make a transition in little over a year, work out what it
means and then set about the task of devising and implementing strategies that
secure a long-term future in a tough regulatory environment. It is still on that
journey. The following issues give some flavour as to what was and is
involved:

● An organization with a public-sector ethos propelled into privatization.
● Two major reorganizations.
● Developing technology that is having a significant impact on the way the
company is run and is scheduled to have a massive impact.

- Substantial headcount reduction.
- From consumer- to customer-service orientation.
- From dependency on the public-sector borrowing requirement (PSBR) to investor relations and competition for capital.
- From incremental pay systems and 'local government style' conditions to merit pay and conditions the free market will bear.
- From a culture of collectivism to the necessity of empowerment and 'bottom-up push'.
- From certainty to the management of uncertainty.

Water – the historical context

The history of water is embedded within our national history. In the fourteenth century the Crown, for instance, granted charters to influential individuals, towns and the Church – not all of which met with approval. In our own area Hull was linked by canals and dykes to surrounding village springs; fresh-water channels were deliberately polluted nightly by village protestors. Before the Industrial Revolution water supplies often reached the population through hollowed-out elm trunks connected by lead pipes to houses and public taps in the streets.

With industrialization, these rudimentary systems became inadequate. Established institutions were no longer able to cope with demand and water – the source of life – became the source of death. This became such a problem that, following Edwin Chadwick's report on 'Sanitary Conditions of the Labouring Population of Great Britain' (1842), Parliament stepped in. There followed the Waterworks Clauses Act and the Public Health Act (1848), paving the way for the control of the nation's water supply to be passed to private companies and a number of municipalities. Even during this era river pollution was made worse by the legalization, in 1847, of the drainage of cesspools into surface water sewers.

The situation went unchecked for many years, leading to heavy pollution; yet local authorities did little, seeking neither financial gain or votes in the solution. Although sewage disposal was given low priority, water supply became a prime target for the bold, creative talents of Victorian engineers. Waterworks and reservoirs were constructed. Water undertakings secured additional quality by purchasing catchment area land and controlling farming practices. Electricity-powered pumps brought advances in distribution, which were matched by improvements in treatment and quality. By the mid-1930s water was supplied by local authorities to most of the population of England and Wales and by statutory water companies to a substantial portion of the remainder. The Water Act of 1945 facilitated the amalgamation of many entities and introduced a waterworks code, which was the basis for the development of the industry until the Water Act of 1973. In 1974 the number of water suppliers had been reduced to under 200 (from 2,000 in 1915 and 950 by 1950) but there were still around 1,400 local authorities responsible for sewerage services.

Like all large water companies, Yorkshire Water has its roots in a multitude of water undertakings, from small companies to parts of local authorities. It was out of this that in 1974 the Yorkshire Water Authority was formed – one of ten regional authorities defined on the basis of river basin catchment areas. One has only to glance at the thick handbooks of union agreements to get a feel for the task our predecessors faced to produce some rationalization; and it has been no mean achievement. The management task in those days was to bring together activities under the generic heading of water undertakings and to produce some semblance of order, typically on a geographical basis. Within a particular area, once established, functional activities such as water collection, treatment and distribution were found. On the sewage side, there was the collection of sewage through a system of sewers – known as sewerage – and sewage treatment. Some of the sewerage activities were (and are) subcontracted back to local authorities. Yorkshire Water Authority had to cope with a heavy burden of inherited and on-going capital expenditure necessary to upgrade a massive infrastructure, parts of which had suffered from a century of neglect.

In addition to the supply of water and sewerage services, the water authorities' responsibilities included resource planning, pollution control, fisheries, land drainage, flood protection and alleviation, recreation and conservation. Local authorities appointed the majority of water authority board members. The chairman and other members were government appointees with responsibility to the Secretary of State for Environment and through to MAFF for land drainage. The Water Act 1983, together with some legislation within the 1973 Act, incorporated the reduction in the maximum permitted size of water authority boards to fifteen members – all government-appointed. The water authorities were also required to make arrangements to get closer to *consumers'* interests; one outcome was the formation of the Water Services Association by the ten authorities. A key issue in 1974 was and is finance; their combined assets of £2.4bn in 1974 were financed by debt of £2.2bn. Money to finance capex was part of the PSBR. For practical purposes, water was a nationalized industry.

The enactment of the Water Act 1989 on 6 July meant that many of the functions of the water authorities passed (with the exception of those of the statutory water companies) to the water service companies. At the same time, certain of the water authorities' other functions to which I have just referred passed to the (new) National Rivers Authority (NRA). Each of the water holding companies is a holding company of a water service company, which, under the Act, has been appointed a water undertaker and sewerage undertaker for water supply and sewerage services in its respective water and sewerage regions; they largely, but do not totally, overlap.

For Yorkshire Water plc, the *regulated* core business is Yorkshire Water Services made up of Customer Services, Water Treatment and Supply, Sewerage, Sewage Treatment and Disposal and Contract Services (organizationally referred to later). The other activities of the company (*non-regulated*) were, until recently, grouped as Yorkshire Water Enterprises Limited. This was established at the time of privatization in order to grow shareholder value in the medium to long term. It mainly consists of an environmental division and a property services company. Each is headed by a board, as is Water Services. The formation of the environmental division usefully illustrates part of the company's business philosophy because it is operating in such areas as industrial waste (not dealt with by our traditional sewage activities) yet utilizing our asset base. After privatization, Yorkshire Water also formed a joint company with Babcock International, called Babcock Water Engineering Limited, to extend the range of its engineering activities and to provide new long-term opportunities for its civil engineering staff; the current massive capital programme will not continue at the same rate indefinitely. Also Yorkshire Water's water engineering skills were combined with Babcock's international contract management expertise, which offer potential to expand overseas.

The core and headquarters organizations now employ around 4,000 people (4,500 at the time of privatization and a peak of 6,500 in the water-authority days) and the enterprise-related side 950. With a 1993 turnover of £481.6m, the PLC is in the top 400 of European companies and is one of Yorkshire's largest. It services 4.4 million domestic and 140,000 industrial and commercial customers, and 1.4bn litres of water are treated every day. Since privatization, capital investment has totalled around £1bn and is planned to continue into the next century as the company maintains its commitment to achieving environmental quality standards and to customer service.

Post-privatization: The essential differences

With a water authority, the responsibility for the undertaking was to Secretaries of State with a latter-day requirement 'to make arrangements for the representation of **consumers'** interests'. Investment was subject to the vagaries of the PSBR. The focus now is much different as a PLC. Accountability is to **customers** as individuals, and through Customer Service Committees, to the official Regulator, the Director General of Water Services who heads the Office of Water Services (OFWAT). There are also, however, accountabilities to a number of other regulatory bodies, such as the Drinking Water Inspectorate and the company must operate within the rigours of legislation typified by the Control of Pollution Act. The legislative regime largely stems from the EC. Access to capital is now through the money markets and there is thus a wholly new dimension to be considered, namely shareholder and investor relations. While the constraints of the PSBR have been left well and truly behind, concepts such as shareholder value have to be addressed and balanced with commitment to service, the issue of being a (regulated) monopoly supplier and the EC legislative position.

These essential differences bring about new opportunities, but also fresh vulnerabilities, which have to be addressed. As we shall see, the impact of tightening regulatory pressures, combined with shareholder expectations, are driving forces behind diversification – additional to the need to seek out ways of making the core business efficient. But the necessity to diversify (as well as the freedom to do so) also brings with it a significant potential for failure as well as success. We could, for example, choose the wrong area of operations or the wrong partner in a joint venture. We could pay the wrong price or hold unrealistic expectations about synergistic benefits. Because the nine other major companies have started their 'commercial existences' from broadly the same starting points, there is less scope to diversify in the UK than a single organization would face in the same situation. Inevitably this leads to attention turning overseas – *an altogether new ball game for a former public utility*. We also had and have to embrace the issue of the acquisition of new skills, which can bring problems. Experience was to show that bringing in potential 'whizzkid commercial types' from outside the industry was to result in failure in some (but not all) cases; in contrast, some home-grown talent was to blossom in the new environment. To add to all this, we have the issue of balancing management time in the correct proportion in order to keep the focus on the core business.

Enter again perhaps at this point what is today more the tendency not only of customer focus, but of militant consumerism. With the increasing awareness brought about by general political debate about privatization, the impact of EC regulations, increased environmental concerns and of the need to make good the substantial under-investment over the years, people are now much more aware. They feel less inclined to overlook the activities of an anonymous water board (yes – we have changed our title!) or some adjunct to the local council. Interesting evidence of this is provided by the substantial increase in claims we are now experiencing from members of the public. They cover loss or damage caused not only by significant incidents such as mains and sewer bursts, but also grazes, torn clothing and damage to car tyres resulting from tripping or running over stop tap boxes, manhole covers and the like.

Not only have we to deal with all the complexities of running a core business properly, we have also to *handle* well the necessity of diversification to which I have just referred. This will (rightly) test our communication skills. For our customers (many of whom are in the lower income bracket) – *and for us too of course* – the immediate focus is domestic; on issues such as water quality and reliability of supply, on charges and our responsiveness as an organization. When we, for instance, look at opportunities abroad, we must not as a management come across as amateur businessmen relishing some new-found commercial freedom funded by captive consumers. It is exceedingly important to stress that, in practice, money connected with the core business is ring-fenced; that which is associated with the development of non-core activities is in no way connected – a point which can be misunderstood. We must therefore portray and explain diversification in terms of its essential benefits.

Survival

The company's business strategy has to integrate these dimensions. For the first time people had to start to take on board the concept of survival both at the business and the personal levels. As a water authority, the culture was one of public service; of a worthwhile job, secure with a good pension and generous severance for those who did not make it. Many would be professionally qualified. Indeed, it would be this sense of professionalism and civil engineering achievement that would drive many on rather than necessarily belonging to a particular organization. It could also be speculated that many may have chosen their careers consciously rejecting the private sector ethic.

Changed circumstances – but how to manage them?

There was no doubting the vastly different conditions in which we found ourselves. Some probably found them threatening and unwelcome; others would think of them as enormously challenging and would revel in the numerous opportunities that lay ahead. Either way, the challenge was to seek out and combine the energies of everyone in the newly defined business strategy. Much of what follows deals with that task.

1980's organization and culture

With a significant amount of investment having been undertaken since 1974, including a water distribution grid, the company was organized into four geographic regions at the time of privatization; this had already come down from eight, including a rivers division. It was a conventional approach with divisional managements; structures by and large mirrored each other. Notwithstanding the search for further efficiencies, an absolutely key issue that had to be confronted was the one of the customer interfaces and customer service. Central billing was in position by 1983 but operational functions were divisionalized.

From a 1990s perspective, aspects of human resources management stood out from what one might have expected to have found in a large, public-sector organization. For instance, in the early to mid 1980s a key management training programme called 'Managing for Productivity' was introduced. It blended psychological theory with the practice of management and focused very much on situational management and employee motivation. It was later incorporated into a Middle Management Development Programme (MMDP). In fact one could detect the beginnings of what today we now refer to as empowerment – though often, as now, to be misinterpreted. While many identified with the message, particularly at the middle levels, there was criticism as to whether or not it was believed in (and practised) by the top strata. In the late 1980s parts of the company began to pick up on the quality movement too, which sat quite naturally with the MMDP. This has been built on and was later to prove very helpful in assisting with the communication of corporate objectives in the core business in 1991.

One 'soft' but significant factor to arise from the 'quality movement' was the fact that many people came forward to train as quality coaches. One began to see the emergence of the quality action team as a means of problem-solving. The particular approach adopted with quality suited the culture. It was safe. It was to a degree systematized though it did not extend throughout the organization. The right words were used and, for those involved, it had a sincerity. However, it inevitably lacked the *driver of survival* found in leading edge commercial organizations. It dealt with issues rather than focus on *job quality*. Though it can be assumed that the majority of people who were involved supported these programmes, I think that there are also those who would observe that significant culture shift was obtained through hard work on the industrial relations front as much as by anything else. Also, in this period, one or two managers not known for their consideration for human beings left the scene.

The development of people was given further impetus by the decision to send directors, over a period of time, on intensive management programmes at top (mostly American) business schools. Earlier, travelling scholarships were introduced and it became possible for anyone in the company to apply to be sponsored for a part-time MBA programme in addition to a full-time 1-year facility. The company also decided to invest in a high-quality development centre process for its senior people. These centres are well regarded by those who go on them. Inevitably, though, there was some resentment about the selection process. Now that there is an attempt to extend them further into the organization, this is less of a problem.

The FD went to Harvard

. . . and shortly after his return he became Managing Director and Deputy Chairman of the PLC. There had been suggestions that, after the activity of privatization (tackled very successfully by the formation of a dedicated privatization team), the company was drifting. This probably was not true but was borne more of a sense of unfulfilled expectation than anything else. Also, the management cadre was unused to exercising the empowerment it sought; there was a tendency to look upwards to 'them' and to wait. We were very much dealing with an underlying culture even though there had been not inconsiderable investment in the soft HR issues.

It is perhaps not unusual for organizations to look for a catchword or a set of letters that captures some 'essential truth' or direction of travel. For us it was CCFF: Commitment, Capability, Flexibility and Focus. With this came the realization that the company depended for its survival on its financial, technical and human resources – each with its dedicated strategy in the context of overall business strategy, which aimed to define the business(es) that the company wished to be in and the desired position/performance level.

Financial strategy aimed to identify the company's financial constraints and opportunities that would both influence, and be influenced by, business strategy. Technology is basically driven by business strategy but may also contribute to the direction of the business and human resources strategies by highlighting commercial opportunities and focusing on the abilities of people in the company. Human resources strategy, it is believed, is a main driver of business strategy, because any business strategy can only be achieved by the skill (capability) and the sustained efforts (commitment) of its people. However, business strategy has major implications in human resource terms, especially in relation to the numbers, quality and competencies required for its achievement.

It is of course tempting to construct a strategy model for the organization, but models can only serve a useful purpose to an extent with the ever accelerating pace of change. For instance, in the period 1955-80, 238 of the original Fortune 500 companies dropped out. In 1980-85, there were another 143. Fifty per cent of the organizations quoted in *In Search of Excellence* do not now qualify and two do not exist. There are many apparent conflicts around: to innovate yet keep costs down; to know the detail but delegate; being lean and mean yet people-centred; fast response and planning for the future. The push for quality is another factor and it is sometimes the case in organizations that the cause of quality improvement has been submerged. Symptoms of poor quality include deviations from standard; indeed the absence of clear standards and the necessity for many corrections to be made. The reasons for this are that quality (the existence of a specification/fitness for purpose/conformance to specification/lack of variation) is seen as a programme not a process and a way of thinking, as something for the 'lower' levels; it can also fall foul of management impatience.

One of the key factors in strategy determination is not only the 'why?' and the consequential 'what?' but the order and priority of what needs to be done. The Burke–Litwin model is helpful in this respect. It is causal and serves as a guide for organizational diagnosis as well as for planned, managed organizational change. The environment box represents the input. The performance box represents the output. The remaining boxes represent the throughput aspects. See Figure 12.1.

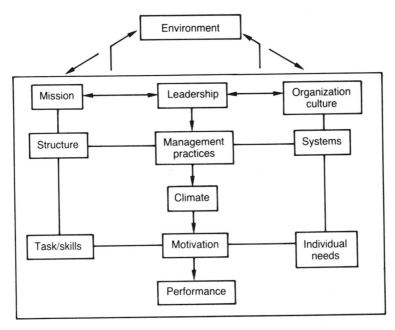

Figure 12.1 *Adapted from the Burke–Litwin model of performance*

One can see from Figure 12.1 that the greatest leverage is to be obtained by acting on the mission/leadership/culture line. A distinction is made between the transformational and the transactional.

Our business, financial, technical and human resource strategies are linked broadly together in the following ways:

Business strategy

- what business?
- what level of
  performance?
- how to achieve it?

Financial strategy

- cash requirements for
  growth?
- financial market
  constraints and
  opportunities?
- how to measure
  performance?

HR strategy

- how to improve
  capability/skill of people?
- how to improve effort/
  commitment of people?
- required competencies?

Technology strategy

- how to deliver
  technology required?
- requirement?
- how to convert
  technology into
  opportunities?

We concluded that in the 1990s we could be sure of two things. Firstly, that the rate of change in the environment in which Yorkshire Water plc operated would tend to increase and that it would be highly unpredictable. The second thing we can be sure about is that there is an increasing complexity about the way in which changes in one part of the politico-economic environment affect other parts. This is amply illustrated in the context of our company's background. Who 5 years ago would have predicted the effects on the concern of the political decision to privatize water authorities? We are likely to remain subject to these forces and with the additional European dimension thrown in as well.

The unpredictable rate of change shows through in each of the key strategic areas as the examples show:

Business strategy   – regulatory uncertainty for the core business
- new standards of service required from the core
  business
- new product/market opportunities for the enterprise
  businesses including acquisitions
- declining prospects for some existing enterprise
  businesses.

Financial strategy — uncertainty about national and international economic prospects, which affect RPI, interest rates, capital costs and income
— the status of the company in the financial markets
— new financing products.

Technology strategy — new IT products in system control
— new telecommunications systems
— advantages in treatment process technologies
— new opportunities in sensing, monitoring and instrumentation.

HR strategy — the interaction of the above three strategic areas on HR
— the legislative dimension within the EC allied to political uncertainty in the UK
— trends in world labour markets (in part influenced by the impact of technology itself).

We concluded that we would succeed only by ensuring that our people possessed a high level of capability allied with commitment and that they were organized in such a way as to provide maximum focus. The objective of our human resources strategy became to improve the capability, commitment and focus of our people. The principles and policies needing to be adopted to fulfil this have to consider 'hard' issues like pay and conditions; they are measurable and usually have a cost. However, the link between the level of pay and conditions, on the one hand, and business performance, on the other, is not a straightforward one to make. Recruitment (internal/external), training and development issues clearly have a bearing on capability and also on commitment. Policies in these areas can be quantified and will have associated costs. The most difficult area in which to define principles and policies is in the area of action designed to improve commitment.

The nature of commitment

It is often to be observed in times of crisis, for example, when one witnesses interviews with military personnel, that commitment is high. (As it happens, tension in the Gulf was high at the time we were looking at our position.) It is tempting to observe that 'it would be nice to have that same level of commitment in any organization'. In many ways it does exist, yet military comparisons are often made with managers who have experience of both environments expressing a preference for the military fighting unit. The reasons given include comradeship (low status differentiation in times of pressure) and a common purpose (survival – unite against a common enemy). Added to this, and applicable in both the military and commercial situations, may also be professionalism (wanting to do a good job), but this force is not necessarily linked to the organization itself. It can be independent and transferable (to other organizations).

Commitment may be defined as the alignment of personal values and objectives with those of the organization. They can be achieved through a combination of a shared sense of purpose, leadership, the craft of management and through support systems. The balance between these elements is not fixed but part of a continuum, and depends on the successful mixing of loose and tight controls. HR strategy must address the twin motivations of survival and professionalism. An aspect of business strategy as far as Yorkshire Water was and is concerned is to make as realistic as humanly possible the survival aspect, since we are at present a regulated monopoly (core business).

Parallels with true free-floating commercialism.

I have referred to the fact of the regulatory environment. Some would say that Regulators are surrogate customers. This is true to some extent – some would say a significant extent. Very important as Regulators are, for they could in reality make or break organizations, there is a danger that regulated organizations 'think regulator' all or most of the time rather than 'thinking customer'. This comment may seem rather strange, but let me develop this theme. I have referred to the survival dimension. Free-floating commercial organizations would offer a product or service to their chosen market. To do so will have required marked research, product design, production, marketing and selling. It would also require keeping in constant touch with the market, which implies *responsiveness and, better still, anticipation*. Thus in this environment, it is possible apparently to do all the right things yet still not come out on top.

We are now well and truly in the world of consumerism which means choice. In fact choice itself has a number of elements such as design, quality, availability, cost and price. This gives rise to the concept of excellence and the capacity to improve. So organizations can be good, sometimes very good, yet that does not guarantee that we, the customers, will buy. There is no certainty and there are therefore no guarantees. The need to survive is born of this process and operating systems such as 'just in time' are tremendous drivers in people management terms. Customer satisfaction is no longer enough: organizations must delight. Think of this when you (say) next buy a car. Thousands of hours and millions of pounds will have been invested to bring it to you. You are courted; you evaluate and then *you decide*. Once that choice is made, there is a winner – but there are also losers, losers who have made substantial investments as well. I do not wish to paint a one-side picture and to suggest that public sector and regulated organizations do not operate under real pressures. In the case of water, for instance, we have very considerable and rightly onerous responsibilities towards public health. We too must seek and obtain customer satisfaction.

We have referenced the customer and employee survival dimensions in discussing comparisons with 'free-floating' enterprises. But there are of course two other sets of stakeholder: the shareholder and the community as a whole. With the move to privatization, the issue of shareholder relations was a totally new dimension the newly formed company had to take on board, both structurally and attitudinally. I return to an earlier point that many people who now find themselves part of privatized organizations may well have self-selected themselves out of the private sector. For them now to have to confront such capitalist issues as the shareholder dimension comes as a shock.

We chose to tackle this through educative articles in our in-house newspaper, by setting up a dedicated annual report and presentation to employees – The Employee Event – and by issuing shares. The manner of the share issue was significant. For 3 years now, the company has decided to issue shares to its employees – but not on a percentage of salary basis. Everyone got the same number irrespective of position or seniority. This came as an unexpected and welcome surprise and served as an introduction to the issues of share ownership and shareholder capitalism. We have also instituted a building society-linked sharesave scheme, which also provides the mechanism for share ownership and there is an executive share option scheme for senior people as well. There is some evidence (yet to become noticeable in our company) that where employees are substantial stakeholders in a company, employee attitudes exhibit substantial business-centred focus. The fact that the company had a large number of unissued shares enabled a start to be made on this aspect of policy. However, timing would be an important factor and we first wished to see some progress on the human resources issues before considering any extension of these measures.

Early attempts at extending commitment

With the immediate thrust of privatization over, the longer-term direction of the company had to be defined. If nothing else, we had to deal with the suggestion of drifting – though some would observe that this is a contradiction in terms in an empowered organization. The Managing Director took his proposals on corporate direction and commitment to the board for approval, which was duly obtained. It was then considered essential that we should invest in a period of consultation with the top managers in the company. This was done by the MD tabling a watershed paper entitled 'Foundations for the

Future' to those same senior managers. It was decided to call one of those top level, 2-day off-site conferences, where this paper was presented, analysed and debated. (In our culture it became known as the Parkway event.) There were, however, some 'givens', and the four primary purposes of the company were included in that category. (These primary purposes appear later in the section on management standards p. 290.) It was the opportunity to explain in some depth the essential differences between a water authority and a privatized plc, the likely impact of regulation, the impact on financing and the significance of the Enterprise activities on the future growth of the company and the share price. The aim was to gain understanding and acceptance for this; we were not voting on business strategy. The other purpose of the conference was to look at implementation issues.

The conference focused on the human resources aspect of the trio of financial, technical and human resources after discussion about the strategic direction of the company – largely to aid understanding. Though the impact of regulation was considered likely to be ever-tightening controls, the management of financial resources was not considered to be a major problem. (Times were to change and, for instance, the company and indeed the whole industry was to get caught up in a robust debate with OFWAT on the cost of capital.) It is worth recording here that our company sees itself as a science-based company and also one which is seeking to exploit the best in automation and control technologies. We have, for instance, formed an alliance with a university and a major software house. What we now call our Management Automation and Control Environment (MACE) initiative is having and is destined to have a major impact on the way we do things, including employment levels and the character of the work itself.

At the conference key values were identified. It was also realized that values in themselves meant very little if behaviour was not altered. In fact behaviours were identified as one of the major factors in obtaining commitment. At the conclusion of the conference there was some debate as to whether we should issue some form of statement or 'rallying call to the troops'. After careful reflection, we decided not to do so – or at least not immediately. There was the feeling that, although the fact of our meeting was not a secret, the issuing of some summit-like communiqué would be seen as lacking realism. Since we were at the time focusing on commitment, it could also have been seen as incompetent. We did however feel that we should do something.

And what then?

The MD felt inspired. He had concluded that to have embarked on this approach to culture change was risky in view of our history but, so far, he felt it had been worth it. Naturally there was a desire to answer the question:

Where do we go from here? We had advocates of what became known as a 30/30/30 strategy. (You can tell that a number of us are ESTJs, for those readers who know something of the Myers-Briggs type indicators!) Our group was about thirty strong and there was an idea that we should each organize (30) similar mini-events, each with thirty attendees and in 30 days reach 900 people. Great! We had cracked it! But were these sessions to be of the same type? We were after all the top echelon. Were we going to tell – or sell? The feeling was that the direction of the company was reasonably understood but that the values needed further examination and clarification before we went on to look at the behaviour side.

One of the issues to emerge was that, however we proceeded from this point, it was crucial to carry with us those not party to the general 'feel good' feeling of those who attended the conference – around 4500 people in fact! After all, we were convinced – or so we thought. 'The problem would be with *them*, the damp-proof course.' While the matter of how we proceeded was undoubtedly a key issue, I have long suspected this reference to the damp-proof course. Though the concern for what those outside the conference would think was sincere, was this reference not a mask for the fact that at best we had acquiescence – or even unexpressed dissent?

It was decided that we would meet again after a few weeks, during which time all the material would be summarized and we could all reflect. Managers were empowered to make holding statements to staff who had witnessed this mass exodus to a local hotel. We did indeed meet again shortly after and many would regard this as less than satisfactory. On reflection, this was to some extent inevitable because we were starting to wrestle with the practicalities of making it all happen. The agenda for this second meeting (both were facilitated by an external consultant whom we respected) focused on a series of initiatives for change, for which handouts were prepared on specific topics such as reward, appraisal and empowerment. Some saw this approach as somewhat prescriptive and a departure from the free-flowing collegiate atmosphere of a few weeks ago. There was possibly some resentment of the preselection of the topics, especially as they included what was for some the touchy subject of reward management. However, some progress was made and the practical meaning of the values and behaviours was filled out a little more. A worthwhile suggestion was that somehow the cultural way forward should incorporate the work already undertaken in parts of the company with quality initiatives. Equally, it has to be said, there was a suspicion in some senior management circles that there was some sort of conspiracy to hang most aspects of change management on the 'quality movement', thereby 'kicking into touch' difficult challenges. However, the quality hook was to prove useful, as I later describe.

It was agreed that further work should be done on specific topics, e.g. on reward, and most important, all present were asked to submit one page on any one of the four issues they felt strongest about. The emphasis was to be on *what to do*. Shortly afterwards, the MD received a number of proposals but the response was by no means universal. Some made proposals and others did not. Was this significant? Did it reflect what in the opinion of some was a prescriptive second meeting? Were people struggling to think precisely how to effect change? Were some very uncomfortable with the issues anyway? Did they believe that this change in approach was genuinely participative or just a facade? Did some actually *want* to be put on the spot, thereby being fully identified with what was to follow (whatever form it took)? Some of these reasons are of course more 'acceptable' than others and it is the task of the leader/leadership group to manage colleagues through this phase.

This does indeed raise other aspects about cultural change, which itself can be driven by a variety of reasons: survival is a fundamental one and this can reflect the need to provide value for money allied to responsiveness to customers. Acquisition is another. Change can be evolutionary or revolutionary. People can adapt and, given changed circumstances, actively help to bring it about. Better still, they can be part of the process of anticipation and, through *bottom-up push*, help initiate change. This requires an empowering organization that listens or a cadre of dominant personalities that will drive things through in any case. Or change can be imposed, and to avoid the obvious dangers of passive or outright resistance, whole managements are eliminated or changed – as can happen post-takeover or when a new chief is appointed.

We allowed a further period of a few weeks for mutual reflection. I say mutual for two reasons: firstly, the senior managers themselves needed to reflect on the experience and, secondly, the MD himself wished to reflect on what had been said over both the initial and follow-up meetings. Many of the managers in the group will have belonged to the 'we are looking for a lead/drifting' camp. Well – they had certainly been involved in what was for them something radical; radical in terms of the concepts contained in the expression of the primary purposes of the company and that we were *in reality* no longer 'talking water authority'; radical too in that as a group, they were being asked to contribute to strategic thinking issues of structure and culture. Many would have been wondering whether this new approach was in fact real. Were they being *told* or *consulted*?

At this juncture it should perhaps be mentioned that the MD (formerly you will recall the FD) had and probably still has a reputation for being the dominant decision-taker and a powerful personality. Many issues, some of them key, tended to await his 'nod'. It could be observed that this suited the culture of collectivism, of passing on and upwards for approval. This type of issue is absolutely fundamental when looking at structural and cultural change. I had noticed that not only was the MD so regarded. A former top man, who had left to take up a senior position in another organization, was often cited and spoken of in affectionate terms – by the current MD, too. What we are talking about here is leadership. In these cases, leadership through the power of personality as well as through technical competence – and also position power. This is not the place to analyse leadership styles and situational leadership in depth, except to say that managements can cause behaviour in all sorts of ways. And so when we are considering how to take an organization forward, we need to realize not only that there could be various internal forces at work, but also how they came to be embedded.

I have referred to survival and acquisition as two examples of drivers of cultural change and therefore introduce the notion of internally driven or externally imposed change. As the art of management has evolved, there can be little doubt these days that people now realize that the organizations that will win are those that *inspire* everyone to want to give of their best. Many by implication associate the generation of this kind of environment with flatter, looser frameworks and the absence of some 'captain on the bridge' shouting orders. While this tendency is undoubtedly to be applauded, I also believe it is grossly misunderstood by many who see empowerment in effect as being allowed to carry on in their own compartments and where outside help is seen as threatening or interefence. The Japanese approach can be similarly misrepresented by passing it off as amongst other things, people-centred. Indeed it is people-centred but it is also disciplined. Great emphasis is placed on planning, disciplined implementation and a commitment to continuous improvement.

Our Managing Director had the choice of imposing change as in the acquisition situation or of investing in an altogether longer and more involved process in order to build that sure foundation. Imposition is attractive and it has its place. More often than not whole tranches of management disappear. In our case, we had elected to go what we supposed to be the more durable route and to move away from our historical collectivism (a collectivism not of the Japanese type).

One associates collectivism with the public sector. Other associations are those of professionalism, 'safety', reliability and service. (This is not a complete list.) Historically, at least, one sees evolution rather than revolution; a kind of solid long-termism lacking in fast and flexible response – excepting in cases of emergency, when responses are often magnificent. This is not to decry some of these virtues and, in any case, we are witnessing radical changes not only through privatizations but also through the establishing of agencies and the Citizen's Charter. To a significant extent therefore people are self-selecting in the jobs/careers they choose and they become part of the culture.

In any organization the nature of leadership is important. Equally, strong, believable people tend to be noticed and to emerge on top. What is important, and never more so in today's organizations, is the propensity of the 'followers'. Are they, for example, by inclination passive or are they made passive? In truth one will find a mixture and today's challenge is to inspire everyone to want to contribute to the full extent of their abilities.

After the reflection

Given the original 30/30/30 idea, we certainly felt that we had to extend the knowledge of what was going on. There was, after all a significant number of senior managers who had not been party to the original discussions and whose 'buy-in' was essential. Indeed they would be able to help shape some of the thinking by virtue of the positions they held. And so another conference was arranged along the lines of the original. As before, there was the opportunity to communicate and explain fully the new business strategy and to start to examine some of its implications, namely the 'onion' concept, of which more later. By then the idea of values and behaviours was not new but they were able to be filled out, and this was one of the benefits of the meeting. We looked at practical issues especially from the point of view of identifying supports and barriers to the change process. There was quite a warm feeling after this meeting and a very natural desire, as with the top team, to *do something*, including publishing some form of charter based on a vision statement. In the end, the consensus was that, since behaviours were a key element in the way forward, we should publish (initially to ourselves) what we termed the Yorkshire Water Management Standards. We had after all agreed that we could all sign up to them. Because the fact of the conference and the generation of the standards represented a significant stage in our culture, I set them out in full.

Yorkshire Water: Management Standards

Background

In the first half of 1991 the Directors and Senior Management of the Company met in a series of meetings triggered by a presentation from the Deputy Chairman outlining his views on the future direction of the Company. This was centred around the four headings of purpose, strategy, values and behaviour. A major result of Parkway was the identification of the core values and key behaviours which managers thought to be relevant to themselves and YW both now and in the future. These values and behaviours were further reviewed in the context of the core business's Total Quality initiatives at a separate meeting and at a specially convened meeting of the new Enterprise organization.

There was significant agreement that the overall purposes of the Company are:

To improve the health and well-being of our customers and the environment by providing outstanding quality of product and service at competitive cost.

To maximize total returns to shareholders in the long run.

To provide employees with opportunities to realize their full potential.

To make a positive contribution to the Yorkshire community.

Central to their fulfilment are the three pillars of human, technical and financial resources and it is our challenge to manage and integrate them successfully. What follows has to do with the HR element and draws largely on the work that managers put in over many hours of discussion. It represents a 'checklist', the YW standard, against which managers should measure themselves and seek to be measured. Hitherto that measurement, and subsequent recognition, has typically been task-based. The creation and sustaining of an enabling change-orientated culture will of necessity need to embody process issues as well.

Core values
Trust, Loyalty, Pride, Honesty, Integrity, Endeavour, Quality Service/Exellence, Competitiveness.

Values are personal to the individual and are frequently displayed in the way a person behaves. In the same way a company displays values in the way it behaves. It is the YW philosophy that its behaviours should be based upon core values. The company further believes that if these values align closely with individual values, then this will be a sound basis on which its human resources can make their full contribution, develop and feel that they 'belong'.

It is believed that the core values and the associated behaviours which follow will find wide support amongst all employees. YW considers that their adoption and practice is a fundamental obligation of all managers.

Behaviours
Whatever values people hold (and to whatever degree) the principal means by which they are lived and transmitted is through behaviour. In fact behaviour is so important that it is possible to devalue certain values through inappropriate behaviour; this could even be accidental in an inattentive moment.

Yorkshire Water expects the following behaviours to be displayed by its managers, aspiring managers and key professional staff. Many such behaviours are not related to level and will form a means of distinguishing one person from another in their life with the company. They have been grouped around four major headings which inter-relate.

Positivity
Commonly summed up as displaying and encouraging a 'can do' attitude. A key way in which this can be developed in others is for managers to invite their staff to seek out and to list the positive points in any situation – even though at times, the positive course may not always be chosen.

A manager will therefore encourage and reward initiative-taking and flexible behaviour and support their staff by conferring on them the confidence to believe in themselves. He/she will always stress the desirability of thinking in terms of constant improvement and live this through his/her actions.

Key Words:	Bold	Opportunity
	'I can'	Promotional
	Initiative	Enjoyment
	Flexibility	Confidence

Empowering
The display of this behaviour is seen as being essential to survival in today's world because organizations will only be competitive and survive if they constantly improve – and they cannot improve sufficiently unless all their employees are contributing to their

full extent; and they cannot do this until they are empowered. Empowering means giving people the tools and the training to do the job and adopting a coaching style. It means allowing them to gain experience where mistakes are turned to advantage thinking in terms of improvement. (Allowing people to make mistakes must be treated with caution and a distinction made with obvious carelessness.) Empowerment is a very visible way in which a manager/an organization confers trust in an individual. Such trust also incurs obligation on the part of the manager and the managed. Authority is delegated and with it, real responsibility *but* ultimate responsibility remains with the manager.

Successful empowerment taps into the often expressed point of view that the person who knows most about the job is the person who is doing it all the time. In the complex world of today, it is also the route towards enabling managers to give time to their wider managerial role.

Key Words: Enabling   Trusting
            Learning   Coaching/Training
            Delegating Accountability
            Supporting Recognition

Communication

Communication is defined as being downwards, upwards and lateral in direction. To be effective it needs to be regular, relevant and two-way. The absence of any one of these characteristics is likely to result in criticisms of poor communication because communication is both real and perceived. The missing link feeds the perception that communication is poor. Communication takes time and managers should recognize that by exhibiting good communications behaviour, and giving up a precious resource – time – they transmit a key value of recognition through which other things are achieved. Questioning and clarifying skills can be used to support the listening process. The informal continuous and formal periodic types of appraisal are also examples of this time commitment. Here again, the adoption of a coaching style is most likely to be successful.

Key Words: Openness   Appropriate for the purpose
            Informing   Means (*verbal*, written, data)
            Listening   Message
            Two-way feedback Management by walking about

Recognition

Recognition is fundamental to good management practice. It can form part of the feedback process and supplies a fundamental human need felt by most of us at some point. Yorkshire Water managers are expected to develop this characteristic in its many forms tailoring their approach to suit the circumstances whilst preserving essential consistency. They are expected to display visibility in appropriate forms as a means of being 'in the know' and keeping in touch with those for whom they are responsible – and with other parts of the organization. This talking to people through management by walking about will again demand the manager's time but as a process is linked to communication, empowerment and positivity.

Reward comes in a number of forms: financial, promotion, recognition by others, tokens, publicity and one-to-one interaction. Successful mixing of these techniques is essential and some will be part of an informal and continuous process. Others are more closely linked to the periodic formal process of appraisal. Yorkshire Water managers are expected to develop appraisal skills as a key element of performance management.

Key words: Reward   Indirect
             Appraisal   Asking opinions
             Stroking   Exposure
             Awareness   Success/failure
             Teams/Individuals   Management by walking about

In Conclusion:

These behaviours are not the only behaviours through which all of the values can be expressed. However, they are those on which we wish to concentrate in the first instance. There is now at senior managers' level significant apparent support for their full-hearted adoption though approaches may well be different in the different parts of Yorkshire Water. We also believe that these behaviours are reflected in the various quality initiatives being introduced throughout the company and that they are mutually reinforcing.

All managers presently have their own particular styles. This means that these values and behaviours are evident in some but not in others – or as may quite widely be the case – are selectively applied. In order that the Company may progress, it is vital that everyone's capabilities are expanded and that they are not restricted by the existing ways of doing things. With this determination, Yorkshire Water expects all its managers to 'sign up' to these standards in the development of our Company.

The onion

The 'onion' concept, to which managers had been introduced at the conference, as you might guess deals with the identification of core business activities and points to (nonetheless important) outer layers of activity that are less central. The use of this concept was of appeal because it enabled us to concentrate on the *focus* aspect of our strategy as well as provide a vehicle for organizational rationalization. However, when we are talking about commitment, it is pretty fundamental to provide people with the reasons for being committed. Participation in suicide is not a very attractive option! In the past we had talked about getting rid of non-core activities and to endeavour to do this in as humane a way as possible. We had even considered subcontracting whole activities to third parties under a system called operational contracting.

As our thinking developed, we sought to modify this approach by going for a process of identifying and setting up separate business units but within the shell of the parent company. Where necessary, they would have limited protected status; but this would only be for a time until they reached critical mass. This approach became a major instrument of strategy as we sought to combine the desire for *focus* with improvements in efficiency and hence *value for money* for our customers. However, equally as important, we sought to achieve the widest possible buy-in from all our staff for the changes that lay ahead. That is not going to occur if the approach is one of rule by fear or if managements take advantage of recessionary conditions. It is long established that one deserves to reap as one sows. One of the disappointing features of the present time in the UK as a whole is that one comes across managements who are opportunist in the treatment of people. Some would no doubt observe 'that it would be nice to have the choice'.

We had that choice and were convinced that it was essential to provide our staff who were to be affected by change with reasons to view the changes positively. What better motivator than success. **A primary measure of success is customer satisfaction, as satisfied customers tend to return.** In human resources terms this was the fundamental operating principle that drove, and drives, our onion concept. To put that across, that the 'onionization' process meant job opportunity as well as some uncertainty, was a major challenge.

Wait and watch

With the publication of the standards, it was time, we thought, to introduce a little breathing space, though, as always, some of us felt impatient. Though managers seemed comfortable that they be asked to sign up to these standards, we wondered whether we had acquiescence rather than acceptance. However, it seemed to us at the time that we were probably proceeding along the right lines, as many a successful company has similar benefits embedded within a charter of existence. Because we had picked up the fact that communication, empowerment and recognition were so important, we issued, in full consultation with senior managers 'Guidelines for the Successful Conduct of Performance Appraisal'.

They were in themselves non-threatening and served to fill in a space in what we hoped would be a 'gestation' period. They were very practically based and did not place managers in a straitjacket. As well as being of practical value, they could also be regarded as having sent a signal of continuing top level interest in moving culture forward. For how could this be achieved without some organized framework for boss- subordinate communication – not the only process of course? The watching process revealed a mixed picture as far as follow-up action to the management conferences was concerned. Though some managers did take the essential messages to their people according to their own 'house styles', others did not. They had sought empowerment but were not yet pushing against the barriers. Few, for instance, appeared to see fit to display and talk about the management standards they had mostly thought were such a good idea a few months previously. As people below the management strata were heard to comment, 'how can we judge management behaviour if we do not know what are the standards?'

Meanwhile the first of the 'onionized' business centres was beginning to establish itself. The activities, pipe-laying and repair, had been placed under the umbrella of the Enterprise organization in order to give a distinct focus and, theoretically, to free it from the more constraining labour management practices of the core business. The new business, which was yet to develop a critical mass, was free to go and get business outside the company. By the same token, the core would be free to purchase not only from Pipeline Services but from the outside market as well, based on quality, delivery and price. (A protected transitional period was allowed.)

Since we are examining structural issues, it is relevant to introduce some timescales. The first Parkway top level conference was held on 28 February 1991, the follow-up on 18 March and the enlarged conference was on 23 April. The Enterprise group held its on 14 May. The appraisal guidelines were published in the Summer. Meanwhile, in June and July, the Managing Director of the core business undertook a series of twenty-one roadshows throughout the region so that everyone in the business could hear the message about values and behaviours first-hand. There was also the opportunity to ask questions. The vehicle for all this was the official launch of the business's Commitment to Quality Campaign. I have referred earlier to the quality 'movement'. It suited the culture to do this and gave it an accessible context.

Because we wanted to try to measure the effects of the culture change process, it was decided as a corporate initiative to run a comprehensive, company-wide, benchmark employee attitude survey in the October–November 1991 timeframe, run by the Institute of Manpower Studies. The focus was on the four key behaviour areas. We deliberately decided not to sample our population but to make it available to all. This was to give everyone the chance to take part. The response rate was over 60 per cent which, given our high proportion of 'blue-collar' staff, was quite encouraging. We saw this initially as a biennial event – possibly settling down to an annual frequency (not yet). The thinking behind it was not only to gather valuable data over time but also to send a signal that we wished to be open and welcomed feedback. Surveys also seemed to be embedded in the culture of a number of leading edge Western companies.

We cannot go into the detail of the results here. However, not surprisingly, we found that the responses to a number of items hinged on level – with generally a more positive attitude higher up the company. Overall the results were not bad. Significant negatives were to do with the need to improve inter-departmental cooperation and – surprise, surprise! – communication, although on a personal basis bosses rated well. It was also clear that we needed to do some work on giving staff recognition. (This was a little surprising in a sense in view of previous activities concerning the 'soft' people skills.) Job and career satisfaction were rated quite highly. Other conclusions were linked to demography with, for example, half the respondents in the manual grades being over 40. We are overdue to run the next survey and the results will be interesting in view of what many will regard as more turbulent times.

The late Autumn of 1991 did not bring much evidence of bottom-up initiatives. What were we expecting? We were certainly looking for more evidence of living the behaviours. Greater knowledge that they even existed would have been a start! It would also have been rewarding to have had some (bottom-up) organization proposals. Impatience was contained but it was decided to give a further pointer and corporate reinforcement to what was begun nearly a year earlier. Using the quality 'tag', our own people and a consultant working together designed a package called 'Leading and Coaching for Quality'. It had several features. it was a toolkit, revisiting and updating the 'Managing for Productivity' programme of the mid-80s. It highlighted the role of the manager as *leader and coach*. It was layered to match seniority levels; and it once again reinforced Parkway. It was rated quite successful but there were murmurings of prescription. . . !

Not only waiting and watching

Apart from these moves on culture development, there were other activities either going on or planned. These covered both expansion and contraction. For example, on the disposals side, after we had moved across from the core into our Enterprise grouping activities centred around direct mailing, we decided that it would be the thing to do to sell the 'business' on. However, of far greater significance have been the development of existing strengths and our extension into new areas of activity. The following examples illustrate this well.

We have recently formed a solid waste management business in partnership with the local authorities of Barnsley, Doncaster and Rotherham. We have worked with health authorities and hospitals to form a clinical waste business based on environmentally friendly incineration. A subsequent acquisition has made us the largest company in clinical waste in the country. We have strengthened and added to our laboratory analysis capability by making two acquisitions of laboratories in Holland. This not only gives us insights into EU regulation and European trends but the potential for substantial extra business via the customers of the acquired laboratories. We are strengthening the relationships we have with industrial customers by working with them in the provision of waste-management consultancy. This can lead to our managing on-site waste treatment, as is, for instance, the case with the large Coca-Cola plant at Wakefield. We are using our expertise in property in partnership with others, for example, in the development of a large shopping complex at Morley near Leeds. And then there is our joint venture with Yorkshire Electricity to produce electricity using wind power on Ovenden and Royd Moors. All of this serves to illustrate the reality of substantial change.

More candidates for onionization

Following the creation of the pipeline business, other candidates, such as our Southern Area maintenance group, emerged. The rationale was the same: develop a critical mass, initially with some protected business from the core but with no long-term guarantees. Others such as our direct mail business were developed later to be sold.

In the Autumn of 1993 the MD decided to give the cause of organization development a further kick – and endeavour to secure ownership – by forming a special 'onion' steering group chaired by the Managing Director of the Enterprise subsidiary. This group was formerly charged with delivery of the strategy. One outcome was to develop a review process as a framework for implementation. The group struggled and felt that it needed to enhance the analytical phase in order to be able to develop soundly based proposals for the future. It was decided in June 1993 to call for the assistance of some international strategy consultants. Their specific brief was to review our actual appraisal processes themselves (including areas then under examination) and to look at operating experiences to date. Their work was extended and, in February 1994, we were about to enter a radical relationship centred on an approach ensuring that bottom-up push.

Some conflicts of interest

There was no doubting the conviction we felt in creating both the pressure and the opportunity of the onion. I believe that we made a mistake in placing management responsibility for the first of the entities we split off with the Enterprise grouping. (They could not then be described as businesses.) Yorkshire Water Enterprises has a very specific brief – namely to contribute 10 per cent of the profit in 5 years and to be the driving force in the growth of shareholder value. The increasing impact of regulation will, it is thought, make it more and more difficult for this to be achieved through core business performance.

The formation and development of the pipe-laying and repair entity, competing with contractors who offer less favourable conditions to their staff, for instance, and placing it in Enterprise, caused conceptual problem. Was Enterprise free to pursue singlemindedly its primary objectives or was it to be some form of 'lifeboat' to help secure the smooth passage of the employee relations' aspects of the strategy? In truth we expected both aspects to be delivered. There are, for instance, those who feel that we can prove that we are/could become better than some contractors with whom we are compared –

including on quality of work. (You cannot readily inspect underground work done on your behalf.) As the process of evaluation continues, it is sobering to note that in one area of our company, we are actually subcontracting operational responsibility for distribution.

All the work that had already gone on was given additional focus through further organization change featuring the formal placing of organization development responsibility with the water company and the establishing of a leadership team. The task is to deliver what is now known as the YW99 vision. The previous Enterprise role lapsed, with the enterprise focus now centring on the environmental business, business development and possibilities overseas.

It is also worth mentioning that the MD wished to deal with another dynamic that had started to set in the core business as a consequence of 'onionization'. As the non-core activities were being identified, there was the suggestion of relief setting in in parts of the core, and that that meant that people were 'safe' and could 'relax'. There were even suggestions of unreasonable behaviour on the part of core staff towards former colleagues who had moved into the new non core entities (purchaser/ provider).

The organization change itself defined even more clearly than before the core functions, and one of the main drivers was cost reduction. *It represented a major effort on our part to manage uncertainty and still does.* A new Contract Services Division has been formed, wholly staffed from inside the company. (There is a cultural risk here – learning new tricks in time – but its very existence serves to demonstrate our commitment to the resourcefulness of our people.) The mission is to improve the operational efficiency of the service areas, which initially comprise electrical, mechanical, building and distribution maintenance. The new division will also identify further outsourcing opportunities and other areas of the 'core' suitable for transfer out. It will, in addition, involve itself in competitive benchmarking – quite a mission!

The principal accountabilities of the members of the YW99 Leadership Team (assisted by an internally recruited change team) well illustrate its fundamental nature:

- The achievement of operational levels of service bounded by regulation but also covering the softer perception issues especially those in customer service.
- The delivery of the contract services objectives (see above).
- The delivery of the necessary technology changes.
- The achieving of substantial operating cost reductions.
- The delivery of the human resources framework and a suitable communications strategy.

Other people issues

I have spent some time talking about commitment and the desire to increase it when many would say that what we need to do will have the inevitable effect of actually reducing it.

But there are other issues too and we are probably unexceptional in this respect. We need to secure the necessary skills in our workforce. While the culture has until now been one of no compulsory redundancy, this policy is unlikely to be sustainable. We must now think in terms not of training *per se* but of employability. (Other companies such as Rover, having gone through the consequences of restructuring, have very successfully introduced the idea of self-development and learning with their Learning Business.) We now have to think in terms not necessarily of *employment and no compulsory redundancy but of employability*. We have, for example, a programme which is now being extended to enable those who want to qualify under the NVQ System and have been doing work to gain the appropriate accreditations.

We also must move forward in the reward area, and are doing so by piloting a merit pay process in our group headquarters office. People are a company's most valuable resource but also one of the costliest. As a most effective former boss of mine once said, 'overheads walk in and around on two feet'. Existing pay structures are too rigid, with too many status differences and few consequences for failure. There is still the 'culture of annual, automatic salary increments' and, to an extent – though survival pressures will change this – a claims culture (towards allowances and expenses). Historically (as I referred to earlier) there has been an expectancy of a job for life and an accompanying tendency of costly buyouts of inadequate performers. Now at last, and post-privatization, things are starting to move rapidly; but let us not kid ourselves – in a free-floating environment events can and do move even faster and with spectacular consequences, as IBM shows.

A new deal for people

The key objectives of a new-deal employment 'compact' have increasingly to become:

- To reduce the expectation of a level of pay that automatically goes with the job. The idea of the going rate (of annual increases) must go. The performance of the company is the primary driver and, within that, individual performance.
- To empower managers toward their people/teams on the basis of that performance.

- To facilitate and encourage long-term employment with the company but not to guarantee it.
- To offer reasonable compensation to those who *genuinely* must go.
- To improve employability.
- To reduce status differences to a necessary minimum.

It is possible to divine a number of positives from this process, as well of course as some negatives, and the human resources leadership is now well into a delivery programme.

Before we leave this area, I would like to say a word about merit pay. One finds generally very firm advocates both for and against merit pay, i.e. the capacity to vary individual base salary with individual performance. It is notable that many successful companies have such a system. I suspect that many more have these systems, say that they believe in them, maybe even in a 'macho' way, but their effectiveness is doubtful. There have furthermore been pieces of research that cast doubt – certainly on the macho school. This has been music to the ears of those who have a vested interest in maintaining the status quo, especially if such people are well positioned on some agreeable median with no at-risk element. One also hears that pay variation militates against the team and is divisive.

When the same academic studies state that 'there is little or no link between pay and performance', they omit to state the converse: that pay variation works against performance. It is essential that we place pay in context. It is very important to most people but as one part of a general HR spectrum. It should not be placed on a pedestal of its own, and by doing so many managements will or have come unstuck. At the policy level, we firmly believe that pay *should support the management process*; the granting of automatic increments notably does not fit in with this philosophy! This said, there are many traps for the unwary in operating merit pay systems; and it is crucial to have realistic expectations for them. It is perfectly possible to introduce team-based objectives in any merit scheme, thus avoiding a common allegation that pay variation is a divisive force. It should, however, be noted that it can be more appropriate, where large numbers of rather similar jobs are to be found, to operate a merit bonus system rather than vary base salary with performance.

The nature of culture

We have examined at some length the interaction of business drivers principally with human resources culture; and in a chapter entitled **Structural issues and challenges** it is I think quite reasonable to do so. But before trying to draw some conclusions, it is worthwhile looking a little more at the nature of culture itself.

Simply expressed, it could be defined as 'the way we do things around here' or the way organizations perceive themselves. In practice, it is probably an amalgam of many dimensions, a number of which interact with each other. And so we would in some cases have – increasingly so these days – core values, these being the basic substance of mission statements. As we have seen, it is the actual behaviours coming from them that are important. These values arise from basic beliefs. Other contributors to culture are more to do with operational management, and include such things as systems and procedures – and these in turn influence attitudes, or can do. Interwoven with all this are customs, beliefs and the 'folklore' of a place, both formal and informal.

Culture therefore has a profound influence on the way things are done and so, when considering culture change (or lest that imply too static a statement, culture development), it is wise to embrace the totality and not structure alone – or dictat. Culture also tends to be expressed in personal terms, often centring on the characteristics of the leader. However it can be just as informative to look at the characteristics of the followers.

Culture change needs to be planned and have defined aims. These aims have their root in the primary purpose of the particular organization, and this is where some diversity is to be expected. Whether we are talking about the (competitive) marketplace or the captive one, there is now some convergence with the increasing focus on customer service and standards of service (Citizen's Charter).

There are various ways in which culture change occurs. Acquisition is one, and here the options of the acquiring company are to integrate or to go for more radical change, depending on the reasons for the acquisition in the first place. For example, do they include access to markets, technology, human or physical assets? Another would be a radical change in the competitive position – either anticipated or sudden. Where organizations have some choice in the matter, at least in so far as pace and timing are concerned, it would be desirable to go through a process of 'unfreezing', making the change and then 'refreezing'. However, it is doubtful today if it is desirable to 'refreeze' totally, as we have to get used to continuous, even discontinuous, change.

The structuring of expectations is a fundamental management task, and it is clearly desirable to try to enthuse the whole workforce. If one sets aside the economic arguments, it is this sentiment that should inform a change strategy. The challenge is to create fresh opportunities (as with our onion) rather than to invite people to participate in their own self-destruction. The task is to promote the need for change and then change the way people feel; to train for new skills and employability, to recognize and celebrate success – above all, to achieve management ownership.

To use consultants or not/pulling it all together

The use of consultants can be legitimate for several reasons, including the provision of expertise, an external perspective, additional resource and as a change agent. While organizations must never be introspective, it is sad sometimes to witness the wasted internal capability and capacity brought about by the failure of organizations to tap into that potential. The adage 'lend me your watch and I will tell you the time' contains some truth, yet it is amazing how many organizations still persist with this internally demotivating approach. And of course the high price tag that inevitably results from the engaging of consultants virtually guarantees attention – at least, for a time.

It is useful here to contrast the approach adopted by many Japanese companies, which notably do not go down this route, preferring instead to tap into the latent reserves of their own people. The Japanese Nemawashi process of consultation and involvement, allied to the Ringi system of sign-off and commitment, are well known. It takes time and can result in the appearance of occasional flat-footedness, as the sale of Rover to BMW possibly has shown. But Japanese chief executives and senior managers are well versed in the fundamentals of motivation and recognize the power in simply 'asking the people'. Action of this type is less likely to follow strict hierarchical lines or consultation with some elite, but will be widely distributed and multi-level, according to the issue under consideration. Corresponding reputations, which are made or broken in the process, are often transitory. But underpinning all of this are thorough investigation and planning, proper training and, following rigorous implementation, a commitment to continuous improvement. (As balancing comments, we should perhaps first record the fact that there generally exist more cooperative arrangements between private enterprise and the state than are to be found, say, in the UK – the so-called 'Japan Inc' approach. Some would be less generous than this and talk of indirect protectionism! Second, the financial system has the reputation of taking the longer-term view.) Let it also be observed that 'Japan Inc' does not always get it right. For instance, the collaboration between the Electronics Industry and the Ministry of Telecommunications on high-definition TV has been wrong-footed by the West's approach to digital signal processing, with its considerable impact on high-speed data highways.

Some might argue that the apparently drawn-out nature of Japanese decision-making processes will increasingly render Japanese companies less competitive in the 'nano-second nineties' and that they will have to change. Only (**only?!**) present market dominance stands in the way. We shall see; for, having achieved such dominance in terms of scale based on quality, reliability, responsiveness and price, the power of the Japanese organization to anticipate and to innovate should not be underestimated. Whole new markets have been created, e.g. the Walkman. Other factors also lie behind this success story, including a commitment to educational excellence, respect for seniority and the inner strength of the family, leading to their own particular brand of collectivism. Add to this the fact that most people in most Japanese organizations would feel empowered has me rushing to examine the implications of national culture on structural change. For in this country at least, I believe that there has been a tendency for there to be wholesale misrepresentation of what empowerment is all about. It has stressed the 'do your own thing element' without the structure and discipline of formality. There is a great danger therefore that while this most critical of driving forces in assisting structural change will be relegated and passed off as a mere 'fad', (national) competitors will have exploited its full potential. Successful implants in this country do, for instance, have this formality, including formality in communications.

It becomes difficult and not a little dangerous to offer up some prescription for structural change and, if I may be forgiven, I am not going to do so. In a recent presentation at an *Economist* conference on 'The Organization of the 21st Century', Professor Don Schultz of Northwestern University was cautious. He likened today's CEOs to the captains of ships when pilots (externally focused) were needed. He spoke of the past being no basis for the future, and therefore of *discontinuous change*. He referenced the necessity for four new management skills:

- New concepts of financial management departing from the desire to make comparisons, referencing only the solid usable assets of an organization.
- From inside out to outside in: the need to focus on customers and other stakeholders.
- Organizational focus, with specialization on high skill level capability in limited arenas.
- Mastery of communication, both internally and externally.

One might add that the increasing attention which many organizations are giving to community affairs picks up at least two of these four.

Schultz concludes by observing that these qualities are not necessarily innate, *but that they can be developed*. They will, he thinks, require more of a right-brain qualitative approach and less of a left-brain quantitative one.

But as well as possessing such skills that will be of assistance in helping them generate the appropriate climate, CEOs must ensure that they are supported by senior managers and staff who have the *nous* to pick up on the essential direction and to support it through the continuous stream of proposals of a 'bottom-up push' type; and who see the opportunities of empowerment and, at the same time, accept the *obligations of management*. Any historical tolerance of inappropriate behaviours can no longer pass unchecked. *Anxiety must be transformed into excitement. I would also observe that one of the greatest barriers to progress is certainty, difficult though this may be to manage in HR terms.*

Hindsight is golden

We have taken 3 years to get where we are today in matters of organization and culture change, post-privatization. It could be argued that this is far too long and that it could only have been possible in a monopolistic situation. Part of this is accounted for in what I have described as the wait and watch phase and part is wrapped up in the self-doubt about Pipeline Services (YPS). Was it to be regarded as a lifeboat or did it make sense to be in the activity at all?

Having identified what was to become YPS as the first of the 'onionized' businesses, we should have treated it (managerially) as a start-up situation and put in (possibly only for a time) some top management. We did not adequately support the operations manager, who made some progress in changing the culture of a particularly 'difficult' depot, and then integrating other depots, as part of a process of gaining 'critical mass'. We placed far too much faith in the hope that it would 'come around' and, in culture terms, it did not provide the beacon for others to follow.

There was no doubting that many of us believed in and believe in the core values and behaviours, including the Managing Director himself. It was a conscious decision to adopt the path we did (foundation paper/ point the way/gestation period/expect inputs) but, on his own admission, the 'softer' approach went against some instincts!

We could have overdone the wait and watch phase. It was probably an inadequate concept. We should have widened and then harnessed the knowledge of a systematic review process, to which we had already been introduced by one of the firms of consultants we employ – the preparation phase in my Japanese comparison. This would have served to widen the involvement, extend ownership and given a structure for so doing.

I have referred to the power of personality and of leadership. We had and have that personality (the MD) and we should have organized a more up-front communication process before or at the same time as the 'Leading and Coaching for Quality' programme. This programme should have been more rigorously followed through, with, possibly, a few management casualties on the way. We should have checked understanding. It was here where we confused empowerment with giving a further lead; and it must be said that the MD wanted to intervene earlier. We might have expected more bottom-up push too, but perhaps we should have sought it more visibly.

With the declaration of the YW99 philosophy and the decision now taken to work with business process re-engineering consultants, we must be determined to catch up. I believe that we have many of the skills required to bring about the desired changes ourselves, and, to a significant extent, it is not necessary to use consultants. The price tag of their engagement is, however, likely to force consideration of what they recommend/do, among other issues. Of coure they are likely to bring fresh perspectives and will have expertise; but it is the requirement to catch up that has become the real driver. Had we been less timid and less tolerant earlier on, we might not be using consultants at all – or at least more for embellishment.

I will, however, always be of the point of view that there is untapped resourcefulness in most workforces and a process of discovery as managers learn how to create *for themselves* the right (often changing) frameworks. Disciplined (sometimes radical, sometimes incremental) change, inspired by celebration of achievement, obligatory communication and the management of dissent are likely to feature in the method.

In conclusion, might I observe without, I think, too much bias, that Yorkshire Water has visited a number of the stops on the journey of organization development. I hope that it will be increasingly successful. As with most organizations these days, time is not now on our side. The original basis of the 'onion', *proactive* in its approach, may yet be solely transformed into a *reactive* programme of dedicated outsourcing in response to relentless regulatory and political pressures.

Managements in any organization seeking to empower must realize that in reality there must be successful mixing of *loose and tight* controls and that this understanding must be shared throughout the workforce in order to derive the benefits. Schultz's new management skills are, I am sure, very relevant, as long as we remember some of the others, including the power of anticipation. We would also do well to remember that applied commonsense will take us a long way, rather than being taken in by one particular tendency or another.

Acknowledgements

I would like to thank Ian Knight and David Verlander of Yorkshire Water Group Staff and Kathryn Brown of Price Waterhouse for reading through and checking my original draft and for their helpful suggestions. I also acknowledge some source material that derives from the Managing Director's Foundation Paper on Human Resources Strategy for the 1990s; from the Water Share Offer Prospectus that was produced for the Privatization of the Water Industry; from various company documents; and from Yorkshire Water's PR Department.

External acknowledgements:

Burke, W Warner and Litwin, George H (1987) *A Causal Model Of Organisation Peformance,* Warner Burke Associates

Fowler, Alan (1993) 'How To Manage Cultural Change,' *Personnel Management Plus*, November.

Georgiades, Nick (1990) 'A Strategic Future For Personnel?', *Personnel Management,* February.

Holdsworth, Sir Trevor (1991) *Strategic Planning Society News,* July-August.

Learning Resources
Centre